ASCENT
CENTER FOR TECHNICAL KNOWLEDGE

D1210652

Autodesk® Civil 3D® 2022
Fundamentals
Part 2

Learning Guide
Imperial Units - 2nd Edition

AUTODESK.
Authorized Publisher

ASCENT - Center for Technical Knowledge®
Autodesk® Civil 3D® 2022
Fundamentals - Part 2
Imperial Units - 2nd Edition

Prepared and produced by:

ASCENT Center for Technical Knowledge
630 Peter Jefferson Parkway, Suite 175
Charlottesville, VA 22911

866-527-2368
www.ASCENTed.com

Lead Contributor: Jeff Morris

ASCENT - Center for Technical Knowledge (a division of Rand Worldwide Inc.) is a leading developer of professional learning materials and knowledge products for engineering software applications. ASCENT specializes in designing targeted content that facilitates application-based learning with hands-on software experience. For over 25 years, ASCENT has helped users become more productive through tailored custom learning solutions.

We welcome any comments you may have regarding this guide, or any of our products. To contact us please email: feedback@ASCENTed.com.

AS-C3D2201-FND2IM-SG2   //   IS-C3D2201-FND2IM-SG2

Contents
Part 1

Preface xiii

In This Guide xvii

Practice Files xix

Chapter 1: The Autodesk Civil 3D Interface 1-1

  1.1 Product Overview 1-2

  1.2 Autodesk Civil 3D Workspaces 1-3
       Start Tab 1-4

  1.3 Autodesk Civil 3D User Interface 1-7

  Practice 1a Overview of Autodesk Civil 3D and the
  User Interface 1-13

  1.4 Autodesk Civil 3D Toolspace 1-19
       Prospector Tab 1-20
       Settings Tab 1-23
       Survey Tab 1-24
       Toolbox Tab 1-24

  1.5 Autodesk Civil 3D Panorama 1-27

  Practice 1b Autodesk Civil 3D Toolspace 1-29

  1.6 Autodesk Civil 3D Templates and Settings 1-37
       Drawing Settings in Detail 1-37

  Practice 1c Autodesk Civil 3D Settings 1-48

  Chapter Review Questions 1-52

  Command Summary 1-53

Chapter 2: Survey, Points, and Linework **2-1**

2.1   **Survey Workflow Overview** **2-2**
Workflow 2-2

2.2   **Survey Figures** **2-3**
Figure Styles 2-3
Figure Prefix Database 2-4

Practice 2a Creating Figure Prefixes **2-6**

2.3   **Styles** **2-7**

2.4   **Points Overview** **2-12**
Point Label Style 2-18

Practice 2b Point Marker Styles **2-25**

2.5   **Point Settings** **2-33**

2.6   **Creating Points** **2-35**

Practice 2c Creating Autodesk Civil 3D Points **2-36**

2.7   **Description Key Sets** **2-37**

Practice 2d Creating a Description Key Set **2-41**

2.8   **Importing Survey Data** **2-46**
Import Points Only 2-46
Duplicate Point Numbers 2-48
Survey Toolspace 2-49
Import Points and Figures Using the Survey Database 2-49

Practice 2e Importing Survey Data **2-55**

2.9   **Reviewing and Editing Points** **2-59**

2.10 Point Reports **2-61**

Practice 2f Manipulating Points and Point Reports **2-63**

2.11 Point Groups **2-67**
Defining Point Groups 2-67

Practice 2g Creating Point Groups **2-74**

2.12 Lines and Curves **2-77**

Practice 2h Beginning a Subdivision Project **2-81**

Chapter Review Questions **2-85**

Command Summary **2-87**

Chapter 3: Surfaces.. 3-1

3.1 **Surface Process** 3-2

3.2 **Surface Properties** 3-8

3.3 **Contour Data** 3-11
Weeding Factors 3-12
Supplementing Factors 3-13
Contour Issues 3-14
Minimizing Flat Triangle Strategies 3-15

3.4 **Other Surface Data**.. 3-16
DEM Files.. 3-16
Drawing Objects 3-16
Point Files 3-16
Point Groups 3-17
Point Survey Queries 3-17
Figure Survey Queries 3-17

Practice 3a Creating an Existing Ground Surface 3-18

3.5 **Breaklines and Boundaries**... 3-26
Breaklines 3-27

Practice 3b Add Additional Data to an Existing Ground Surface 3-33

3.6 **Surface Editing**.. 3-41
Line Edits 3-43
Point Edits 3-43
Simplify Surface 3-44
Smooth Contours 3-45
Smooth Surface 3-46
Copy Surface 3-47
Surface Paste.. 3-47
Raise/Lower Surface 3-47
Adjusting Surfaces Through Surface Properties 3-48
Copy Deleted Dependent Objects.. 3-48

3.7 **Surface Analysis Tools**.. 3-49
Viewing a Surface in 3D.. 3-49
Surface Preview in the Prospector....................................... 3-50
Quick Profile 3-52

Practice 3c Surface Edits 3-53

3.8 **Surface Labels**... 3-65
Contour Labels 3-66
Spot and Slope Labels 3-66

3.9 **Surface Volume Calculations**.. 3-67
Volumes Dashboard.. 3-67
Bounded Volumes 3-67
Volume Reports 3-68
Grid Volume or TIN Volume Surface.................................... 3-68

3.10 Surface Analysis Display **3-69**

Analysis Settings 3-71

Analysis Data Display 3-72

Practice 3d Surface Labeling and Analysis **3-73**

Chapter Review Questions **3-79**

Command Summary **3-82**

Chapter 4: Project Management **4-1**

4.1 **Design Development** **4-2**

4.2 **Templates** **4-3**

Creating Template Files 4-3

4.3 **Managing Styles** **4-4**

Import 4-4

Drag and Drop Method 4-4

Purge 4-6

Reference 4-6

4.4 **Styles in Depth** **4-9**

4.5 **Online Maps Service** **4-12**

Practice 4a Autodesk Civil 3D Styles **4-14**

4.6 **Autodesk Civil 3D Projects** **4-23**

Single-Design Drawing Projects 4-23

Multiple Drawings Sharing Data Using Shortcuts 4-23

Autodesk Docs Design Collaboration 4-24

Multiple Drawings Sharing Data with Autodesk Vault 4-24

4.7 **Sharing Data** **4-25**

4.8 **Using Data Shortcuts for Project Management** **4-26**

Update Notification 4-28

Removing and Promoting Shortcuts 4-29

Data Shortcut Workflow 4-29

Workflow Details 4-30

Advantages of Data Shortcuts 4-31

Limitations of Data Shortcuts 4-31

Practice 4b Starting a Project **4-32**

Practice 4c Manage File Sizes with Data Shortcuts **4-38**

Chapter Review Questions **4-49**

Command Summary **4-51**

Chapter 5: Alignments **5-1**

5.1 **Roadway Design Overview** **5-2**

5.2 **Autodesk Civil 3D Sites** **5-3**

5.3 **Introduction to Alignments** **5-4**
    Criteria-Based Design 5-6
    Alignment Types 5-7
    Alignment Segment Types 5-8

Practice 5a Creating Alignments from Objects **5-10**

5.4 **Alignments Layout Tools** **5-16**
    Alignment Editing 5-18

Practice 5b Creating and Modifying Alignments **5-19**

5.5 **Alignment Properties** **5-25**
    Station Control Tab 5-25
    Design Criteria Tab 5-25

5.6 **Labels and Tables** **5-27**
    Alignment Point Labels 5-27
    Independent Alignment Labels 5-31
    Alignment Table Styles 5-33

Practice 5c Alignment Properties and Labels **5-34**

Chapter Review Questions **5-42**

Command Summary **5-43**

Chapter 6: Profiles **6-1**

6.1 **Profiles Overview** **6-2**
    Repositioning and Deleting Profile Views 6-3

6.2 **Create a Profile View Style** **6-4**

6.3 **Create Profiles from Surface** **6-12**

6.4 **Create Profile View Wizard** **6-14**

Practice 6a Working with Profiles Part I **6-19**

6.5 **Finished Ground Profiles** **6-27**

6.6 **Create and Edit Profiles** **6-29**
    Superimposing Profiles 6-30
    Transparent Commands 6-31
    Assigning Profile Band Elevations 6-33
    Profile Segment Types 6-34
    Profile Labels 6-34

Practice 6b Working with Profiles Part II **6-37**

Practice 6c Working with Profiles Additional Practice **6-47**

Chapter Review Questions **6-54**

Command Summary **6-55**

Chapter 7: Assemblies **7-1**

7.1 Assembly Overview **7-2**
Assemblies 7-2
Subassemblies 7-3
Subassembly Composer 7-6

7.2 Modifying Assemblies **7-8**
Attaching Subassemblies 7-8
Detaching Subassemblies 7-11
Copying Assemblies 7-11
Modifying Subassemblies 7-11
Select Similar Subassemblies 7-12
Getting More Information on Subassemblies 7-13

Practice 7a Creating Assemblies **7-14**

Practice 7b (Optional) Creating Assemblies Additional Practice **7-21**

7.3 Managing Assemblies **7-25**
Identifying Assemblies 7-25
Sharing Assemblies 7-26

Practice 7c Managing Assemblies **7-27**

Chapter Review Questions **7-35**

Command Summary **7-36**

Chapter 8: Corridors **8-1**

8.1 Creating a Corridor **8-2**
Target Mapping 8-4
Corridor Frequency 8-5

8.2 Corridor Properties **8-6**
Information Tab 8-6
Parameters Tab 8-6
Codes 8-7
Feature Lines 8-8
Slope Patterns 8-8
Corridor Contextual Ribbon 8-9
Exporting Corridors 8-9

Practice 8a Creating Corridors **8-11**

8.3 Designing Intersections **8-25**
General Tab 8-26
Geometry Details Tab 8-27
Corridor Regions Tab 8-27

Practice 8b Intersections **8-29**

8.4 **Roundabouts** **8-41**
    Roundabout Standards 8-41
    Creating Roundabouts 8-41
    Heads Up Display 8-45

Practice 8c Roundabout with Corridor.................................... **8-46**

8.5 **Corridor Section Review and Edit** **8-51**

Practice 8d Corridor Section Editor **8-54**

8.6 **Corridor Surfaces**.. **8-56**
    Overhang Correction 8-57
    Surface Boundaries 8-57

Practice 8e Corridor Surfaces **8-58**

8.7 **Sample Line Groups** **8-64**
    Modifying Sample Line Groups 8-67

Practice 8f Creating Sample Lines **8-68**

8.8 **Section Volume Calculations**... **8-73**
    Earthwork Volumes 8-73
    Mass Haul 8-74
    Material Volumes 8-74
    Quantity Takeoff Criteria 8-74
    Define Materials 8-75

Practice 8g Compute Materials **8-76**

Chapter Review Questions... **8-87**

Command Summary **8-89**

Index **Index-1**

Contents
Part 2

Preface xiii

In This Guide xvii

Practice Files xix

Chapter 9: Grading 9-1

    9.1 Grading Overview 9-2

    9.2 Feature Lines 9-4
        Feature Line Contextual Tab.. 9-4
        Elevation Editor 9-5

    Practice 9a Creating Feature Lines 9-7

    9.3 Create Design Surfaces from Feature Lines 9-19

    Practice 9b Create the Interim Design Surface 9-21

    9.4 Grading Tools 9-23
        Grading Creation Tools Toolbar.................................... 9-23

    Practice 9c Create Grading Groups................................ 9-24

    9.5 Modifying Autodesk Civil 3D Grading.......................... 9-34
        Grading Styles... 9-34
        Feature Line Labels 9-34
        Grading Criteria 9-34
        Grading Criteria Set 9-35
        Grading Volumes 9-36

    Practice 9d Modify Grading and Calculate Volumes 9-37

    Chapter Review Questions.. 9-48

    Command Summary 9-49

Chapter 10: Pipe Networks 10-1

    10.1 Pipes Overview.. 10-2

    10.2 Pipes Configuration 10-4

Practice 10a Configuring Pipe Networks 10-15

10.3 Creating Networks from Objects 10-23

Practice 10b Creating Pipe Networks by Objects 10-25

10.4 The Network Layout Toolbar.. 10-28

Practice 10c Creating Pipe Networks by Layout............................ 10-30

10.5 Network Editing.. 10-37
    Pipe (and Structure) Properties... 10-37
    Swap Part.. 10-38
    Connect/Disconnect From Part 10-38

Practice 10d Editing Pipe Networks 10-39

10.6 Annotating Pipe Networks 10-45
    Pipe Networks in Sections 10-46
    Pipe Network Reports and Tables 10-47

Practice 10e Annotating Pipe Networks... 10-48

10.7 Pressure Pipe Networks 10-54

Practice 10f Create a Pressure Pipe Network................................ 10-62

Chapter Review Questions.. 10-78

Command Summary 10-79

Chapter 11: Plan Production 11-1

11.1 Final Design... 11-2

11.2 Plan Production Tools 11-3
    Overview for Plan/Profile Sheets 11-3
    Overview for Section Sheets... 11-4
    More Information 11-4

11.3 Plan Production Objects 11-5
    View Frames 11-6
    View Frame Groups 11-6
    Match Lines 11-6

11.4 Plan Production Object Edits.. 11-7
    Name.. 11-7
    Description 11-7
    Object Style.. 11-7
    View Frame Geometry Properties Edits.. 11-8
    Match Line Geometry Properties Edits 11-9

Practice 11a Plan Production Tools - View Frames 11-10

11.5 Creating Sheets.. 11-18

Practice 11b Plan Production Tools - Sheet Generation 11-19

11.6 Section Views 11-24
    Section View Wizard 11-24

Practice 11c Plan Production Tools - Sections **11-27**

11.7 Sheet Sets **11-35**
Sheet Set Manager Palette 11-36
Structuring Sheet Sets 11-37
Editing Sheet Sets... 11-37
Sheet Set Manager Properties... 11-39

Practice 11d Plan Production Tools - Sheet Sets **11-41**

Chapter Review Questions **11-52**

Command Summary **11-54**

Chapter 12: Quantity Takeoff and Visualization **12-1**

12.1 Civil 3D Multi-view Blocks **12-2**

Practice 12a Adding Detail to Drawings **12-6**

12.2 Pay Items **12-10**

Practice 12b Integrated Quantity Takeoff **12-12**

12.3 Visualization **12-21**

12.4 3D Navigation Tools **12-23**
ViewCube 12-23
Steering Wheel 12-26

12.5 Managing Views in 3D **12-29**

12.6 Corridor Visualization **12-33**
Line of Sight Analysis 12-34

12.7 Share **12-37**

Practice 12c Visualizing Corridors **12-39**

Chapter Review Questions **12-45**

Command Summary **12-46**

Appendix A: Additional Information **A-1**

A.1 Opening a Survey Database **A-2**

A.2 Point Cloud Surface Extraction **A-3**
Attach Point Cloud A-3
Surfaces from Point Clouds A-8

Practice A1 Create a Point Cloud Surface **A-12**

A.3 3D Solid Surface from TIN Surface **A-14**

Practice A2 3D Surface Solids and Label Adjustments **A-16**

A.4 Design Data **A-21**
Parcel Size A-21
Road Design Criteria A-22

Appendix B: Project Explorer..**B-1**

    B.1 Introduction to the Project Explorer..............................**B-2**

    B.2 Project Explorer User Interface **B-4**

    Practice B1 Project Explorer Interface **B-9**

    B.3 Civil 3D Object Management..**B-13**

    Practice B2 Edit Civil 3D Pipe Objects **B-18**

    B.4 Reports and Object Sets **B-24**

    Practice B3 Reports and Object Sets **B-26**

    Chapter Review Questions..**B-33**

    Command Summary **B-34**

Appendix C: Parcels..**C-1**

    C.1 Introduction to Parcels **C-2**
        ROW Parcel C-4
        Parcel Style Display Order C-4
        Parcel Properties...C-6
        Parcel Labels and Styles...C-7
        Create Parcels from Objects C-8
        Creating Right-of-Way Parcels.....................................C-8

    Practice C1 Create Parcels from Objects...........................**C-9**

    C.2 Creating and Editing Parcels by Layout Overview **C-17**

    C.3 Creating and Editing Parcels **C-20**
        Freehand...C-22
        Slide Line C-22
        Swing Line...C-22
        Free Form Create...C-22

    Practice C2 Create Parcels by Slide Angle **C-24**

    C.4 Renumbering Parcels **C-29**

    Practice C3 Rename/Renumber Parcels **C-30**

    C.5 Parcel Reports...**C-37**

    C.6 Parcel Labels **C-39**

    C.7 Parcel Tables **C-42**

    Practice C4 Reporting On and Annotating the Parcel Layout **C-44**

    Chapter Review Questions..**C-51**

    Command Summary **C-53**

Index **Index-1**

Preface

The *Autodesk® Civil 3D® 2022: Fundamentals* guide is designed for Civil Engineers and Surveyors who want to take advantage of the Autodesk® Civil 3D® software's interactive, dynamic design functionality. The Autodesk Civil 3D software permits the rapid development of alternatives through its model-based design tools. You will learn techniques enabling you to organize project data, work with points, create and analyze surfaces, model road corridors, create parcel layouts, perform grading and volume calculation tasks, and lay out pipe networks.

Topics Covered

- Learn the Autodesk Civil 3D 2022 user interface.

- Create and edit parcels and print parcel reports.

- Create points and point groups and work with survey figures.

- Create and manage styles and label styles.

- Create, edit, view, and analyze surfaces.

- Create and edit alignments.

- Create data shortcuts.

- Create a Civil 3D template drawing.

- Create sites, profiles, and cross-sections.

- Create assemblies, corridors, and intersections.

- Create grading solutions.

- Create gravity fed and pressure pipe networks.

- Perform quantity takeoff and volume calculations.

- Use plan production tools to create plan and profile sheets.

Prerequisites

- Access to the 2022.0 version of the software, to ensure compatibility with this guide. Future software updates that are released by Autodesk may include changes that are not reflected in this guide. The practices and files included with this guide might not be compatible with prior versions (e.g., 2021).

- Experience with AutoCAD® or AutoCAD-based products and a sound understanding and knowledge of civil engineering terminology.

Note on Software Setup

This guide assumes a standard installation of the software using the default preferences during installation. Lectures and practices use the standard software templates and default options for the Content Libraries.

Configuration Changes

The following configuration changes need to be made to ensure the practices run smoothly. For more information on making these configuration changes, consult the Civil 3D help menu.

- Set the *Template* file location to **C:\Civil 3D Projects\Ascent-Config**, as shown below.

- Set the *Pipe Catalog* location to **C:\Civil 3D Projects\Ascent-Config\Pipes Catalog**, as shown below.

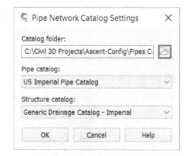

- Set the *Pressure Pipe Catalog* location to **C:\Civil 3D Projects\ Ascent-Config\Pressure Pipes Catalog\Imperial**, as shown below.

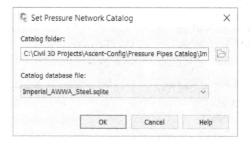

Students and Educators Can Access Free Autodesk Software and Resources

Autodesk challenges you to get started with free educational licenses for professional software and creativity apps used by millions of architects, engineers, designers, and hobbyists today. Bring Autodesk software into your classroom, studio, or workshop to learn, teach, and explore real-world design challenges the way professionals do.

Get started today - register at the Autodesk Education Community and download one of the many Autodesk software applications available.

Visit www.autodesk.com/education/home/

Note: Free products are subject to the terms and conditions of the end-user license and services agreement that accompanies the software. The software is for personal use for education purposes and is not intended for classroom or lab use.

Lead Contributor: Jeff Morris

Specializing in the civil engineering industry, Jeff authors training guides and provides instruction, support, and implementation on all Autodesk infrastructure solutions.

Jeff brings to bear over 20 years of diverse work experience in the civil engineering industry. He has played multiple roles, including Sales, Trainer, Application Specialist, Implementation and Customization Consultant, CAD Coordinator, and CAD/BIM Manager, in civil engineering and architecture firms, and Autodesk reseller organizations. He has worked for government organizations and private firms, small companies and large multinational corporations and in multiple geographies across the globe. Through his extensive experience in Building and Infrastructure design, Jeff has acquired a thorough understanding of CAD Standards and Procedures and an in-depth knowledge of CAD and BIM.

Jeff studied Architecture and a diploma in Systems Analysis and Programming. He is an Autodesk Certified Instructor (ACI) and holds the Autodesk Certified Professional certification for Civil 3D and Revit.

Jeff Morris has been the Lead Contributor for *Autodesk Civil 3D: Fundamentals* since 2019.

In This Guide

The following highlights the key features of this guide.

Feature	Description
Practice Files	The Practice Files page includes a link to the practice files and instructions on how to download and install them. The practice files are required to complete the practices in this guide.
Chapters	A chapter consists of the following - Learning Objectives, Instructional Content, Practices, Chapter Review Questions, and Command Summary.
	• **Learning Objectives** define the skills you can acquire by learning the content provided in the chapter.
	• **Instructional Content**, which begins right after Learning Objectives, refers to the descriptive and procedural information related to various topics. Each main topic introduces a product feature, discusses various aspects of that feature, and provides step-by-step procedures on how to use that feature. Where relevant, examples, figures, helpful hints, and notes are provided.
	• **Practice** for a topic follows the instructional content. Practices enable you to use the software to perform a hands-on review of a topic. It is required that you download the practice files (using the link found on the Practice Files page) prior to starting the first practice.
	• **Chapter Review Questions**, located close to the end of a chapter, enable you to test your knowledge of the key concepts discussed in the chapter.
	• **Command Summary** concludes a chapter. It contains a list of the software commands that are used throughout the chapter and provides information on where the command can be found in the software.
Appendices	Appendices provide additional information to the main course content. It could be in the form of instructional content, practices, tables, projects, or skills assessment.

Practice Files

To download the practice files for this guide, use the following steps:

1. Type the URL *exactly as shown below* into the address bar of your Internet browser, to access the Course File Download page.

   Note: If you are using the ebook, you do not have to type the URL. Instead, you can access the page simply by clicking the URL below.

   ## https://www.ascented.com/getfile/id/ceratocentronPF

   Note: If you are completing the optional practices in Appendix A, you will need to download the point cloud file from the URL below.

   ## https://www.ascented.com/getfile/id/ceratochilusPF

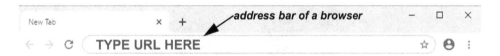

2. On the Course File Download page, click the **DOWNLOAD NOW** button, as shown below, to download the .ZIP file that contains the practice files.

   DOWNLOAD NOW ▶

3. Once the download is complete, unzip the file and extract its contents.

   The recommended practice files folder location is:
   C:\Civil 3D Projects

   Note: It is recommended that you do not change the location of the practice files folder. Doing so may cause errors when completing the practices.

Stay Informed!

To receive information about upcoming events, promotional offers, and complimentary webcasts, visit:

www.ASCENTed.com/updates

Chapter 9

Grading

Nearly every civil engineering project requires grading the terrain to create the correct slope and drainage. In this chapter, you will use feature lines and grading objects and groups to create a finished ground surface. Then, you will check the balance of the cut and fill quantities on the newly created surface.

Learning Objectives in This Chapter

- Create feature lines and grading objects to design the finished ground.
- Display the finished ground correctly by modifying grading objects using styles, feature line labels, and grading criteria.

9.1 Grading Overview

Autodesk® Civil 3D® grading uses objects called *feature lines* and *grading groups*.

- Feature lines are complex, linear 3D objects that define a string of known elevations, such as the perimeter of a proposed pond. Feature lines can be created by converting AutoCAD® lines, arcs, or polylines. Grading feature lines can also be exported from Corridors by selecting the *Modify* tab> Corridor panel and launching the **Feature Lines from Corridor** command.

- Parcel lines double as feature lines, and can be edited directly using the Feature Line Elevation Editor. Parcel lines in the extents of a grading group are also automatically added to the surface, even if they are at elevation 0. (You can avoid this by locating feature lines and parcels in separate sites.)

- The feature lines can be created from an alignment. They can also be dynamically linked to the alignment or corridor model from which they were created.

- The Autodesk Civil 3D software can calculate the position of one feature line based on another, such as a pond bottom calculated at a specific slope and elevation below the perimeter. Distance, slope, and surface parameters used in solutions are assigned using *grading criteria*.

- *Grading groups* are collections of these solutions that form a contiguous whole, such as the detention pond shown in Figure 9–1.

Figure 9–1

- Grading groups can be used to generate Autodesk Civil 3D surfaces. Tools are also available for calculating grading group volume, and adjusting grading groups to check the balance of cut and fill material.

- Surfaces created from grading groups (as well as corridor surfaces) display in the Toolspace, *Prospector* tab and can be adjusted using normal surface editing tools, such as **Add** or **Delete Surface Point** or **Swap Edge**. These edits are maintained and dynamically reapplied if the grading group is modified.

- Feature lines and grading groups are organized by site. Any feature lines added in the perimeter of a grading group, within the same site, are automatically added to the grading group.

- Feature lines can also be site-less. This provides more flexibility on how feature lines can be used and how they interact with each other.

- Feature lines can be used to create Corridor models.

- Feature lines can also be extracted from corridor links.

9.2 Feature Lines

Feature Line Contextual Tab

The *Feature Line* contextual tab (shown in Figure 9–2), contains commands to edit and modify feature lines. These commands include tools to edit feature line elevations and feature line geometry, such as **Break**, **Trim**, **Extend**, and **Fillet** (which creates a true 3D curve).

Figure 9–2

There are multiple ways of creating feature lines, such as:

- **Create Feature Lines from Objects**

- **Create Feature Lines from Alignment** (linked or unlinked)

- **Create Feature Lines from Corridor** (linked or unlinked)

- **Create Feature Lines from Stepped Offset**

These commands are available in the *Home* tab>Create Design panel, expanded **Feature Line** flyout, as shown in Figure 9–3.

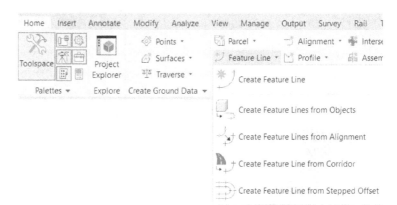

Figure 9–3

Linking feature lines to alignments or corridors makes the feature lines uneditable. This can have advantages in that as the alignments or corridors change, the feature lines will automatically update. However, the inability to edit the feature line (e.g., using Break, Trim, Extend, and Fillet) often makes this option less attractive.

Hint: Updating Feature Lines

If feature lines derived from corridors are unlinked, you can always update the feature lines to the new corridor elevations through the feature line contextual ribbon.

Elevation Editor

The Grading Elevation Editor vista (shown in Figure 9–4), enables you to add, modify, or vary the elevations of a feature line. The feature line data is organized into rows; each row lists the data for a specific vertex.

Station	Elevation(R...	Elevation(Actual)	Length	Grade Back	Grade Ahead	Elevation Derived From
0+00.00	0.50'	247.94'	27.57'		1.81%	Relative to Surface
0+27.57		248.44'	282.02'	-1.81%	2.00%	Absolute Elevation
3+09.58		254.08'	76.44'	-2.00%	-3.00%	Absolute Elevation
3+86.03		251.79'	176.77'	3.00%	-3.27%	Absolute Elevation
5+62.79		246.00'	176.77'	3.27%	-2.73%	Absolute Elevation
7+39.56		241.18'	76.44'	2.73%	-3.00%	Absolute Elevation
8+16.00		238.89'	282.02'	3.00%	3.21%	Absolute Elevation
10+98.02	0.50'	247.94'		-3.21%		Relative to Surface

Figure 9–4

-  **(Select a Feature Line Or Lot Line):** Enables you to change the feature line that you are editing.

- **(Zoom to):** Zooms in to a highlighted vertex.

- **(Quick Profile):** Creates a quick profile along the feature line.

- **(Raise/Lower):** Raises or lowers all of the feature line vertices by the elevation entered in the edit field on the right.

- **(Raise/Lower Incrementally):** Changes the elevations by the elevation increment entered (the default is 1).

- **(Set Increment):** Sets the increment value.

- **(Flatten Grade or Elevations):** Enables you to flatten selected vertices to a specified grade or single elevation.

- ⊹ **(Insert Elevation Point):** (Green) Adds an elevation control to the feature line. Elevation points provide an elevation control without creating a new vertex. These points are Z-controls without X- or Y-components.

- ⊹ **(Delete Elevation Point):** (Red) Removes elevation points.

- ⊹ **(Elevations from Surface):** Takes the elevations of all of the vertices from the surface if no rows are selected. If a row is selected, it only takes the surface elevation for that vertex.

- ⊹ **(Reverse the direction):** Changes the direction of the feature line by reversing the order of its points.

- ▦ **(Show Grade breaks only):** Only displays rows for vertices where there is a change to grade.

- ▦ **(Unselect All Rows):** Clears selected vertices. With no rows selected, the **Raise/Lower** commands apply to all rows.

- **(Select from List):** When elevations are set to be relative to a surface, select the surface that is in control using the drop-down list, as shown in Figure 9–5.

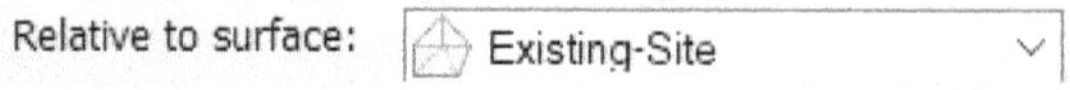

Relative to surface: △ Existing-Site ∨

Figure 9–5

- ▦ **(Select from the drawing):** Select the controlling surface (for Relative to surface) from the drawing.

You can edit the elevations of a feature or parcel line before or after it becomes part of a grading group.

Practice 9a

Creating Feature Lines

Practice Objectives

- Create feature lines from a drawing object, corridor, and referenced object.
- Create a feature line using design data.

The first step in grading is to establish an interim design surface based on existing site conditions. In this practice, you will define feature lines from the parcel boundary and corridors, from which you will create a surface. Next, feature lines defining design features are created, to be used for grading purposes to meet the interim design surface.

For the Grading drawings, the completed corridors, the Ascent Place knuckle and cul-de-sac target alignments, the Mission Avenue alignment, and the Existing-Site surface have been referenced through Data Shortcuts.

Task 1 - Create a feature line for western edge based on existing surface elevations

To establish an interim design surface, you will create a feature line from an existing polyline along the western and southern edges of the school parcel. Then, you will create one feature line from the southern edge of the Jeffries Ranch Rd corridor, as shown in Figure 9–6.

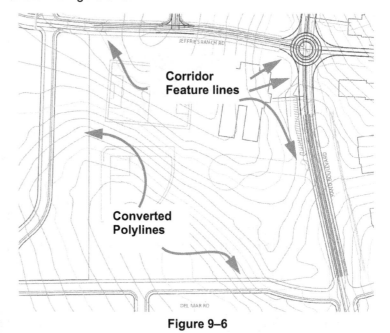

Figure 9–6

The other corridor feature lines will be added, trimmed, and joined together to form one feature line. This is beyond the scope of this exercise simply because it is too time-consuming. You will, however, join the polyline feature line with the corridor feature line.

1. Open **GRD1-A.dwg** from the *C:\Civil 3D Projects\Working\ Grading* folder.

See the Project Management for how to work with Data Shortcuts.

2. Hover the cursor over the Data Shortcuts and review the tooltip which displays, shown in Figure 9–7. Ensure that your Data Shortcuts are set so the **Working Folder** is set to *C:\Civil 3D Projects\Data Shortcuts\Fundamentals* and the **Data Shortcuts Project Folder** to *Ascent-Development*. If required, right-click on Data Shortcuts to set the **Working Folder** and **Data Shortcuts Project Folder**.

Figure 9–7

3. Select the preset view **Grad-South.**

4. In the *Home* tab>Create Design panel, expand **Feature Line** and select (Create Feature Lines from Objects), as shown in Figure 9–8.

Figure 9–8

5. When prompted to *select the object,* pick the cyan polyline as indicated in Figure 9–6 (above) and press <Enter> to finish the selection.

6. In the Create Feature Lines dialog box, do the following (as shown on the right in Figure 9–9):

- For the *Site*, click on 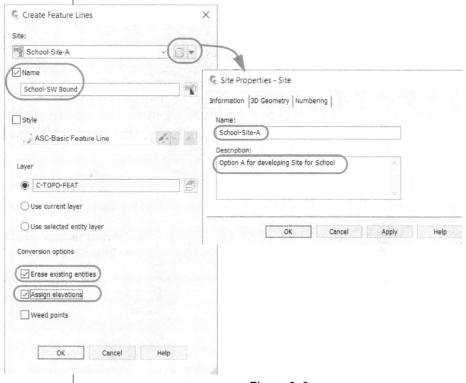 (New Site) to create a new site.
- In the Site Properties dialog box, for the *Name*, enter **School-Site-A**.
- For the *Description*, enter **Option A for developing Site for School**.
- Click **OK** to close the Site Properties dialog box.

7. In the Create Feature Lines dialog box, do the following (as shown on the left in Figure 9–9):

- Check the **Name** box and name the feature line *School-SW Bound.*
- Leave the **Style** box unchecked to keep the default style.
- In the *Conversion options* area, select **Erase existing entities** and **Assign elevations**.
- Click **OK** to continue.

Figure 9–9

8. In the Assign Elevations dialog box that opens, ensure the following are set, as shown in Figure 9–10:

- *From surface:* toggled on and set to **Existing-Site**
- *Insert intermediate grade break points:* **checked**
- *Relative elevation to surface:* **unchecked**

Figure 9–10

9. Click **OK** to close the Assign Elevations dialog box.

10. You will note that the cyan polyline has now changed to a green feature line. When you select it, you will see a series of round grips, which are the intermediate grade break points, and square grips, which are the vertices of the feature line, as shown in Figure 9–11.

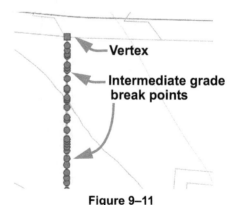

Figure 9–11

11. Save the drawing

Task 2 - Extract feature line from corridor.

In this task, you will create a feature line from the southern edge of the Jeffries Ranch Rd corridor to form the northern edge of the School design surface.

1. Continue to work in the previous drawing.

2. Zoom and pan to the southwest edge of the **Jeffries Ranch Rd** corridor, as shown in Figure 9–12.

3. In the *Home* tab>Create Design panel, expand **Feature Line** and select ![icon] (Create Feature Lines from Corridor).

4. Select the **Jeffries Ranch Rd** corridor. The *Code Set Style* has been set to **ASC-All Codes - No Display**, so you will need to select one of the parallel segments of the road, which are the links, as shown in Figure 9–12.

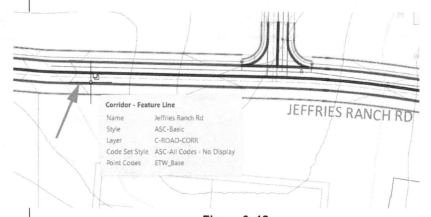

Figure 9–12

5. When prompted to select the corridor feature line, hover over the various parallel links and note how they turn red and their code appears as a tooltip. Select the southernmost one, which is **P2**, as shown in Figure 9–13. Press <Enter> to finish the selection.

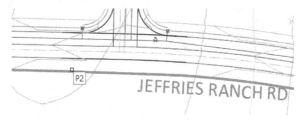

Figure 9–13

6. In the Extract Corridor Feature Lines dialog box that opens, click the **Settings** button to open the Extract Corridor Feature Lines Settings dialog box, then set the following (as shown in Figure 9–14):

- *Dynamic link to corridor:* **unchecked**
- *Apply Smoothing:* **unchecked**
- *Name:* **checked** and type the name **FL - <[Corridor Name]> South Edge**

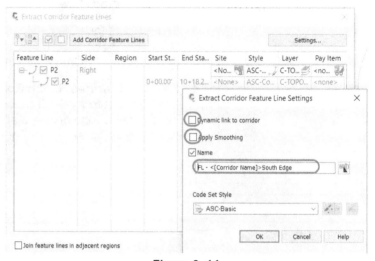

Figure 9–14

7. Click **OK** to close the Extract Corridor Feature Lines Settings dialog box, then click **Extract** to close the Extract Corridor Feature Lines dialog box.

8. Save the drawing.

Task 3 - Create a feature based on design elevations.

In this task, you will create a feature line for the baseball field whose elevations and slopes have been pre-calculated to ensure correct drainage. Based on the required drainage for the baseball field, the critical points have been established, as shown in Figure 9–15. Use these points to create a feature line.

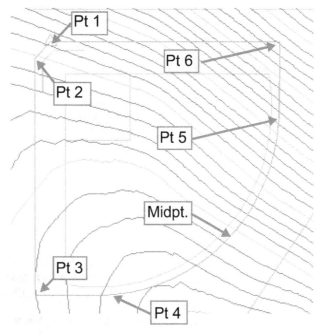

Figure 9–15

1. Continue working with the drawing from the previous practice or open **GRD1-B.dwg** from the *C:\Civil 3D Projects\Working\ Grading* folder.

2. Select the preset view **Grad-Baseball**.

3. In the *Home* tab>Create Design panel, expand **Feature Line** and select   (Create Feature Line).

4. In the Create Feature Lines dialog box, set the site to **School-Site-A** (if necessary) and name the feature line **Baseball**, then accept all of the other defaults. Click **OK** to close the dialog box and start creating the feature line.

Use the Endpoint Osnap to pick these points.

5. When prompted for the feature line points, select the end point **Pt1** (as shown above in Figure 9–15). At the *Specify elevation or [surface]:* prompt, type **S** (for Surface) and press <Enter>.

6. In the Select Surface dialog box, select **Existing-Site** from the drop-down list. Select **Relative elevation to surface:** and type **0.50'**, as shown in Figure 9–16. This will tie the feature line vertex to the surface and keep it 6 inches higher than the surface, even when the surface elevation changes.

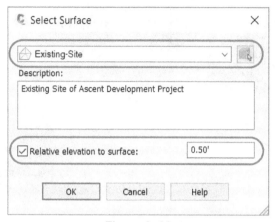

Figure 9–16

7. When prompted for the next point, select point **Pt2**, as shown previously in Figure 9–15.

8. You are prompted to *Specify grade or [SLope/Elevation/ Difference/SUrface/Transition] <0.00>:*. Type **D** and press <Enter> to give it the difference in elevation.

9. Now you are prompted to *Specify elevation difference or [Grade/Slope/Elevation/Surface/Relativetosurface/ Transition]:*. Type **0.5** and press <Enter>. This will make this vertex 6" higher than the previous one.

10. Select **Pt 3** and type **G** to specify the grade. Type 2 for the grade. You need not enter the percent symbol (%). This will make the elevation at this vertex at a 2% grade up from the last vertex.

11. Pick **Pt 4** and type **T** for Transition. This means you will defer specifying an elevation at this time.

12. Next, type **A** and press <Enter> to start an arc. Select **Pt 5**. When prompted for the elevation, simply press <Enter> (for the default is Transition from the last choice); you will continue to defer.

13. After **Pt 5**, type **L** and press <Enter> to return to straight lines.

14. At **Pt6**, type G (for Grade), and type -3 (negative three) and press <Enter>. This means that from the vertex elevation of Pt3, the grade through Pt4 and Pt5 to Pt6 will be 3% lower.

15. Type **C** to close the feature line and press <Enter> to exit the command.

16. In Model Space, select the feature line that you just created and in the contextual tab>Modify panel, select **Edit Elevations** to toggle on the Edit Elevations panel, and then select **Elevation Editor**, as shown in Figure 9–17.

Figure 9–17

17. In the Grading Elevation Editor vista (shown in Figure 9–18), you can change the feature line design.

18. Add an elevation point by clicking ↳ (Insert Elevation Point), as shown in Figure 9–18.

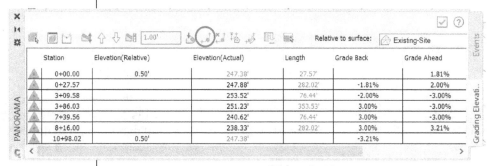

Station	Elevation(Relative)	Elevation(Actual)	Length	Grade Back	Grade Ahead
0+00.00	0.50'	247.38'	27.57'		1.81%
0+27.57		247.88'	282.02'	-1.81%	2.00%
3+09.58		253.52'	76.44'	-2.00%	-3.00%
3+86.03		251.23'	353.53'	3.00%	-3.00%
7+39.56		240.62'	76.44'	3.00%	-3.00%
8+16.00		238.33'	282.02'	3.00%	3.21%
10+98.02	0.50'	247.38'		-3.21%	

Figure 9–18

19. When prompted to *Specify Point:*, select the midpoint between **Pt4** and **Pt5**, as shown previously in Figure 9–15. In the dialog box, type **246.0'** for the Elevation, as shown in Figure 9–19, then click **OK**.

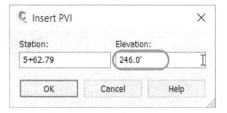

Figure 9–19

---

20. Note the new entry in the Elevation Editor for this new Elevation Point, which has a green circle as its designation (compared to the green triangles for the Points of Intersection (PI)), as shown in Figure 9–20.

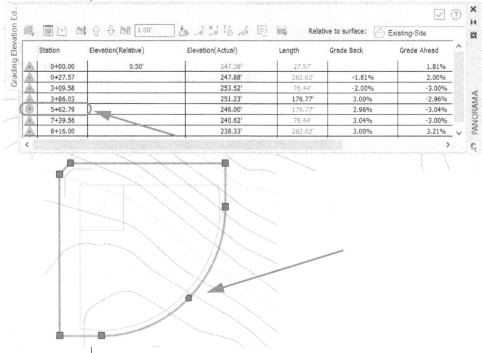

Figure 9–20

21. Feel free to experiment with the Elevation Editor by changing the values in any of the cells and notice how the other cells update. Also note that you cannot change the actual elevation of the first (and last) point, since it is relative to the surface.

22. Close the Elevation Editor, then save the drawing.

Task 4 - Create more feature lines for the school building footprint and soccer field.

In this task, you will create feature lines for the soccer field and for the school footprint. You will establish the elevations of these feature lines after the interim design surface is built later in this chapter, rather than using the Existing-Site as you had done in the previous task.

1. Continue working with the drawing from the previous task or open **GRD1-C.dwg** from the *C:\Civil 3D Projects\Working\ Grading* folder.

2. Select the preset view **Grad-Soccer.**

3. In the *Home* tab>Create Design panel, expand **Feature Line** and select (Create Feature Lines from Objects).

4. When prompted to *select the object*, type **X** (for XREF), select the outermost rectangle around the soccer field (as shown in Figure 9–21), and press <Enter>.

Figure 9–21

5. Name the feature line **Soccer**.

6. Do NOT select **Assign elevation** or **Weed points**. You will assign the elevations later.

7. Click **OK** to create the feature line.

8. Save the drawing.

9. Select the preset view **Grad-School**.

Do not work too hard on getting the rectangle perfect; you will be using a different one later.

10. Draw a rectangle similar to the one shown in Figure 9–22.

11. In the *Home* tab>Create Design panel, expand **Feature Line** and select (Create Feature Lines from Objects).

12. When prompted to *select the object*, select the rectangle you just drew and press <Enter>.

Figure 9–22

13. Name the feature line **School-footprint**.

14. Check the **Erase existing entities** box.

15. Do NOT check **Assign elevation** or **Weed points**. You will assign the elevations later.

16. Click **OK** to create the feature line.

17. Save and close the drawing.

9.3 Create Design Surfaces from Feature Lines

A common practice in land development is to create an interim base surface for design purposes. For hilly, irregular project sites with many natural grade changes and topologies, it can be a challenge to provide preliminary design grading directly to the existing site. An interim surface can be used to make it easier to come up with design proposals, as can be seen in the quick profile of both the existing grade and the interim design grade in Figure 9–23.

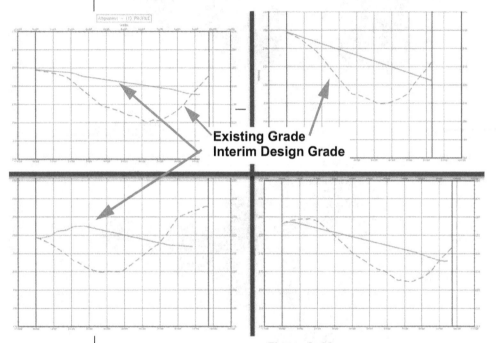

Existing Grade
Interim Design Grade

Figure 9–23

The interim surface will intersect the existing surface at the project site's boundary. If the boundary is a corridor, extracted feature lines from the corridor are used to create the interim surface. If the boundary is open space, a feature line created with elevations from the existing ground will be used.

The result is a less complex grading surface, which is often flatter with lesser elevation changes. Compare the existing surface in Figure 9–24 with the interim design surface in Figure 9–25.

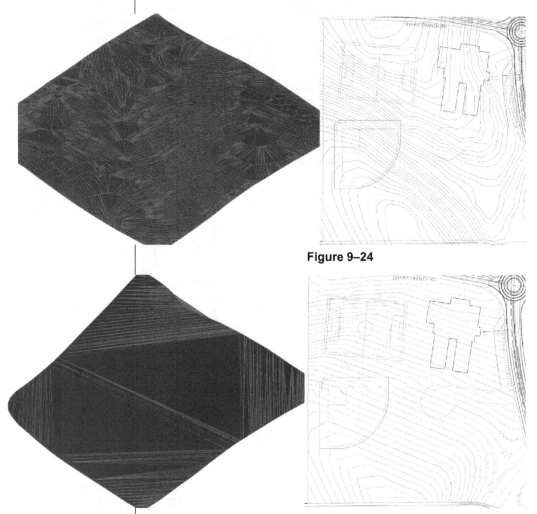

Figure 9–24

Figure 9–25

In practice, it is recommended that an interim design grade be refined with other features deemed necessary for the final design. Such features may include streams and waterways, proposed pathways, etc.

The first step of creating such feature lines has been done in the previous practices. The next step is to create a interim surface with these feature lines. With such an interim design grade, preliminary grading of building pads, parking lots, irrigation or retention ponds, and sports fields can be done and studied.

Practice 9b

Create the Interim Design Surface

Practice Objective

- Create grading objects to design the finished ground and display the finished ground contours.

In this next drawing, the boundary feature line has been completed. More corridor feature lines were extracted, but not linked. Then, the feature lines were trimmed and the endpoint vertices were adjusted to meet other endpoint vertices from other feature lines, both in elevation and location (by using the Endpoint Osnap). Finally, the feature lines were joined together, as shown in Figure 9–26. The name of the resulting feature line is **School-Site Boundary**.

Figure 9–26

1. Open **GRD1-D.dwg** from the *C:\Civil 3D Projects\Working\ Grading* folder. Do not continue from the previous drawing.

2. In the Toolspace, *Prospector* tab, select **Surfaces**, right-click, and select **Create Surface**.

3. In the Create Surface dialog box, set the following (as shown in Figure 9–27):

- *Type*: **TIN surface**
- *Name*: **IDG**
- *Description*: **Interim Design**
- *Style*: **ASC-Contours 2' and 10' (Design)**
- *Render Material:* **Sitework.Planting.Grass.Thick**

Figure 9–27

4. Click **OK** to accept the changes and close the dialog box.

5. Expand the *IDG* surfaces collection and the *Definition* collection.

6. Select the **Breaklines** data element, right-click, and select **Add...**.

7. In the Add Breaklines dialog box, enter **Boundary from feature lines** for a description and leave all other options as default.

8. Click **OK**.

9. Select the perimeter feature line, as shown in Figure 9–26 above, and press <Enter> to finish the selection.

10. The surface is built. You may have to regenerate the drawing to see it.

11. Select the **Existing-Site** surface and in the Surface Properties, set the surface style to **ASC-Border Only**.

12. Save the drawing.

9.4 Grading Tools

Grading Creation Tools Toolbar

Grading groups are created and edited using the Grading Creation Tools toolbar (as shown in Figure 9–28), which is accessed in the *Grading* tab>Create Grading panel.

Figure 9–28

Some of the more commonly used tools include:

- (Set the Grading Group): Enables you to consolidate grading objects into a single collection to generate a grading group surface for volume computations.

- Grade to Distance **(Criteria drop-down list):** Enables you to select specific criteria in a given criteria set.

- (Create Grading): Generates a grading solution from the currently selected criteria.

- (Edit Grading): Enables you to change the grading parameters after a solution has been generated.

- (Grading Volume Tools): Opens the Grading Volume Tools toolbar, which provides cut and fill information about the grading group, and adjustment tools.

Practice 9c | Create Grading Groups

Practice Objective

* Create grading objects to design the finished ground and display the finished ground contours.

Task 1 - Create a grading object that grades to a surface.

The baseball field will have a grade of 4% for 10', then a 10' buffer going up 1.5' in elevation, and then grade to the existing site surface.

1. Continue working with the drawing from the previous practice or open **GRD1-E.dwg** from the *C:\Civil 3D Projects\Working\ Grading* folder.

2. Select the preset view **Grad-Baseball**. The dark green feature line created in the last practice should be displayed.

3. In the *Home* tab>Create Design panel, expand  Grading and select **Grading Creation Tools**, as shown in Figure 9–29.

Figure 9–29

4. In the Grading Creation Tools, click  (Set Grading Group), as shown in Figure 9–30.

Figure 9–30

5. Select **School Site-A** and click **OK**.

6. In the Create Grading Group, type **Sports** as the name. Do not select the **Automatic surface creation** option, as shown in Figure 9–31. Click **OK**.

Figure 9–31

7. On the left in the Grading Creation Tools, click (Set Target Surface), as shown in Figure 9–32. Select **IDG** and click **OK**.

Figure 9–32

8. In the Grading Creation Tools toolbar, set the grading criteria to **Grade to Distance**, as shown in Figure 9–33.

Figure 9–33

9. In the Grading Creation Tools, click  (Create grading), as shown in Figure 9–34.

Figure 9–34

10. When prompted:

   - To *select the feature*, select the dark green feature line outlining the baseball field.
   - Pick a point to the outside of the feature line for the side to grade.
   - Select **Yes** to apply it to the entire length, and press <Enter>.
   - Type **10** to specify the distance of 10 feet, and press <Enter>.
   - Select **Grade** to specify a format of grade.
   - Type (negative) **-4** to grade down 4% from the feature line, and press <Enter>.

11. In the Grading Creation Tools, set the grading criteria to **Grade to Relative Elevation**, as shown in Figure 9–35.

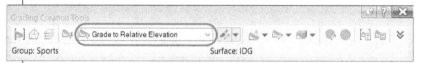

Figure 9–35

12. In the Grading Creation Tools, click  (Create grading), as before.

13. When prompted:

- To *select the feature*, select the dark green feature line outlining the 10' buffer you just created around the baseball field.
- You no longer need to select the side since there is already grading on one side.
- Select **Yes** to apply it to the entire length, and press <Enter>.
- Type (negative) **-1.5** for the Relative Elevation, and press <Enter>.
- Select **Slope** to specify a format of slope.
- Type (negative) **-3** to grade down at a 3:1 slope from the feature line, and press <Enter>.

14. In the Grading Creation Tools toolbar, set the grading criteria to **Grade to Surface**, as shown in Figure 9–36.

Figure 9–36

15. Click  (Create grading).

16. When prompted:

- To *select the feature*, select the outer-most dark green feature line created with the last grading object.
- Select **Yes** to apply it to the entire length.
- Press <Enter> through the remaining prompts, accepting the defaults, which is **Slope** format of *2:00:1* for both cut and fill conditions.
- Close the Grading Creation Tools toolbar.

17. Save the drawing.

Task 2 - Create an infill.

Playing fields are graded for drainage. Grassed surfaces usually have a 1% to 2% minimum slope. The baseball field that you will be working on has a 2% slope across the field with a 4% slope surrounding it, then it steps down 1.5' at a gradual 3:1 slope before turning into a 2:1 slope out to daylight in both cut and fill situations.

If you have difficulty spotting the diamond shape grips, zoom in closer and regenerate the drawing to increase their size.

1. Select one of the grading objects that you created in Task 1 by selecting one of the green or red diamond grips. In the *Grading* contextual tab>Modify panel, click (Grading Group Properties).

2. In the *Information* tab, select the **Automatic Surface Creation** option. Accept the defaults in the Create Surface dialog box and click **OK**. Select the **Volume Base Surface** option and select **IDG** as the base surface, as shown in Figure 9–37. Click **OK**.

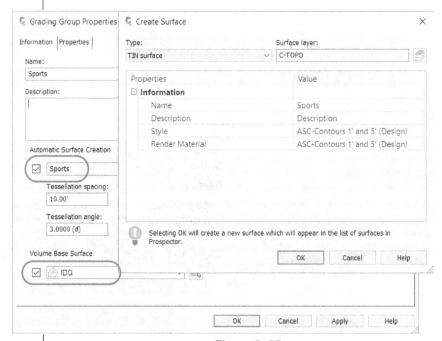

Figure 9–37

3. Save the drawing. (Before opening the Object Viewer in the next step, it is always prudent to save the drawing.)

4. Select the baseball field surface (select one of its contour lines) and also select one of the grading diamond grips.

5. In the *Surface* contextual tab, click 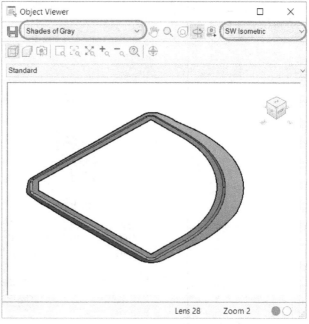 (Object Viewer). Set the view direction to **SW Isometric** and the style to **Shades of Gray**. Note the hole in the surface, as shown in Figure 9–38. Press <Esc> twice to close the Object Viewer and release the selection.

Figure 9–38

Alternatively, within the Grading Creation Tools toolbar, select Create Grading Infill.

6. In the *Home* tab>Create Design panel, expand  (Grading) and click **Create Grading Infill**, as shown in Figure 9–39.

Figure 9–39

7. Pick a point in the middle of the baseball field grading object and press <Enter>. Contours should fill in the middle, as shown in Figure 9–40.

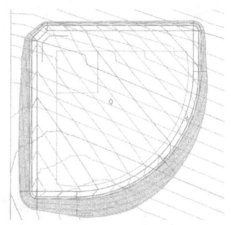

Figure 9–40

Note that the ball field is all in cut format, because you based the elevations on the **Existing-Site** surface, but you graded to the **IDG** surface. You need to raise the grading incrementally until you have a condition that suits the side better.

8. Select the original feature line, as shown in Figure 9–41. From the *Feature Line* contextual tab, launch the Elevation Editor.

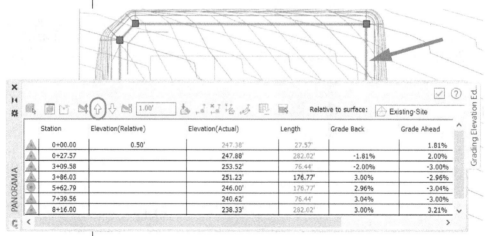

Station	Elevation(Relative)	Elevation(Actual)	Length	Grade Back	Grade Ahead
0+00.00	0.50'	247.38'	27.57'		1.81%
0+27.57		247.88'	282.02'	-1.81%	2.00%
3+09.58		253.52'	76.44'	-2.00%	-3.00%
3+86.03		251.23'	176.77'	3.00%	-2.96%
5+62.79		246.00'	176.77'	2.96%	-3.04%
7+39.56		240.62'	76.44'	3.04%	-3.00%
8+16.00		238.33'	282.02'	3.00%	3.21%

Figure 9–41

9. Click the Up arrow to raise the feature line by 1 foot. Note the entire grading raises since it is all connected. The elevations in the Elevation Editor also update.

10. Click the Up arrow two more times and note the changes.

11. For the *Elevation (Relative)* for Station 0+00, type in **10** and press <Enter>. Close the Elevation Editor.

12. Once again, check out the surface with the Object Viewer as you did before. Now you can clearly see the infill, as shown in Figure 9–42.

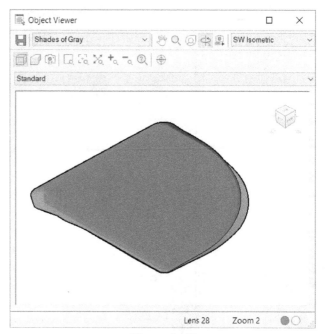

Figure 9–42

13. Save the drawing.

Task 3 - Grade the soccer field.

---

1. Select the preset view **Grad-Soccer**.

2. Select the feature line shown in Figure 9–43. From the *Feature Line* contextual tab, launch the Elevation Editor.

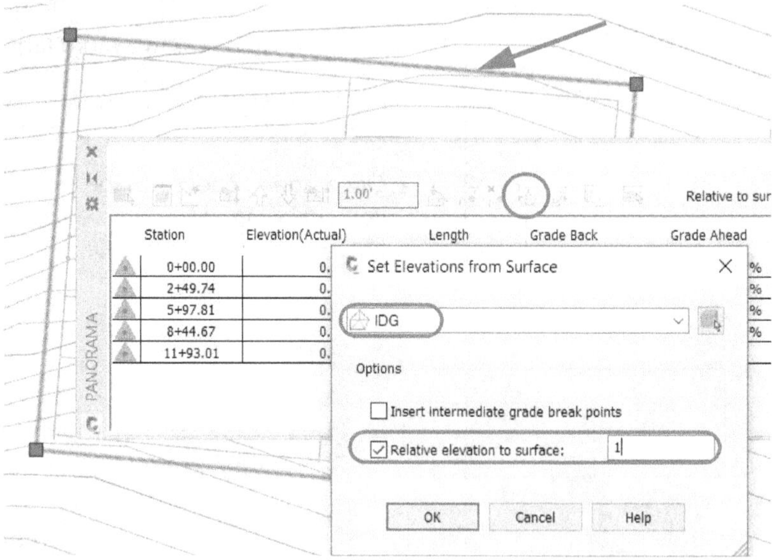

Figure 9–43

3. Click (Elevations from surface). In the Set Elevations from Surface dialog box, select **IDG** for the surface and set it relative to surface by **1.00'**, as shown above in Figure 9–43.

4. Click (Flatten Grade or Elevation). In the Flatten dialog box, select **Constant Elevation**, as shown in Figure 9–44.

Figure 9–44

5. Click **OK** to close the Flatten dialog box.

6. Close the Elevation Editor.

7. With the feature line still selected, launch the (Grading Creation Tools) from the *Feature Line* contextual tab>Launch Pad panel (right-hand side).

8. Do the following:

   - Ensure that the *Grading Group* is set to **Sports**.
   - Ensure the *Surface* is set to **IDG**.
   - *Grade to Distance* to the outside at a distance **10'** at a grade of (negative) **-4** for the entire length.
   - *Grade to Surface* for the entire length at the default values.

9. Create a grading infill for the soccer field as you have done earlier.

10. Save the drawing.

11. Select the preset view **Grad-School**.

12. Select the school footprint feature line.

13. From the *Feature Line* contextual tab, launch the Elevation Editor. Click (Elevations from surface) from the *Feature Line* contextual tab. In the Set Elevations from Surface dialog box, select **IDG** for the surface and set it relative to surface by **2.00'**.

14. You will not be grading this feature line just yet, so for now, just save the drawing.

9.5 Modifying Autodesk Civil 3D Grading

Grading Styles

A grading style defines how the grading solution displays in the drawing window. The components of a grading style include the grading marker (by default, a diamond shaped grip) for selecting the grading solution, slope patterns, and solution's layers and their properties.

Feature Line Labels

Feature lines have their own family of labels, which can be accessed in the *Annotate* tab>Add Labels panel, by expanding Feature Line and selecting the **Add Feature Line Labels** command (e.g., a label indicating grade and distance).

Grading Criteria

Grading methods (to a surface, at a specific distance and slope, etc.) are organized inside Autodesk Civil 3D drawings as grading criteria. Criteria include the grading method, slope projection, and conflict resolution properties, as shown in Figure 9–45.

- The *Grading Method* properties define what to grade to. Targets can include *Surface*, *Elevation*, *Relative Elevations*, or *Distance*. If the method uses a distance, you need to specify a default distance. If the method is to a surface, you can specify whether it is only for cut or fill, for both cut and fill, or for a distance. Each setting changes the information that the Grading Method needs to complete its task.

- The *Slope Projection* properties assign the format of the slope (e.g., slope or grade) and the default values.

- The *Conflict Resolution* properties define how to resolve problem areas, such as internal corners that overlap.

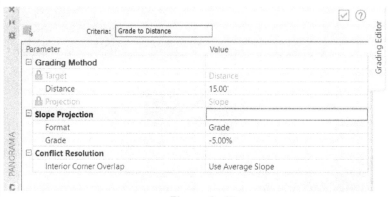

Figure 9–45

Grading Criteria Set

Criteria sets are collections of grading criteria that are useful to group together for a specific task. For example, you can create different sets for residential or commercial site grading, etc. These sets (and the criteria within them) can be found in the Toolspace, *Settings* tab under the *Grading* collection.

In this training guide, you only work with the Basic criteria set provided in the default Autodesk Civil 3D templates.

Modifying Grading

To modify an existing grading object, select the diamond grip at the center of the grading object and click 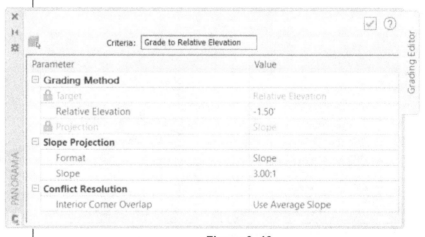 (Edit Grading) or

(Grading Editor) in the *Grading* contextual tab>Modify panel.

*If you have problems finding the diamond grip, zoom out and **REGEN** the drawing. This will resize the diamond grips.*

The **Edit Grading** command enables you to make changes to the grading object using the Command Line and similar prompts to when you first created the grading object. The **Grading Editor** opens the Panorama window in which you can modify any part of the grading parameters without needing to go through the full list of options as you would using the **Edit Grading** command. The Grading Editor Panorama is shown in Figure 9–46.

Parameter	Value
⊟ **Grading Method**	
🔒 Target	Relative Elevation
Relative Elevation	-1.50'
🔒 Projection	Slope
⊟ **Slope Projection**	
Format	Slope
Slope	3.00:1
⊟ **Conflict Resolution**	
Interior Corner Overlap	Use Average Slope

Criteria: Grade to Relative Elevation

Figure 9–46

Grading Volumes

The Grading Volume Tools toolbar (shown in Figure 9–47) displays the volume for all or selected grading solutions in a group. One tool raises or lowers all of the members of a grading group by an incremental value. The icon at the far right forces the group or selected grading solution to determine which elevations it needs for balance. Balance is a design that creates as much excavation material as required to fill in depressions in the design area.

- The volumes in the Grading Volume Tools toolbar are dynamically linked to the grading objects.

- Grading volumes change when editing one or all of the grading group objects.

Figure 9–47

Practice 9d

Modify Grading and Calculate Volumes

Practice Objective

- Modify a grading group using the Grading editor and **Grading Volume** tools.

Task 1 - Modify the grading criteria of a grading object.

For safety reasons, it has been decided to extend the 4% grade encompassing the baseball field from 10' to 15' before starting the 1.5' drop and the steep 2:1 slope going out to daylight. The grade will also change from 4% to 5%. You can accomplish this change using the Grading Editor.

1. Continue working with the drawing from the previous practice or open **GRD1-F.dwg** from the *C:\Civil 3D Projects\Working\Grading* folder.

2. Select the preset view **Grad-Baseball**.

If you have difficulty spotting the diamond shape grips, zoom in closer and regenerate the drawing to increase their size.

3. Select the diamond representing the 4% slope for 10 feet grading object, as shown in Figure 9–48. In the *Grading* contextual tab>Modify panel, click ✦ (Grading Editor).

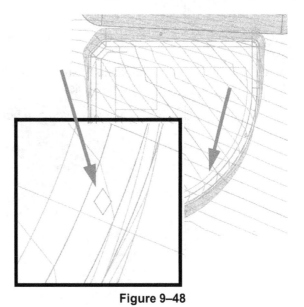

Figure 9–48

Note: *Pausing after changing each value ensures that the computer can process the changes, and can help to avoid crashing.*

4. In the Grading Editor Panorama, set the *Distance* to **15'** and the *Grade* to **-5%**, as shown in Figure 9–49. Click ☑ to accept the changes.

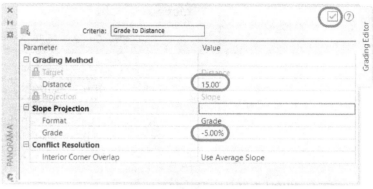

Figure 9–49

5. Save the drawing.

Task 2 - Calculate and balance the volume of a grading group.

In this task, you will calculate the volume of the grading group, and then adjust the elevation of the entire group to balance the volume across the grading area.

1. Select any one of the diamonds representing one of the grading objects in the Sports grading group. In the *Grading* contextual tab>Grading Tools panel, click ▨ (Grading Volume Tools).

2. Zoom out so you see both the soccer and baseball fields.

You may have to select Entire Group for the display to populate.

3. Expand the **Grading Volume Tools** by clicking

   (Chevron). Select **Selection** (if not already selected) to include it in the calculation, as shown in Figure 9–50.

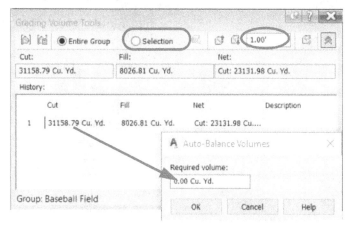

Figure 9–50

4. In the Grading Volume Tools, click (Automatically raise/lower to balance). You want to balance the field, so keep the **Required Volume** at *0.00.* In the drawing, you will note that only the baseball field was changed.

5. Select **Entire Group** so that both fields will be manipulated. Leave the elevation change increment at **1.00'** and click

   (Raise selected grade features) three times, each time noting the updated volume, then lower it twice by clicking

   (Lower selected grade features), as shown in Figure 9–51.

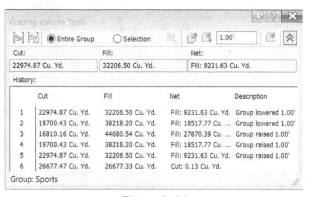

Figure 9–51

6. Save the drawing.

Task 3 - Create the FG surface.

1. In the Toolspace, *Prospector* tab, select **Surfaces**, right-click, and select **Create Surface**.

2. In the Create Surface dialog box, set the following (as shown in Figure 9–52):

    - *Type*: **TIN surface**
    - *Name*: **FG**
    - *Description*: **Final Design Surface**
    - *Style*: **ASC-Contours 2' and 10' (Design)**
    - *Render Material:* **Sitework.Planting.Grass.Thick**

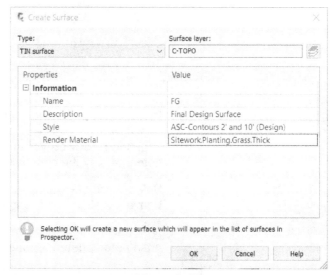

Figure 9–52

3. Click **OK** to accept the changes and close the dialog box.

4. Expand the *FG* surfaces collection and the *Definition* collection.

5. Right-click on **Edit** and select **Paste Surface...**.

6. In the Select Surface to Paste dialog box, select the following surfaces, as shown in Figure 9–53:

- **IDG**
- **Jeffries Ranch Rd-Top**
- **Roundabout (Jeffries Ranch - Rand Blvd) Top**
- **Sports**

Figure 9–53

7. Click **OK** to close the Select Surface to Paste dialog box.

8. The surfaces are built, but the pasting order is incorrect, as shown on the left in Figure 9–54.

Figure 9–54

(The image on the right shows the surfaces after they have been rebuilt correctly.)

9. For clarity's sake, set the surface style of all surfaces except for **FG** to **_No Display**. An easy way to do this is to select the surfaces in the surfaces preview area in the Prospector, then right-click on the *Style* header and select **Edit...**, as shown in Figure 9–55.

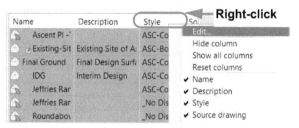

Figure 9–55

10. Select the **FG** surface in the list, right-click, and select **Surface Properties**.

11. In the lower half of the *Definition* tab, rearrange the paste order by selecting a surface and using the arrows on the left to move them. They need to be in the order the surfaces were created, as shown in Figure 9–56:

- **Roundabout (Jeffries Ranch - Rand Blvd) Top**
- **IDG**
- **Jeffries Ranch Rd-Top**
- **Sports**

Figure 9–56

12. Click **OK** to close the Surface Properties dialog box. When prompted, choose to rebuild the surfaces.

13. The surfaces are rebuilt correctly now, as shown on the right in Figure 9–54 (above).

14. With the **FG** surface still selected, in the *Surface* contextual tab>Modify panel>Add Data drop-down list, select **Breaklines**.

15. Enter **School-FL** as a description, leave all other options as their defaults, and click **OK** to close the Surface Properties dialog box.

16. Select the feature line around the school and press <Enter> to finish your selection.

17. Rebuild the surface, if needed. The surface now has a platform for the school, but no organized grading, as shown in Figure 9–57. Where the feature line intersects the surface, a hard edge is produced, like a fold in the surface.

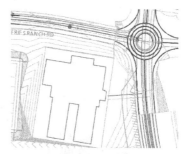

Figure 9–57

18. Save the drawing. (Before opening the Object Viewer in the next step, it is always prudent to save the drawing.)

19. Check out the surface with the Object Viewer as you did before. You can now clearly see the infill, as shown in Figure 9–58.

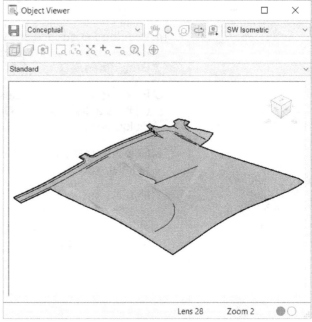

Figure 9–58

20. For initial planning purposes, this will suffice. A lot more work will need to be done to refine the final ground, such as proper grading around the school and correcting the jagged contours in the southeast corner.

Task 4 - (Optional) Create a volume surface.

Now that you have a primarily final surface, you can get an idea of the overall volumes for the entire site. You already discovered finding the volumes of grading groups or individual grading objects, this will calculate the volumes of the extents of the final ground you have established.

1. In the *Analyze* tab>Volumes and Materials panel, click

     (Volumes Dashboard).

2. Click  (Create new volume surface) to create a new volume surface, as shown in Figure 9–59.

Figure 9–59

3. In the Create Surface dialog box, set the following, as shown in Figure 9–60:

- *Name:* **Vol-School Site**
- *Description:* **Volume of EG-FG for school site**
- *Style:* **ASC-Cut and Fill Banding 1' Intervals**
- *Base Surface:* **Existing-Site**
- *Comparison Surface:* **FG**

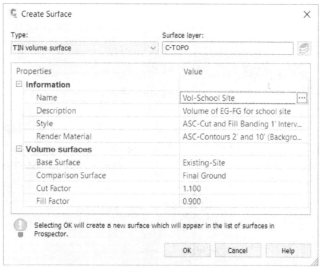

Figure 9–60

4. Click **OK** to close the Create Surface dialog box. The new volume surface is displayed in a series of green and red blotches. The reason is the intervals for the elevation ranges are too small.

5. Select the volume surface and launch **Surface Properties**.

6. On the Analyze tab of the Surface Properties dialog box, do the following, as shown in Figure 9–61:

- Set *Create ranges by:* to **Range interval with datum**.
- Set the number of intervals to **5**. Note: Do not press <Enter> when entering 5 as this will close the dialog box.

- Click 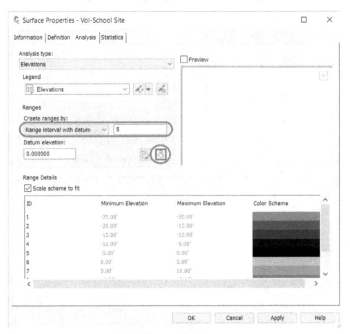 (Run Analysis) to run the analysis.

Figure 9–61

A Cut / Fill table could also be generated, which would be useful.

7. Click **OK** to close the Surface Properties dialog box. The surface will rebuild, as shown in Figure 9–62.

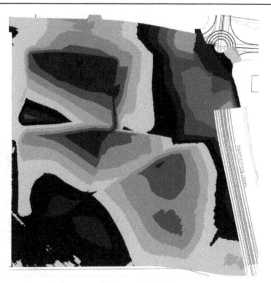

Figure 9–62

8. Save the drawing.

9. (Optional) Save the drawing as **<Your Initials>-Grading-Complete.dwg** in the *C:\Civil 3D Projects\References\ DWG\Proposed* folder.

See the Project Management for how to work with Data Shortcuts.

10. Update the relative paths of the referenced drawings in the alert box.

11. (Optional) Add the FG surface to the project as a surface Data Shortcut.

Chapter Review Questions

1. When creating a feature line from objects, which of the following cannot be used to create a feature line?

   a. Lines or arcs

   b. Circles

   c. Polylines or 3D polylines

   d. XREF

2. How do you ensure that you do not create a hole in the middle of your surface when using grading objects to create the finished ground contours?

   a. Grade to the inside.

   b. You cannot prevent holes in grading group surfaces.

   c. Create infill.

   d. Balance the Volumes.

3. What is the best method of editing a grading object without needing to go through each prompt?

   a. Grading Editor

   b. Edit Grading

   c. Delete the grading object and recreate it.

   d. Grip edit the resulting feature lines.

4. The grading object and the feature line have to be in the same site to be able to work together.

   a. True

   b. False

5. In the Grading Elevation Editor, you can edit...

   a. Grading Objects

   b. Finished Ground Profiles

   c. Pipe Structures

   d. Feature Lines

Command Summary

Button	Command	Location
	Auto Balance	• **Contextual Toolbar:** Grading Volume Tools
	Create Feature Line	• **Ribbon:** *Home* tab>Create Design panel • **Command Prompt:** drawfeatureline
	Create Feature Lines from Corridor	• **Ribbon:** *Home* tab>Create Design panel • **Command Prompt:** createfeaturelinefromcorridor
	Create Feature Line From Objects	• **Ribbon:** *Home* tab>Create Design panel • **Command Prompt:** createfeaturelines
	Edit Elevations	• **Contextual Ribbon:** *Feature Line* tab> Modify panel
	Edit Grading	• **Contextual Ribbon:** *Grading* tab> Modify panel • **Command Prompt:** editgrading
	Elevation Editor	• **Contextual Ribbon:** *Feature Line* tab> Edit Elevations panel • **Command Prompt:** gradingeleveditor
	Grading Creation Tools	• **Ribbon:** *Home* tab>Create Design panel • **Command Prompt:** gradingtools
	Grading Editor	• **Contextual Ribbon:** *Grading* tab> Modify panel • **Command Prompt:** gradingeditor
	Grading Volume Tools	• **Contextual Ribbon:** *Grading* tab> Grading Tools panel • **Command Prompt:** gradingvolumetools
	Lower Grading Features	• **Contextual Toolbar:** Grading Volume Tools
	Raise Grading Features	• **Contextual Toolbar:** Grading Volume Tools

Pipe Networks

In this chapter, you will learn how to create pipe networks for both gravity-fed pipes and pressurized pipes. You will also learn how to create and apply rules to gravity-fed pipes to ensure that they meet design specifications. Then, you will annotate the pipe networks to communicate the full design intent to contractors and other stakeholders.

Learning Objectives in This Chapter

- List the types of utility networks that can be designed in the Autodesk Civil 3D software.
- Configure pipe network and pressure pipe network settings.
- Create pipe networks from objects in the drawing or external reference file.
- Create and edit pressure or gravity fed pipe networks using various tools.
- Communicate important design information about pipe networks by adding labels to plan and profile views and creating reports.

10.1 Pipes Overview

The Autodesk® Civil 3D® software's utility design system is often referred to as Autodesk Civil 3D Pipes.

- You can create pipe networks in Autodesk Civil 3D drawings to represent storm sewers, sanitary sewers, pressure pipes, etc. Autodesk Civil 3D networks can model multiple, connected trunk lines and laterals as part of the same system.

- In the Autodesk Civil 3D software, pipes are geared for gravity flow systems (sewers) and pressurized pipes (water). Electrical ducts, and similar types of conduit can also be modeled, but require special attention.

- Gravity flow systems can be categorized as *Drainage* or *Sanitary*, with the default categorization being *Undefined.*

- Pipes are created in plan view interactively or by converting other linework into pipes (including 2D and 3D polylines and feature lines). Pipes can also be imported from an AutoCAD® Map 3D® software's industry model and through Autodesk LandXML.

- Pipe networks can be created from customized part lists, styles, and rules that can help lay them out (and display them) appropriately.

- Once created, pipe networks can be displayed in profile and section views. Pipes can be edited in plan or profile, and using layout tools, such as the Grid View vista (a spreadsheet-like view of pipe network pipes and structures). Changes made in plan, profile, or Grid View automatically update all other displays.

- The Autodesk Civil 3D software includes an interference check utility to search for possible conflicts between pipe networks only. If interference checking is required of other objects, Autodesk Navisworks is required.

- The Autodesk Civil 3D software includes hydrology or hydraulic (H&H) calculators with the Autodesk Storm and Sanitary Analysis program, Hydraflow Express, the Hydraflow Hydrographs, and the Hydraflow Storm Sewer applications available in the *Analyze* tab. These programs run outside of Autodesk Civil 3D but are included in the overall package. Without these applications, the system is set up to automate the drafting of utility systems, but not to analyze them or suggest pipe sizes.

- Many 3rd party H&H applications also support the Autodesk LandXML transfer of networks configured in the Autodesk Civil 3D software. Therefore, a conceptual layout might be created in the Autodesk Civil 3D software, exported to an .STM file for analysis and adjustment, and then reinserted into the Autodesk Civil 3D software using Autodesk LandXML or the .STM file format.

- You can also perform some of these H&H analysis tools directly within Civil 3D.

- This Fundamentals course does not cover any of these external H&H applications or the analysis which can be done within the Autodesk Civil 3D program.

- The system variable **PipeNetworkSyncMode** controls how the synchronization of data-referenced pipe networks behaves when you open a host drawing. It determines if the pipe networks are always updated or updated only on demand, or if only modified or new pipe parts are updated.

10.2 Pipes Configuration

The Toolspace, *Settings* tab contains values and styles affecting pipe networks. The *Parts Lists* and *Pipe Rules* are the most important settings. Parts Lists contain typical pipes, fittings, appurtenances, and structures for a utility. Pipe Rules trigger error alerts if pipes/structures are not created in accordance with predefined constraints, such as the minimum or maximum pipe length or slope.

Edit Drawing Settings

The Edit Drawing Settings dialog box contains values affecting the pipe layout layers (e.g., pipe networks, fittings, profiles, and section views).

Pipe Network Feature Settings

The Pipe Network Edit Feature Settings dialog box contains values that assign styles, set the pipe network naming convention, set the default pipe and structure rules, and set the default location for pipe and structure labels. To open the Edit Feature Settings dialog box, right-click on Settings in the *Pipe Network* collection, and select **Edit Feature Settings**. The dialog box is shown in Figure 10–1.

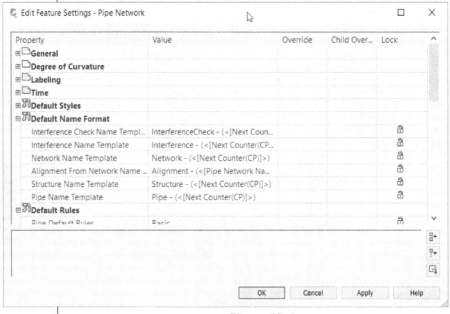

Figure 10–1

Pipe Catalog

The Autodesk Civil 3D software includes standard catalogs in both Imperial and Metric units. Catalog specifications define the size and shape of the underground structures and pipes for sanitary or storm gravity systems.

- The *Imperial Pipes* folder contains **Imperial Pipes.htm**, which displays the components of the Pipe catalog.
- The Pipe catalog includes circular, egg, elliptical, and rectangular shapes. For each pipe shape, the catalog includes inner and outer pipe diameters and wall thicknesses.

Pipe catalog components can be edited by selecting **Modify> Pipe network>Parts List>Part Builder**.

Structure Catalog

The Structure catalog includes specifications for inlets, junction structures (circular, rectangular, or eccentric) with or without frames, and simple junction shapes (rectangular or circular). Additional structures can be created by using the Infrastructure Parts Editor. This is a separate program that runs outside of Civil 3D. The Structure catalog consists of tables and lists that define allowable sizes, thicknesses, and heights.

Pressure Pipe Catalog

The Pressure Pipe Catalog contains configuration files for many different types of pressure pipes, materials, fittings, and appurtenances. Furthermore, additional parts can be created by using the Infrastructure Parts Editor. This is a separate program that runs outside of Civil 3D.

Pipe Network Parts Lists

While the catalogs are shared between multiple projects (and multiple users), each Autodesk Civil 3D drawing can contain any number of Part Lists that are specific to that drawing.

Part Lists are populated with pipes and structures from the catalog and are organized for a specific task (such as Sanitary Sewer and Drain).

- Parts Lists are in the Toolspace, *Settings* tab under the *Pipe Network* collection and *Pressure Network* collection, as shown in Figure 10–2.

- To display a parts list, right-click on its name and select **Edit**.

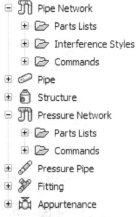

Figure 10–2

The Pipe Network parts list has typical pipe sizes in the *Pipes* tab and typical structures in the *Structure* tab, as shown in Figure 10–3. If required, you can change a pipe or structure size list, or add a new part type.

An important setting for each tab is *Rules*. This is discussed in greater detail later in this chapter.

Render Material affects how the pipes and structures display in 3D.

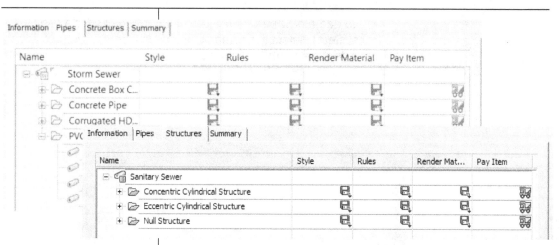

Figure 10–3

- To add a pipe size or structure size, select the part type heading, right-click, and select **Add a part size**. Then select a new part size from the size list, as shown in Figure 10–4.

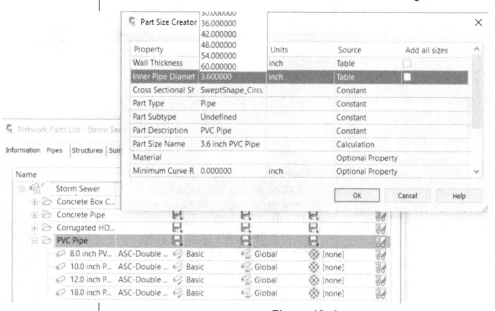

Figure 10–4

- To add a new part family (e.g., concrete pipes for a sanitary system), select the name of the part list, right-click, and select **Add a part family**. Then select a new part family from the list of available parts in the catalog, as shown in Figure 10–5.

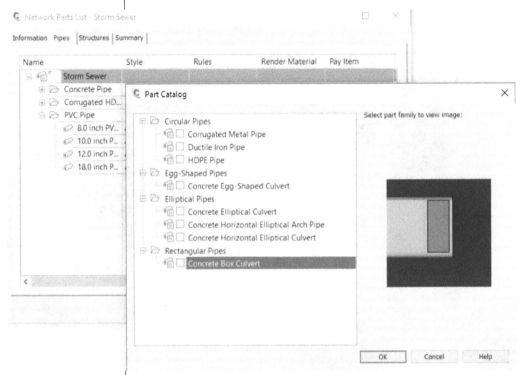

Figure 10–5

The *Pressure Network* parts list has typical pipe sizes in the *Pressure Pipes* tab, typical fitting sizes in the *Fittings* tab, and typical appurtenance sizes in the *Appurtenances* tab, as shown in Figure 10–6. If required, you can change any of the size lists, or add a new part type. *Render Material* affects how the various parts display in 3D.

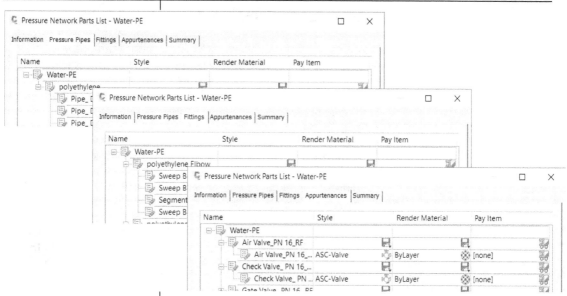

Figure 10–6

Pipe and Structure Styles

The pipe style defines how a pipe displays in plan, profile, and section views. The most used tab of a Pipe Style is the *Display* tab. By toggling on or off the Component display, a style affects how a network displays in the drawing window (e.g., as a single or double line), its layer name, and color.

A structure style defines how a structure displays in plan, profile and section views. The plan settings include the plan view symbol and how a structure displays in profile and section views (the outline of the 3D shape).

Pipe styles include the **Clean up Pipe to Pipe Intersections** option for networks, where one pipe connects to another (rather than to a structure). This enables the pipes to seem to join together. For this option to work, the pipes must be connected with a *null* structure.

Pipe and Structure Rules

Since pipes and structures often need more than one rule applied to them, individual rules are organized into collections called **rule sets**. Then the rules are prioritized from most important to least important by organizing the order in which they display in the list. You can have different sets for different types of pipe, sizes, and/or systems.

- Pipe rules define minimum/maximum slopes, cover, minimum/maximum pipe segment length, how pipes of different sizes align and how they are truncated when attached to a structure.

- Pipe rule sets are located in the Toolspace, *Settings* tab, in the *Pipe Rule Set* collection, as shown in Figure 10–7. To display or edit a rule set, right-click on it and select **Edit**.

Figure 10–7

- Structure rules define the across structure drop's default value, maximum value, maximum pipe size and the sump depth.

- Structure rule sets are located in the Toolspace, *Settings* tab, under the *Structure Rule Set* collection.

Pressure Networks do not use rules. They have other means of checking for conformity to design conditions.

Some pipe and structure rules directly control the layout of new pipes and structures, such as minimum and maximum slope. Some rules are checks that are made after creation, such as maximum pipe length. Rules, such as maximum pipe length, do not prevent you from creating a pipe that is over the maximum length. However, if a pipe is over the maximum length, you are prompted with a warning in the Toolspace, *Prospector* tab and in the Pipe Network vistas, as shown in Figure 10–8.

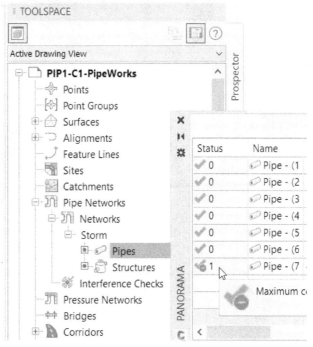

Figure 10–8

Reapplying Pipe Rules

Structure Invert Out elevations are automatically calculated based on the given rules when the structure is first created. Therefore, if new connecting pipes are added to a structure below the lowest invert, the outlet is not automatically lowered until you click ⬚ (Apply Rules) in the *Modify* tab>Pipe Network>Modify panel. An example is shown in Figure 10–9.

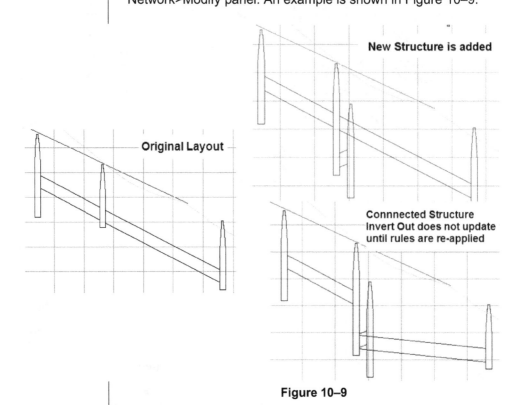

New Structure is added

Original Layout

Connnected Structure Invert Out does not update until rules are re-applied

Figure 10–9

Pipe Layers

Unlike most Autodesk Civil 3D objects, pipe network layers typically need to be manually reassigned when a pipe network is created. Layers need to be assigned for pipes and structures in plan, profile, and section views. For example, the default Autodesk Civil 3D templates automatically map to layers appropriate for storm drainage structures when using the Pipe Network Creation Tools and water structures when using the Pressure Pipe Creation Tools. The Pipe Network Layers dialog boxes are shown in Figure 10–10.

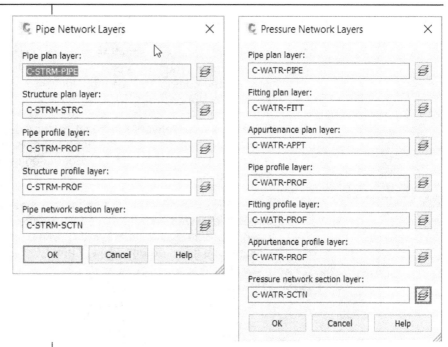

Figure 10–10

If creating a sanitary sewer line, each one needs to be remapped to layers specific to sanitary sewer utilities, such as the examples shown in Figure 10–11.

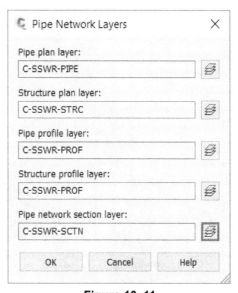

Figure 10–11

Pressure Pipe Parts Lists

As with the Pipe and Structure catalogs, pressure pipes can be shared among multiple projects (and multiple users). They can contain any number of Pressure Network Parts Lists that are specific to that drawing.

Each Pressure Network Parts List can contain multiple catalogs for different materials, allowing for one pressure network to have a combination of parts with different materials, as shown in Figure 10–12.

When parts of a catalog are used within a network, the *Status* states it is **In Use** and there is a lock symbol. If no parts are used, the *Status* states it is **Loaded** with a green checkmark. This means it can be unloaded at any time.

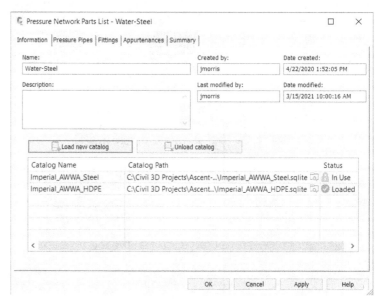

Figure 10–12

Practice 10a | Configuring Pipe Networks

Practice Objective

- Create a new reference template for pipe networks with settings for your organization.

Task 1 - Review the storm drain parts list and rules.

Before creating a network, you should become familiar with the configuration you are about to use. While you have already attached a reference template for the styles, now that you are working on pipe networks, you need to create and attach another reference template for pipes.

1. Start a new drawing from **ASC-Base-Styles.dwt**. In the *C:\Civil 3D Projects\Ascent-Config* folder, save the file as **XXX-Pipe-Styles.DWG** (substitute your initials for XXX) in the same folder.

2. In the Toolspace, *Settings* tab, expand the *Pipe Network* collection, expand the *Parts Lists* collection, right-click on the *Storm Sewer* part list and select **Edit...**.

3. In the *Pipes* tab, the parts list currently contains a large number of concrete pipes. They are all assigned to use the Basic rule set and a pipe style that displays double lines in plan view, as shown in Figure 10–13.

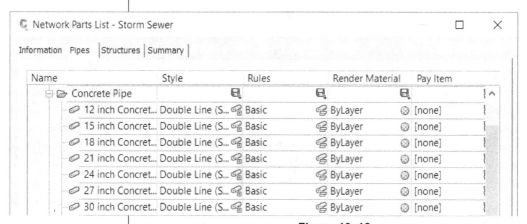

Figure 10–13

4. You don't need all these sizes. Click on the ones you want to remove, right-click and select **Delete**, as shown in Figure 10–14 (note that you can only do this one at a time). Ensure that you keep the 12", 15", 21", 30", and 60" parts.

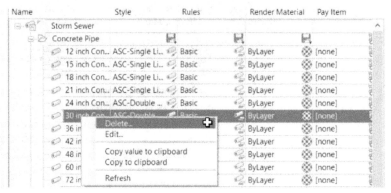

Figure 10–14

5. Change the Styles of the smaller diameter pipes to be Single Lines. Select the pipes up to size 21" and select 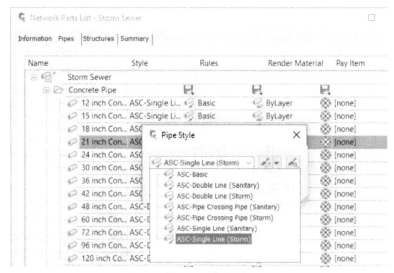 (Pipe Style) and select *ASC-Single Line (Storm)* from the list, as shown in Figure 10–15. (You can only select one at a time.)

Figure 10–15

6. Delete the **Concrete Elliptical Culvert** type (if present) by right-clicking on it and selecting *Delete....* Confirm that you want to delete this Pipe Type.

7. To add another Pipe type, under **Network Parts List - Storm Sewer**, right-click on **Storm Sewer** and select **Add part family…**, as shown in Figure 10–16.

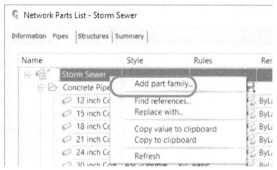

Figure 10–16

8. In the Parts catalog, select **PVC Pipe**, as shown in Figure 10–17. Click **OK** to close the dialog box. Note that the Pipe Parts already in your Parts List do not show in this list.

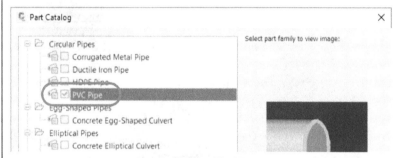

Figure 10–17

9. To add sizes to the part family, select **PVC Pipe**, right-click, and select **Add part size…**, as shown in Figure 10–18.

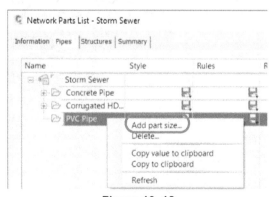

Figure 10–18

10. Select and add the pipe sizes: **8**, **10**, **12**, and **18**. Note that you cannot select all four of these sizes. You will need to add each one separately. To add part sizes, you can select individual sizes in the Value drop-down list (or select the checkbox in the *Add all sizes* column to add all of the available sizes), as shown in Figure 10–19. Ensure that the part Material is set to **PVC**. Click **OK** to add each one.

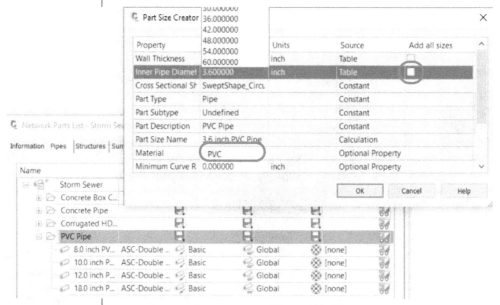

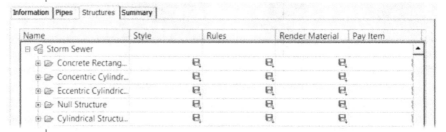

Figure 10–19

11. Change the Pipe Styles of the 8.0" and 10.0" PVC pipes to **ASC-Single Line (Storm)** as you had done previously.

12. Select the *Structures* tab. The parts list includes a number of headwalls of different sizes, and catch basins and manholes. Each of these is assigned styles and rules specific to each type, as shown in Figure 10–20.

Information	Pipes	Structures	Summary			
Name		Style	Rules	Render Material	Pay Item	
⊟ Storm Sewer						▲
⊞ Concrete Rectang...						
⊞ Concentric Cylindr...						
⊞ Eccentric Cylindric...						
⊞ Null Structure						
⊞ Cylindrical Structu...						

Figure 10–20

13. As you did with the Pipes, add a Structure Part Family by right-clicking on Storm Sewer and selecting the **Concrete Flared End Section**, as shown in Figure 10–21.

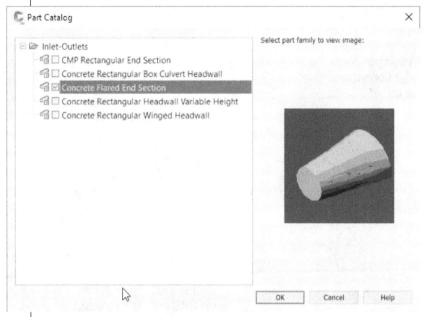

Figure 10–21

14. Add **12"** as the part size and click **OK** to exit the Part Catalog.

15. Click **OK** to exit.

16. In the Toolspace, *Settings* tab, expand the *Structure* collection, expand the *Structure Rule Set* collection, right-click on the **Basic** rule set and select **Edit...**, as shown in Figure 10–22.

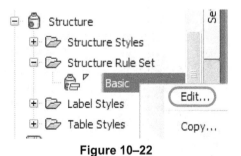

Figure 10–22

Using the arrows at the right side of the Rules tab enables you to prioritize the rules. The rules are processed sequentially from bottom to top. Therefore, place the most important rule at the top of the list.

For this Manhole, in the **Maximum pipe size check** rule you can use a maximum pipe diameter of **4'**. In the Pipe Drop Across Structure rule, you can have elevations based on **Inverts** and a drop across the manhole of **0.10'** with a **3'** maximum interior drop, as shown in Figure 10–23.

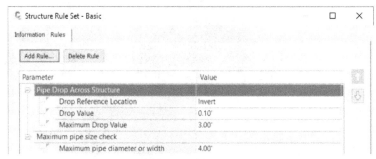

Figure 10–23

17. Review and click **Cancel** to exit without changes.

Task 2 - Review a pressure network parts list.

---

1. Continue working with the drawing from the previous task or open **C:\Civil 3D Projects\Ascent-Config\ ASC-Pipe-Styles-1.dwg**

2. In the Toolspace, *Settings* tab, expand the *Pressure Network* collection, expand the *Parts Lists* collection, right-click on the **Water-Steel** part list and select **Edit...**, as shown in Figure 10–24.

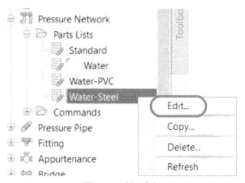

Figure 10–24

If you get an error about a missing catalog, consult the Configuration Changes section in the Preface for proper configuration.

3. In the *Pressure Pipes* tab, review the available pipe sizes. To the right of the ductile iron family, select the disk to change all of the styles to **ASC-Double Line (Water)**, as shown in Figure 10–25.

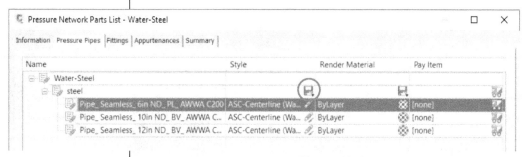

Figure 10–25

4. In the *Fittings* tab, review the available fittings. To the right of each family, select the disk to change all of the styles to **ASC-Fitting**, as shown in Figure 10–26.

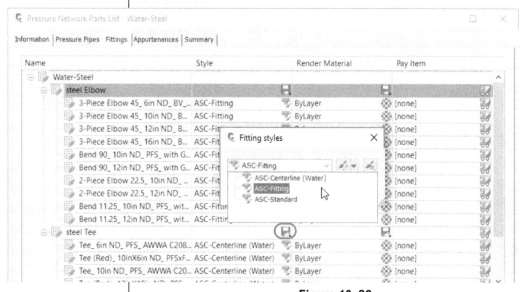

Figure 10–26

5. In the *Appurtenances* tab, review the available valves. To the right of each family, select the disk to set the style to **ASC-Valve**, as shown in Figure 10–27.

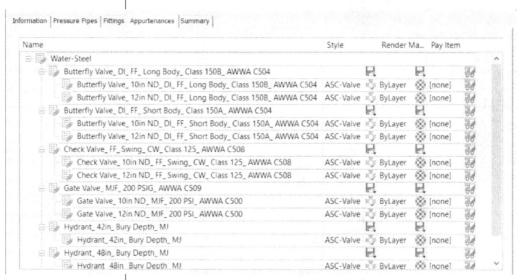

Figure 10–27

6. Click **OK** and save the drawing.

10.3 Creating Networks from Objects

In addition to creating networks by layout, a pipe network can be created from a 2D or 3D object, including:

- AutoCAD lines, arcs, and 3D polylines

- AutoCAD 2D polylines and 2D spline polylines

- Civil 3D alignments

- Civil 3D feature lines

- XREFs of any of these listed objects

In the *Home* tab>Pipe Network panel, and click (Create Pipe Network from Object) to start the creation of a pipe network. Next you are prompted to select the object or type **X** and press <Enter> to select objects from an external reference file. Once selected, a flow arrow displays along the pipe network. The flow is set to the direction in which you drew the original entity but you can reverse the direction by selecting **Reverse**. To leave the flow directions set as is, press <Enter> or select **OK**. A Create Pipe Network dialog box opens enabling you to:

- Name the network.
- Set the parts list.
- Select the default pipe and structure to use.
- Set the surface and alignment to reference.

- You can also clean up the drawing as you create the network, by selecting the **Erasing existing entity** option (if the entity is not part of an XREF), as shown in Figure 10–28.

Figure 10–28

Practice 10b

Creating Pipe Networks by Objects

Practice Objective

- Create a pipe network from objects already in the drawing or external reference file.

In a production environment, the line assignment for utilities is often based on the offsets from the Right-Of-Ways boundary. Based on the tools available in the Network Layout Tools toolbar, it is easier to use the AutoCAD tools to lay out the utility line assignments and then convert it to a pipe network. In this task, you will review the process of converting a line assignment to a pipe network.

1. Open **PIP1-A.dwg** from the *C:\Civil 3D Projects\Working\ PipeNetworks* folder.

See the Project Management for how to work with Data Shortcuts.

2. Hover the cursor over the Data Shortcuts and review the tooltip which displays, shown in Figure 10–29. Ensure that your Data Shortcuts are set so the **Working Folder** is set to *C:\Civil 3D Projects\Data Shortcuts\Fundamentals* and the **Data Shortcuts Project Folder** to *Ascent-Development*. If required, right-click on Data Shortcuts to set the **Working Folder** and **Data Shortcuts Project Folder**.

Figure 10–29

The *C:\Civil 3D Projects\Ascent-Config\ASC-Pipe-Styles.DWG* file has been attached as a Reference Style to the drawing, which is similar to the one you created in the previous task.

3. Select the preset view **Pipe-Create**. In the *Home* tab>Create Design panel, expand **Pipe Network**, and click (Create Pipe Network from Object).

4. When prompted to select the object, select XREF in the command option. When prompted to select the XREF object, select the storm line (the red line at the center of the road), as shown in Figure 10–30.

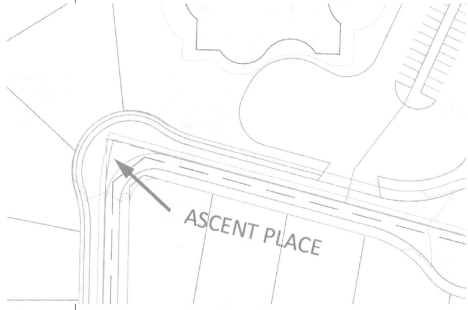

Figure 10–30

5. To ensure that the pipe slopes from the cul-de-sac to the intersection to the south, select **Reverse** to reverse the default flow direction. Press <Enter> to continue.

6. In the Create Pipe Network from Object dialog box, do the following, as shown in Figure 10–31:

- For *Network name*, type **Storm** (you do not want to call it Ascent-Storm because this network will also serve Jeffries Ranch Rd in the next practice).
- In the *Network parts list*, select **Storm Sewer**.
- For *Pipe to create*, select **12.0 inch PVC Pipe**.
- For *Structure to create*, in the **Cylindrical Structure Slab Top Circular Frame** structure family, select **Slab Top Cylindrical Structure 15 dia**.
- For *Surface name*, select **FG**.
- For *Alignment name*, select **Ascent Pl**.
- Clear the **Use vertex elevations** option.
- Click **OK** to accept the selection and close the dialog box.

To find the PVC section, go to the bottom of the list, and then expand it to find the proper size.

Figure 10–31

The Autodesk Civil 3D software has created a Pipe network based on the rules and values entered in the **Create Pipe Network from Objects** dialog box. After you have completed building the network, you will go back and make adjustments to the design inverts, slopes, and part sizes.

7. Save the drawing.

10.4 The Network Layout Toolbar

The Network Layout Tools toolbar contains commands for creating pipe networks by layout (interactively, similar to creating an alignment by layout) and for editing them after creation. This toolbar is opened by selecting *Home* tab>Pipe Network panel, and clicking ⬚ (Pipe Network Creation Tools) or selecting *Modify* tab>Pipe Network panel, and clicking ⬚ (Edit Pipe Network).

Hint: Editing Pipes

If you want to modify or add to a pipe network that you have already defined, use ⬚ (Edit Network) instead of Pipe Network> ⬚ (Create Pipe Network by Layout), as this creates a new network.

The toolbar commands are shown in Figure 10–32.

Figure 10–32

- ⬚ **(Pipe Network Properties):** Enables you to review and edit the properties of a pipe network. These include the default labeling, layers, and default parts list to be used.

- ⬚ **(Select Surface):** Enables you to select a surface model to calculate rim elevations and pipe invert elevations. This can be changed while laying out pipes and structures.

- ⬚ **(Select Alignment):** Enables you to specify an alignment to lay out components by station and offset. The selected alignment can be changed while laying out pipes and structures. The alignment is used only for Quantity Take Off.

- ⬚ **(Parts List):** Enables you to change the current parts list, even in the middle of a layout.

- **38 x 6 x 37 inch Concre** ∨   **24 x 24 inch Concrete** ∨ **(Structure and Pipe drop-down lists):** Enables you to select the next type of structure or pipe to add.

- **(Create flyout):** Enables you to select to lay out pipes only, structures only, or both pipes and structures. When laying out pipes, you graphically select the location of the next structure (or pipe end point if laying out pipes only).

- **(Toggle Upslope/Downslope):** Controls the direction of the next pipe to be laid out in gravity flow networks.

- **(Delete Pipe Network Object):** Enables you to delete a pipe or structure from the network. (**Note:** It is NOT recommended to use the AutoCAD Erase command to delete Pipe Network Objects.)

- **(Pipe Network Vistas):** Opens a grid view where pipes and structures can be reviewed and have their properties edited. Here you can assign meaningful names to pipes and structures (such as **DMH-1**), which can be included in labels.

- **(Undo):** Enables you to undo the last pipe network edit.

Connecting Pipes and Structures

When creating or editing networks with the Network Layout Tools toolbar, you can connect new pipes to previously created structures (within the same network) by hovering the cursor over that structure until the tooltip image displays, as shown in Figure 10–33. Do not place the pipe until you see this tooltip. If doesn't appear, go to the edge of the structure. When displayed, click to connect the new pipe to the structure, otherwise the pipe and structure will be disconnected.

Figure 10–33

New pipes and structures can also be used to divide an existing pipe into two pipes. To do so, hover the cursor over the connection point until the tooltip image displays, as shown in Figure 10–34.

Figure 10–34

Practice 10c | Creating Pipe Networks by Layout

Practice Objective

- Create a gravity fed pipe network by layout.

Task 1 - Create a pipe network by layout.

In this task, you will continue adding to the network using Autodesk Civil 3D's **Pipe Network** creation tool. You will not create a new pipe network for Jeffries Ranch Rd; rather, you will be extending the Storm network you created in the previous practice.

You will insert manholes based on Figure 10–35. The first structure, **pt1**, is located at station 11+00 of Jeffries Ranch Rd. The next structure, **pt2**, is located at the beginning of the curve, **pt3** is at the intersection of Jeffries Ranch Rd and Ascent Pl, and **pt4** is at a station of 0+098.87m along the Jeffries Ranch Rd alignment. Use the information shown in Figure 10–35 as a guide as you complete the following steps.

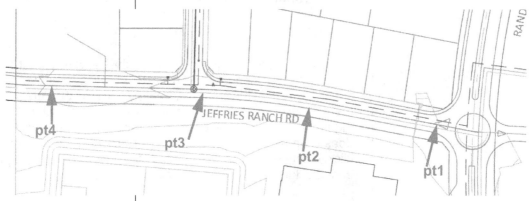

Figure 10–35

1. Continue working with the drawing from the previous task or open **PIP1-B1.dwg** from the *C:\Civil 3D Projects\Working\ PipeNetworks* folder.

2. Select the preset view **Pipe-Create**.

3. In Model Space, select a part in the STORM network. In the contextual tab>Modify panel, click 📝 (Edit Pipe Network), as shown in Figure 10–36.

Figure 10–36

4. In the Network Layout Tools - STORM toolbar, shown in Figure 10–37:

- Click ⌐⌐ (Alignment) and select **Jefferies Ranch Rd**.
- Select **68 x 6 x 57 inch Concrete Rectangular Headwall** for the manhole structure.
- Select **12.0 inch PVC Pipe** for the Pipe part.
- Toggle the slope to **Upslope**.

To find the PVC section, go to the bottom of the list, and then expand it to find the proper size.

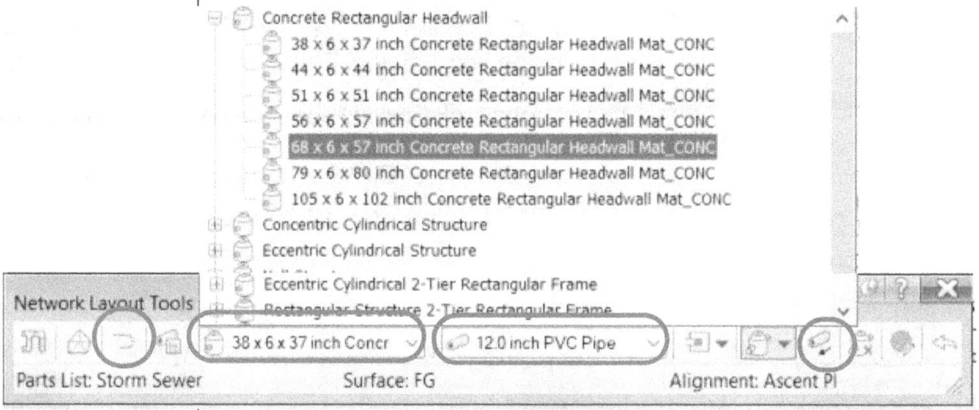

- Click 🗄 (Draw Pipe and Structure).

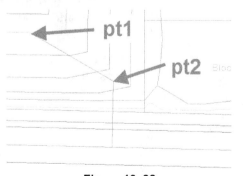

Figure 10–37

5. The Autodesk Civil 3D software prompts you for the locations of the structures. Select end point **pt1** and then select an approximate location near point **pt2** for the next structure location, as shown in Figure 10–38.

Figure 10–38

6. In the Network Layout Tools - STORM toolbar, select **Cylindrical Structure Slab Top Circular Frame>Slab Top Cylindrical Structure 15 dia 18 dia Frm 4 FrHt 4 Slab 3 Wall 4 Floor** for the manhole structure.

7. Toggle the slope to **Downslope**, as shown in Figure 10–39. Leave the Pipe selection as is.

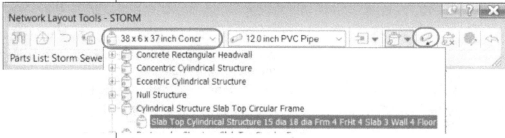

Figure 10–39

8. In the Command Line, you are be prompted for a structure insertion point. Select **Startpoint** for a new starting point.

9. The Autodesk Civil 3D software prompts you for the locations of the structures. Click ⌐◻ (Station Offset) in the *Transparent* tab, as shown in Figure 10–40.

Figure 10–40

10. When prompted for an alignment, select the **Jeffries Ranch Rd** alignment (select an alignment label if it is difficult to select the alignment centerline). Type **1100'** for the station and type **0** for the offset. Press <Esc> to exit the **Transparent command** while remaining in the **Pipe Layout** command. Refer to Figure 10–35 at the start of this exercise.

11. Use the **end point** Osnap to select **pt2** for the next structure, as shown previously in Figure 10–35.

12. When prompted for the next structure, select **Curve** in the command options to draw a curved pipe. When prompted for the end of curve, select the manhole structure at the intersection of Jeffries Ranch Rd and Ascent Pl, as shown in Figure 10–41.

A symbol should display indicating that you are tying into a manhole. In Figure 10–41, the symbol is red; on your screen, it will be yellow.

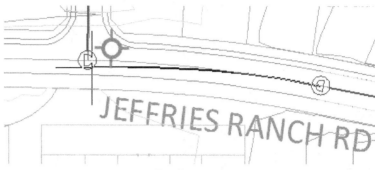

Figure 10–41

You now want to use a different pipe size.

13. In the Network Layout Tools - STORM toolbar, expand the drop-down list and select **18.0 inch PVC Pipe**, as shown in Figure 10–42.

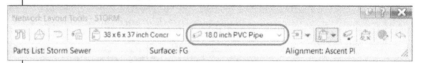

Figure 10–42

14. At the prompt for the end of curve, type **L** and press <Enter> to draw a line. When prompted to select the next structure location, click (Station offset). When prompted for an alignment, select the **Jeffries Ranch Rd** alignment (select an alignment label if it is difficult to select the alignment centerline). Type **324'** for the station, and type **0** for the offset. Press <Esc> to exit the command and press <Enter> to exit the prompt for the insertion point of a structure.

You have made a design change and decided to insert a manhole east of the original intended location, as shown in Figure 10–43. This requires you to make further adjustments to the network later in this chapter.

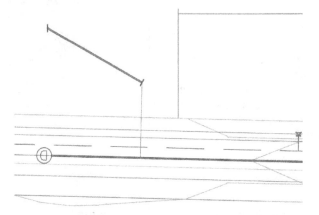

Figure 10–43

15. Close the Network Layout Tools toolbar by clicking the **X**.

16. Save the drawing.

Task 2 - View pipe network in profile view.

---

1. Continue working with the drawing from the previous task or open **PIP1-B2.dwg**.

2. Draw a window from left to right around the pipes to select the last three pipes and four structures that you created in the last task, as shown in Figure 10–44. If the *Pipe Networks* contextual tab does not appear, press <Esc> to clear the selection set, then pick the three pipes and four structures individually.

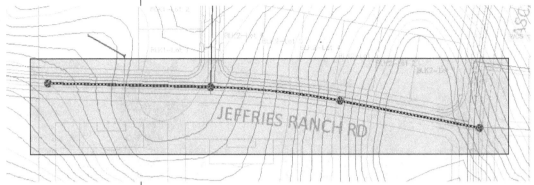

Figure 10–44

3. In the *Pipe Networks* contextual tab>Network Tools panel, click (Draw Parts in Profile).

4. When prompted to select the profile view, select the Jeffries Ranch Road profile view to the right of the site plan. Press <Esc> to release the selected pipe network parts.

5. Because you only selected certain network parts to be added to the profile, you will now review the parts that are relevant to this profile view. Select the profile view and in the contextual tab>Modify Views panel, click (Profile View Properties), as shown in Figure 10–45.

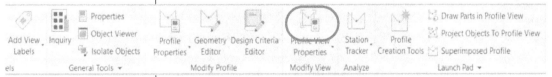

Figure 10–45

Note that your numbers might be slightly different. The key is that not all pipes and structures will be checked.

6. In the Profile View Properties - Jeffries Ranch Rd dialog box, in the *Pipe Networks* tab, ensure that only the following parts are enabled, as shown in Figure 10–46:
   - **Pipe - 5**, **6**, and **7**
   - **Structure - 4**, **7**, **8**, and **9**

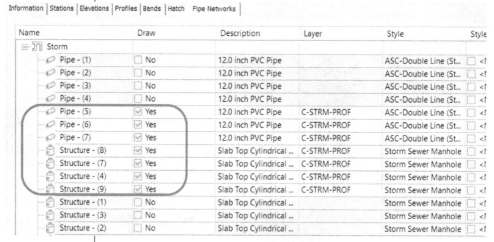

Figure 10–46

7. Click **OK** to close the dialog box and apply the changes.

8. Save the drawing.

10.5 Network Editing

You can edit pipe networks by graphically changing the components' locations in plan or profile views, using tabular fields in the Toolspace, *Prospector* tab and Grid View, and using the Object Properties dialog boxes. All of the commands are available in the shortcut menu that displays after you have selected and right-clicked on a part in plan. (Some, but not all, are available in profile.)

Pipe (and Structure) Properties

The Properties dialog box lists the object's name, dimensions, material, rotation angle, sump depth, etc., as shown in Figure 10–47. Those displayed in black can be edited directly, while those displayed in gray are calculated by the software.

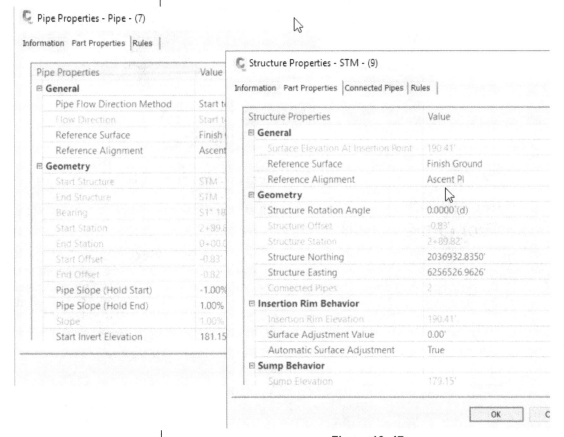

Figure 10–47

Swap Part

The **Swap Part** command exchanges one part for another from the same parts list, but in a different size. When starting the command, the Autodesk Civil 3D software opens the Swap Part Size dialog box, which contains all of the part sizes from the parts list, as shown in Figure 10–48.

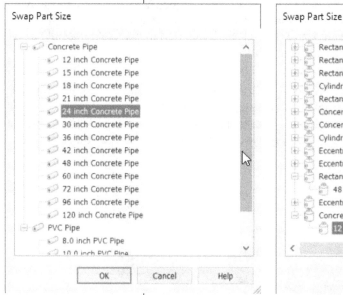
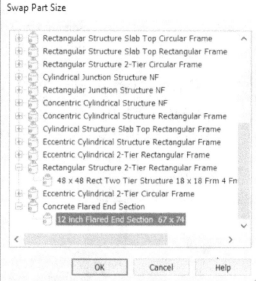

Figure 10–48

Connect/ Disconnect From Part

The **Disconnect From Part** command detaches a selected object from its connected part. Once detached, you can move the selected object and any of its remaining attached items to a new location.

Whether the **Disconnect From Part** or **Connect To Part** command displays in the shortcut menu depends on the state of the selected object. For example, if the object is a structure attached to pipes, the shortcut menu only displays **Disconnect From Part**. If the object is a pipe that is not connected to any other object, the shortcut menu displays **Connect To Part**.

> **Hint: Project Explorer**
>
> The new Project Explorer offers alternatives to editing structure and pipe properties, providing additional flexibility and improvements. For more information, see *Appendix B: Project Explorer*.

Practice 10d | Editing Pipe Networks

Practice Objective

- Edit the gravity fed pipe networks graphically and using the Network Layout Tools toolbar.

Task 1 - Modify a pipe network.

1. Continue working with the drawing from the previous task or open **PIP1-C.dwg** from the *C:\Civil 3D Projects\Working\ PipeNetworks* folder.

2. Select the preset view **Pipe-Edit.**

3. Select the headwall structure shown in Figure 10–49.

    - In the *Pipe Networks* contextual tab>Modify panel, click
      (Swap Part).
    - Select **12 inch Flared End Section** and click **OK** to close the dialog box.

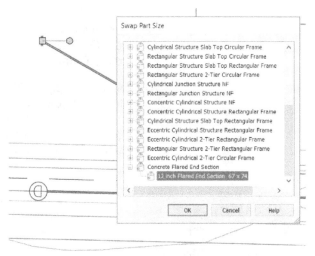

Figure 10–49

4. Select the same structure again. In the *Pipe Networks*

    contextual tab>Modify panel, click (Structure Properties). Change the style of this structure to **Flared End Section** and click **OK** to close the dialog box.

5. Select the same structure again. Note the grips. The square grip enables you to relocate the structure and end of the pipe, while the circular grip enables you to rotate the structure. Select the circular, rotation grip and rotate the structure as shown in Figure 10–50.

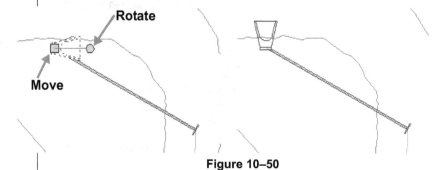

Figure 10–50

6. Press <Esc> to exit the selection.

7. Select the headwall on the opposite end of the pipe. In the *Pipe Networks* contextual tab>Modify panel, click 🖾 (Edit Pipe Network).

8. In the Network Layout Tools toolbar, click 🖾 (Delete Pipe Network Object) and select the south headwall. Press <Esc> to end the **Delete** command.

9. To connect the pipe to the STORM network, select the pipe structure, and select the south east grip to stretch the pipe. Hover the cursor over the manhole on Jeffries Ranch Rd until the connect to structure image displays, as shown in Figure 10–51. Click to accept the connection.

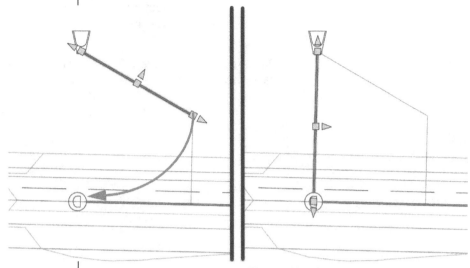

Figure 10–51

10. This pipe connection may throw off the sump depth of the structure and will need to be adjusted in the profile view. If necessary, click on the long structure in the profile view and click on the triangular grip at the bottom of the structure. The tooltip reveals its current elevation. Type in **172.68** and press <Enter> for the proper elevation, as shown in Figure 10–52.

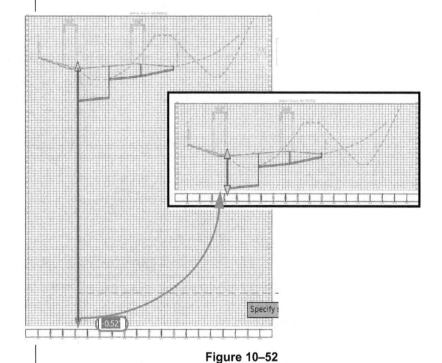

Figure 10–52

11. In Model Space, select the manhole structure that is south of the headwall structure. In the *Pipe Networks* contextual tab> Modify panel, click 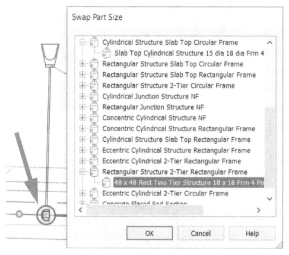 (Swap Part). In the parts list, expand **Rectangular Structure 2-Tier Rectangular Frame**, and select **48 x 48 Rect Two Tier Structure 18 x 18 Frm**, as shown in Figure 10–53. Click **OK**. Then, press <Esc> to release the part. The original round structure is replaced with a square structure.

Swap Part Size

- Cylindrical Structure Slab Top Circular Frame
  - Slab Top Cylindrical Structure 15 dia 18 dia Frm 4
- Rectangular Structure Slab Top Circular Frame
- Rectangular Structure Slab Top Rectangular Frame
- Rectangular Structure 2-Tier Circular Frame
- Cylindrical Junction Structure NF
- Rectangular Junction Structure NF
- Concentric Cylindrical Structure NF
- Concentric Cylindrical Structure Rectangular Frame
- Cylindrical Structure Slab Top Rectangular Frame
- Eccentric Cylindrical Structure Rectangular Frame
- Eccentric Cylindrical 2-Tier Rectangular Frame
- Rectangular Structure 2-Tier Rectangular Frame
  - 48 x 48 Rect Two Tier Structure 18 x 18 Frm 4 Fr
- Eccentric Cylindrical 2-Tier Circular Frame
- Concrete Flared End Section

OK   Cancel   Help

Figure 10–53

12. In Model Space, select the pipe that is connected to the headwall structure. In the *Pipe Networks* contextual tab> Modify panel, click (Swap Part). In the parts list, select **24" Concrete Pipe**. Press <Esc>. Note the Single Line Pipe Style, which you set up in the Storm Parts List customization.

Task 2 - Rename pipe network parts.

When creating the Pipe network, the Autodesk Civil 3D software assigned names to each part. In this task, you will rename these parts so that they conform to company standards.

1. Select the preset view **Pipe-Create**.

2. In the *Modify* tab, select **Pipe Network**.

3. In the *Pipe Networks* tab>Modify panel, expand the drop-down list and select **Rename Parts**.

4. At the prompt to select network parts to rename, select the **manhole structure** at the intersection of Jeffries Ranch Rd and Rand Blvd (by the roundabout), and then select the **Flared End Section** that empties into the pond. The software will select all of the pipes and structures between the selected structures. Then select the **manhole structures** at the end of the cul-de-sac. Note that all of the parts between are also selected. Press <Enter> to end the selection.

Note that your numbers might be slightly different.

5. You have selected 11 structures and 9 pipes, as shown in the dialog box in Figure 10–54. Complete the following:

- For *Structure name template*, type **ST-<[Next Counter(CP)]>** (No space before and after the dash).
- For *Starting number*, type **1**.
- For *Pipe name template*, type **PI- <[Next Counter(CP)]>** (No space before and after the dash).
- For *Starting number*, type **1**.
- In the *Name conflict options* area, select **Rename existing parts**.

If this is to be a standard naming convention, then these settings can be made in the XXX-Pipe-Styles template and will be available to all drawings.

- Click **OK** to accept the changes and close the dialog box.

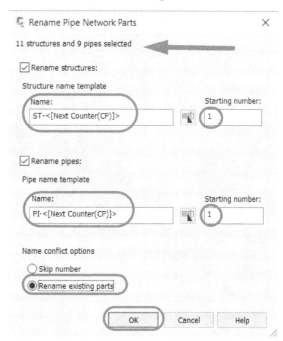

Figure 10–54

---

6. In the Status Bar, toggle on the **Quick Properties** icon, as shown in Figure 10–55. You will use it to edit the structure name.

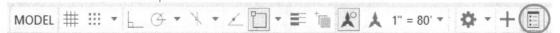

Figure 10–55

7. In Model Space, select the **Flared End Section** structure. In the Properties palette, change the *Name* to **Flared End Section**, as shown in Figure 10–56.

Figure 10–56

8. Save the drawing.

10.6 Annotating Pipe Networks

As with other Autodesk Civil 3D labels, pipe network plan and profile labels are all style-based. A pipe label style can contain an extensive list of pipe network properties. The labels are scale- and rotation-sensitive and use the same interface for creating or modifying styles.

- The Autodesk Civil 3D software can label pipes and structures as you draft them or later as required.

- In the *Annotate* tab>Add Labels panel, expand **Pipe Network** and select **Add Pipe Network Labels...** or expand **Add Pressure Network** and select **Add Pressure Network Labels** to label individual objects or an entire network. The Add Labels dialog box is shown in Figure 10–57.

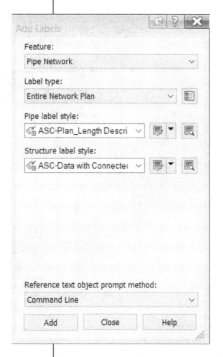

Figure 10–57

Most pipe labels annotate the length and slope of a specific pipe. If you have pipe bends and would rather not label each individual segment as a separate pipe, select the **Spanning** label type. It enables you to select multiple pipes that should be given a single label, which can include overall length, slope, and other properties.

Parts in a network can be renumbered quickly and easily by selecting **Modify>Pipe Network>Modify (panel)>Rename Parts**. Another method is to renumber each one manually using the Pipe Network vistas view, which can be accessed in the Network Layout Tools toolbar, as shown in Figure 10–58. Labels automatically display the new part label.

Figure 10–58

Pipe Networks in Sections

To display pipe networks in sections, they need to be included as a data source for the sections' sample line group. If a sample line group has been created before a pipe network, they are not automatically included. To include them, open the sample line group's Properties dialog box, select the *Sections* tab, and click **Sample more sources...**, as shown in Figure 10–59.

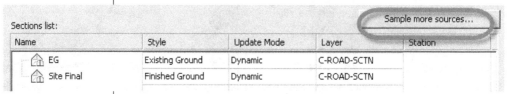

Figure 10–59

Pipe Network Reports and Tables

Pipe reports are available in the Toolspace, *Toolbox* tab (**Home>Palettes>Toolbox**), as shown in Figure 10–60.

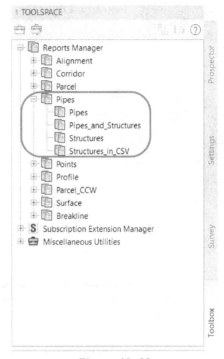

Figure 10–60

Pipe tables can be created inside drawing files using **Annotate> Add Tables>Pipe Network>Add Structure and Annotate> Add Tables>Pipe Network>Add Pipe**.

> **Hint: Project Explorer**
>
> The new Project Explorer offers alternatives to creating tables and reports, providing additional flexibility and improvements. For more information, see *Appendix B: Project Explorer*.

Practice 10e | Annotating Pipe Networks

Practice Objective

- Communicate important design information about pipe networks by adding labels to plan and profile views and creating reports.

Task 1 - Annotate pipe networks.

1. Continue working with the drawing from the previous practice or open **PIP1-D.dwg**.

2. Select the preset view **Pipe-Create**.

3. In the *Annotate* tab>Labels & Tables panel, select **Add Labels**, as shown in Figure 10–61.

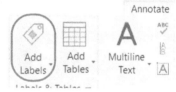

Figure 10–61

4. In the Add Labels dialog box, set the following parameters, as shown in Figure 10–62:

- *Feature:* **Pipe Network**
- *Label type:* **Entire Network Plan**
- *Pipe label style:* **ASC-Plan_Length Description and Slope**
- *Structure label style:* **ASC-Data with Connected Pipes (Storm)**

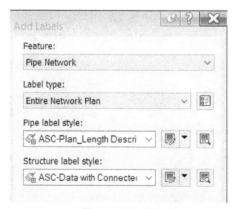

Figure 10–62

5. Click **Add**. When prompted, select any part in the **Storm network**.

6. Save the drawing.

Task 2 - Add labels to parts in the profile view.

1. If necessary, in the *Annotate* tab>Labels & Tables panel, select **Add Labels**.

2. In the Add Labels dialog box, set the following parameters, as shown in Figure 10–63:

   - *Feature:* **Pipe Network**
   - *Label type:* **Entire Network Profile**
   - *Pipe label style:* **ASC-Profile_Length Description and Slope**
   - *Structure label style:* **ASC-Data with Connected Pipes (Storm)**

Figure 10–63

3. Click **Add**.

4. When prompted, select any of the network parts in the profile view, and click **X** to close the dialog box.

5. Save the drawing.

Task 3 - Create a Structure table.

1. In Model Space, select any Storm Pipe network part. In the *Pipe Networks* contextual tab>Labels & Tables panel (shown in Figure 10–64), expand  (Add Tables) and select **Add Structure**.

Figure 10–64

2. In the Structure Table Creation dialog box, for *Table style*, select **Structure with Pipes**. Select **Dynamic** and accept all of the other defaults. Click **OK** to close the dialog box, as shown in Figure 10–65.

Figure 10–65

3. Zoom to an open space and insert the table, as shown in Figure 10–66.

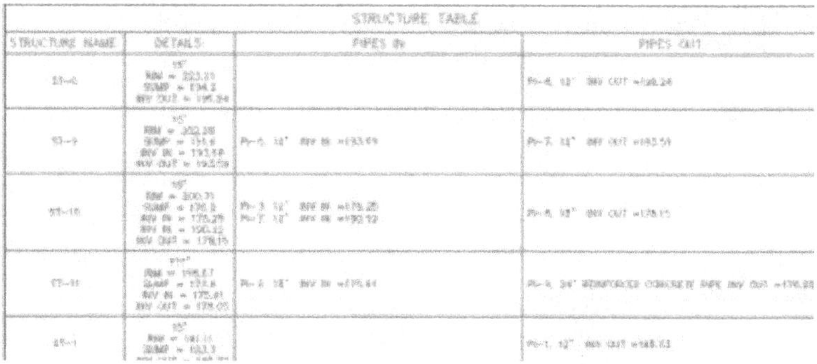

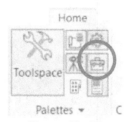

STRUCTURE TABLE

Figure 10–66

4. Save the drawing.

Task 4 - Generate a pipe network report.

1. In the *Home* tab>Palettes panel, click ⬚ (Toolbox), as shown in Figure 10–67.

Figure 10–67

2. In the Toolspace, *Toolbox* tab, expand the *Reports Manager* collection, expand the *Pipes* collection, and select **Pipes_and_Structures**, as shown in Figure 10–68. Right-click and select **Execute**.

Figure 10–68

3. In the Export to XML Report dialog box, accept the defaults because you only have one network. Click **OK**.

4. Type **Pipes** for the name and ensure that the file format is **HTML**. Click **Save**. If prompted to overwrite the file, select **Yes**. The report displays as shown in Figure 10–69.

ASCENT

123 Main Street

Suite #321

Technical Knowledge, State 01234

Pipes and Structures Report	**Client:** Client Company
Project Name: C:\Users\jmorris\AppData\Local\Temp\PIP1-D1-PipeWorks_1_28680_5d8cc3ff.sv$	**Project Description:**
Report Date: 4/22/2020 3:46:17 PM	**Prepared by:** Preparer

Pipe Network: STORM
Pipes

Name	Shape	Size (in)	Material	US Node	DS Node	US Invert (ft)	DS Invert (ft)	2D Length (ft) center-to-center edge-to-edge	% Slope
P-1 (STORM)	Circular	D:12.00		St-1 (STORM)	St-2 (STORM)	185.73	181.98	374.56 373.31	1.00
P-2 (STORM)	Circular	D:12.00		St-2 (STORM)	St-3 (STORM)	181.88	181.25	63.03 61.78	1.00
P-3 (STORM)	Circular	D:12.00		St-3 (STORM)	St-10 (STORM)	181.15	178.25	289.83 288.58	1.00
P-9 (STORM)	Circular	D:24.00	Reinforced Concrete Pipe	St-12 (STORM)	St-11 (STORM)	157.71	188.28	98.43 96.43	-31.06
P-6 (STORM)	Circular	D:12.00		St-8 (STORM)	St-9 (STORM)	196.24	193.69	255.17 253.92	1.00
P-7 (STORM)	Circular	D:12.00		St-9 (STORM)	St-10 (STORM)	193.59	190.92	266.23 264.98	1.00

Figure 10–69

5. Save the drawing.

10.7 Pressure Pipe Networks

Pressure Pipe Networks are used for designing and laying out pressurized systems, such as water networks. There are three types of pressure pipe network objects: Pipes, Fittings, and Appurtenances. You can create Pressure Pipes from existing objects (e.g., lines, arcs, 2D/3D polylines, splines, feature lines, alignments, survey figures, etc.), or by layout.

Pressure Pipes

To start the Pressure Pipe Layout command, in the *Home* tab> Create Design panel, expand **Pipe Networks** and click

(Pressure Network Creation Tools). This opens the Create Pressure Pipe Network dialog box, as shown in Figure 10–70. In it, you can type a name and description, set the parts list to use, and the surface and alignment to reference. You can also set label styles for pipes, fittings, and appurtenances so that they receive labels as you layout the pressure network.

Figure 10–70

Once in the command, the *Pressure Network Plan Layout* contextual tab displays, as shown in Figure 10–71.

Figure 10–71

The reference surface and alignment that were set up during creation display in the Network Settings panel along with the current parts list. The Cover setting is also found in the Network settings panel and specifies the minimum depth the network should be below the selected surface. Ideally, you would select a finished ground surface. In the Layout panel, you can select the pipe material to use.

Pressure pipes can be laid out by themselves or with bends

Using the ☐ Add Bends Automatically (Add Bends Automatically) checkbox, in the *Layout* tab automatically places fittings that are included in the Pressure Networks parts lists.

Editing Pressure Networks

When selecting a part of a pressure pipe network *with a single click*, you select the underlying control alignment, which has the same name as the pipe run. The same the *Pressure Network Plan Layout* contextual tab displays (as shown previously in Figure 10–71).

The glyphs that appear are similar to the alignment glyphs, along with a special one as shown in Figure 10–72:

- Triangular Grip: Extending the pipe.

- Plus sign Grip: adding to the pipe run.

- Square Grip: move the pipe parallel to itself.

- Triangular Up Grip: move the PVI

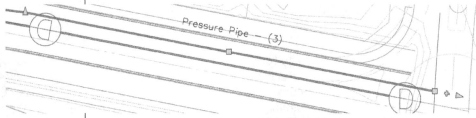

Figure 10–72

The first pick selects the alignment of the pipe run, the second click selects the pipe part.

Fittings

Fittings enable you to specify the T's and other bends to layout a pressurized utility network. Additional fittings can be added to the Autodesk Civil 3D software using the parts catalog. To add additional fittings to a network in the drawing click 🛠 (Add Fitting) in the *Pressure Network Plan Layout* tab>Insert panel.

When configuring the fittings, you can specify the *allowable deflection* in degrees, as shown in Figure 10–73. This can be thought of as "wiggle room" within the fixture and is different for each material.

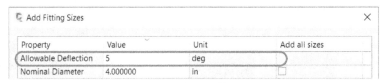

Figure 10–73

Included in the Pressure Pipes catalogs are the following fittings:

- Elbows (90, 60, 45, and 30 degrees)

- Tees

- Reducers

- Couplings

- Caps

The glyphs that appear when selecting the fitting (by clicking on it twice) are as follows, as shown in Figure 10–74:

- Arrow Grip: flip or mirror the fitting.
- Diamond Grip: move the fitting along the pipe.

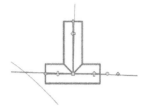

Figure 10–74

Branch Fittings

When pipes of different pipe runs intersect, there is a Branch Fitting tool (⊤) to connect them. If the appropriate fitting (such as a Tee fitting) is found within the parts list, it will connect the pipes appropriately. If there is no proper part in the parts list, Civil 3D will get as close as it can with the parts available.

Appurtenances

Appurtenances are valves, which can be added in the same manner as fittings. Click ⊠ (Add Appurtenance) in the *Pressure Network Plan Layout* tab>Insert panel.

Included in the Pressure Pipes catalogs are the following appurtenances:

- Gate Valves
- Butterfly Valves
- Air Valves
- Hydrants (above and below ground)
- Shut Off Valves
- Check Valves
- Globe Valves

Pressure Pipe Styles

In the fitting and appurtenance styles, you can choose to display the parts as boundaries, catalog-defined blocks, or user-defined blocks. For parts drawn in profile views, you can add masks to hide underlying geometry, you can add hatching to the parts, and you can crop the pipes at the extent of the profile view.

Pipe Runs

Pressure pipe networks are divided into Pipe Runs, which are branches to the overall network. Pipe runs can be added to profile views. Pipe runs are listed in the Prospector within the pressure pipe network.

You can create pipe runs using the following methods, as shown in Figure 10–75:

- By picking points designating the ends of the pipes.

- Selecting objects (lines, plines) to convert to a pipe run.

- Selecting existing pressure pipe parts.

Figure 10–75

Each pipe run also creates a miscellaneous alignment with the same name as the pipe run, which is listed in the Prospector, as shown in Figure 10–76.

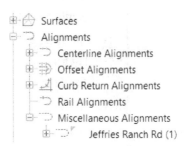

Figure 10–76

When laying out a pipe run, you have the option to use the Compass, which can assist in determining the optimal route of the pipe run. You can toggle the compass's visibility and snapping features in the *Pressure Network Plan Layout* contextual tab>Compass panel, as shown in Figure 10–77. By using the drop-down list in that panel, you can also select the color and the size of the compass. By default, the color is yellow, so if you work on a light background, you may want to select a darker color.

Figure 10–77

When the compass snapping is enabled, the bends in the pipe run are determined by the angles of the elbows in the parts list. These are marked in the compass, as shown Figure 10–78. In this situation, elbows of 11.25, 22.5, 45, and 90 degrees are available.

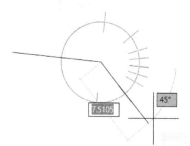

Figure 10–78

Once a pipe run is defined, you can modify it with the standard Civil 3D grips. The triangular grip at the end of an open pipe is for lengthening the pipe, whereas the **+** (plus) grip allows you to add on to the pipe run. You can also add or remove bends or points of intersection (PIs) on existing runs by using the corresponding tools in the *Pressure Network Plan Layout* contextual tab>Layout panel, as shown in Figure 10–79.

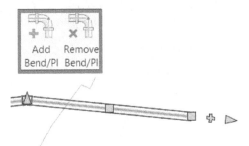

Figure 10–79

Swap Pressure Parts

Similar to gravity fed pipe networks, pressure pipe networks have the option to exchange one part for another, but in a different type, part family, or size. To start the command, select the part, right-click, and select **Swap Pressure Part.** The Swap Pressure Network Parts dialog box displays as shown in Figure 10–80.

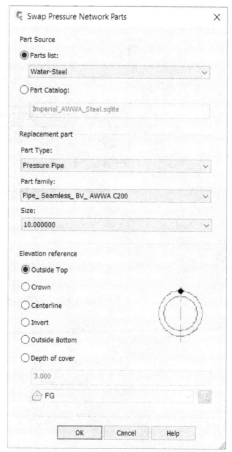

Figure 10–80

Practice 10f | Create a Pressure Pipe Network

Practice Objective

*   Create and edit a pressure pipe network.

Task 1 - Create a pressure pipe network.

In this task, you will create a water network using the **Pressure Pipe Network** commands.

1. Continue working with the drawing from the previous practice or open **PIP1-E1.dwg** from the *C:\Civil 3D Projects\Working\ PipeNetworks* folder.

2. Ensure that your Pressure Pipe Catalog is set correctly to **Imperial_AWWA_Steel.sqlite.** You do this by going to the *Home* tab>expanded Create Design panel and clicking **Set Pressure Pipe Catalog**, as shown in Figure 10–81.

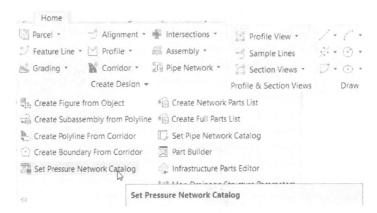

Figure 10–81

3. In the Set Pressure Network Catalog dialog box, ensure the *Catalog folder* path is set to *C:\Civil 3D Projects\ Ascent-Config\Pressure Pipes Catalog\Imperial*, and select **Imperial_AWWA_Steel.sqlite**, as shown in Figure 10–82.

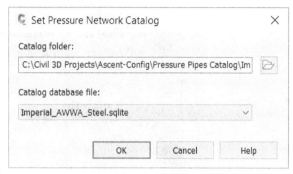

Figure 10–82

4. Select the preset view **Pipe-Create**.

5. In the *Home* tab>Layers panel, click (Layer Freeze). Select any Storm Sewer pipe network label (layer: C-STRM-TEXT) and press <Enter> to end the command.

6. The proposed water line has been sketched on the Base-Proposed-Engineering XREF drawing as a blue dashed line just north of the storm sewer along Jeffries Ranch Rd. A branch of proposed water line extend up Ascent Place, to the east of the road's center line.

7. In the *Home* tab>Create Design panel, expand **Pipe Network** and click (Pressure Network Creation Tools).

8. In the Create Pressure Pipe Network dialog box, set the following, as shown in Figure 10–83:

- *Network Name*: **Water**
- *Pipe Run Name*: **Jeffries Ranch Rd**
- *Parts List:* (use drop-down list) **Water-Steel**
- *Pipe Size*: Leave as is (you'll change it later)
- *Reference surface:* (use drop-down list) **FG**
- *Cover:* **3.00'**
- *Reference alignment:* (use drop-down list) **Jeffries Ranch Rd**
- *Pressure pipe label style*: (use drop-down list) **ASC-Name Only**

Figure 10–83

9. Click **OK** to accept the selection and close the dialog box.

10. In the *Pressure Network Plan Layout* contextual tab>Pipe Run panel, set the pipe size and material to **Pipe_Seamless_12in ND_BV_AWWA C200**, as shown in Figure 10–84.

Figure 10–84

11. Ensure that **Add Bends Automatically** is checked in the *Pressure Network Plan Layout* contextual tab>Pipe Run panel.

12. Toggle the compass's snapping feature **OFF** in the *Pressure Network Plan Layout* contextual tab>Compass panel, as shown in Figure 10–85. When snapping is toggled off, there is no blueish sheen under the icon.

Figure 10–85

13. Use the **Endpoint** object snap to select the points along the dashed blue lines north of the storm sewer, as shown in Figure 10–86.

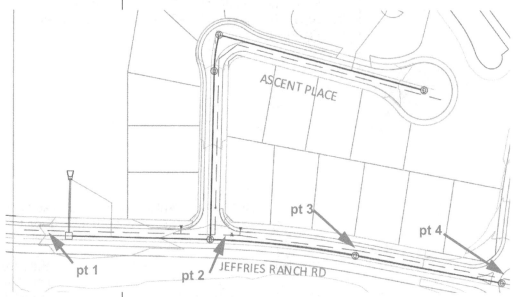

Figure 10–86

14. The second point is to the east of the Tee intersection of the blue reference lines.

15. The third point is above and slightly to the west of the storm sewer's second manhole.

16. The fourth point is at the roundabout of Rand Boulevard and Jeffries Ranch Road.

17. Press <Enter> to end the command, click the green

    checkmark ( ) to close the pressure pipe contextual ribbon, and save the drawing.

18. Expand the **Alignments>Miscellaneous Alignments** branch in the Prospector and note the new miscellaneous alignment that has been created with the same name as the pipe run, as shown in Figure 10–87.

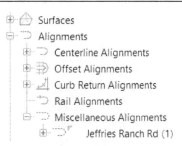

Figure 10–87

Task 2 - Place fittings and add a pipe run.

1. Continue working with the drawing from the previous task or open **PIP1-E2.dwg**.

2. Select one of the pressure pipes you created in the previous task. In the *Pressure Network Plan Layout:Water* contextual tab>Layout panel, expand the Fitting drop-down list and select **Tee (Red)_ 12inX10in ND_ PFSxFF_AWWA C208_ with Gasket SBR_ AWWA C111**, as shown in Figure 10–88.

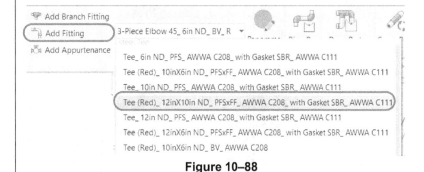

Figure 10–88

3. Click (Add Fitting).

4. Select the point where the blue dotted lines intersect, as shown in Figure 10–89. Wait until you see the Broken Pipe glyph ( ). Press <Esc> to end the command.

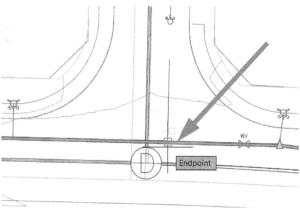

Figure 10–89

5. If the fitting is set in the wrong rotation or location, select it by clicking it twice and pick the down arrow grip to flip the fixture.

6. You need to slide the fitting towards the left, so it is centered on the blue vertical line, as shown in Figure 10–90.

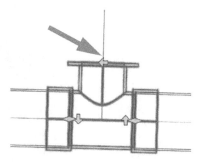

Figure 10–90

7. After placing the fitting, note that you need to extend the pressure network along Ascent Pl.

8. In the *Pressure Network Plan Layout:Water* contextual tab> Pipe Run panel, expand the Add New Pipe Run drop-down list and select **Create New Pipe Run**, as shown in Figure 10–91.

Figure 10–91

9. In the Create Pipe Run dialog box, enter the following, as shown in Figure 10–92:

- *Pipe Run name*: **Ascent Place**
- *Parts list:* **Water-Steel**
- *Pipe size:* **Pipe_ Seamless_ 10in ND_BV_ AWWA C200**
- *Cover:* **3.00'**
- *Reference alignment:* **Ascent Pl**

Figure 10–92

10. Toggle the compass's snapping feature **ON** in the *Pressure Network Plan Layout* contextual tab, Compass panel.

11. Select the ☑ Add Bends Automatically (Add Bends Automatically) checkbox.

12. Hover over the tee fitting that you placed until the fitting tooltip image and the Endpoint grip display, as shown in Figure 10–93. Click to accept the connection and start the new pipe.

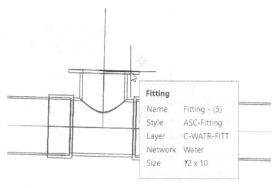

Figure 10–93

13. Use the **Endpoint** object snaps to help you select the next point **pt2**, as shown in Figure 10–94.

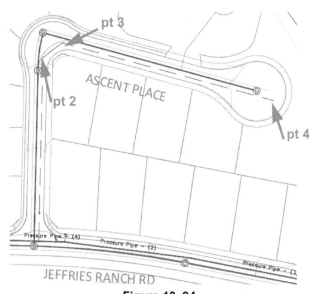

Figure 10–94

14. With the Compass snapping enabled, note that you cannot exactly match the blue reference line, but you can get close. Turn off the Osnaps and pick a point to line up with the next reference segment, as shown in Figure 10–95.

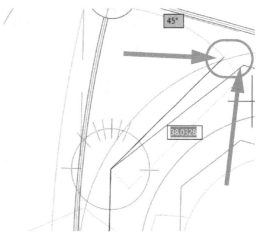

Figure 10–95

15. When you pick the next point, you will see there is no way you can match the bearing of the reference line with the compass snapping, as shown Figure 10–96.

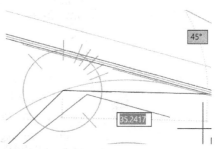

Figure 10–96

16. Turn OFF the compass snapping, then pick the endpoint of the reference line in the cul-de-sac, as marked pt4 in Figure 10–94.

17. Press <Esc> to finish the pipe run.

18. Save the drawing.

Task 3 - Add pipe runs for hydrants and add appurtenances.

1. Continue working with the drawing from the previous task or open **PIP1-E3.dwg**.

2. Select the preset view **Pipe-Intersection**.

3. Select any pressure pipe object in the drawing. In the *Pressure Network Plan Layout:Water* contextual tab> Pipe Run panel, expand the Add New Pipe Run drop-down list and select **Create Pipe Run from Object**, as shown in Figure 10–97.

Figure 10–97

4. Type **X** to be able to pick the line that is part of the XREF.

5. Select the short blue line running between the hydrant symbol and the water main in the eastern portion of the intersection. Ensure that the direction arrow is pointing northward; if needed, type **R** to reverse the direction. See Figure 10–98.

6. In the Create Pipe Run from Objects dialog box, set the following, as shown in Figure 10–98, and then click **OK**:

Simply replace the text "Pipe Run" with "Hydrant".

- *Pipe Run name:* **Hydrant - (<[Next Counter(CP)]>)**
- *Pipe size:* **Pipe_ Seamless_ 6in ND_ BV_ AWWA C200**
- *Reference surface:* **FG**
- *Reference alignment:* **Jeffries Ranch Rd** (NOT Jeffries Ranch Rd(1))
- *Horizontal offset distance:* **0.000**
- *Cover:* **3.00'**

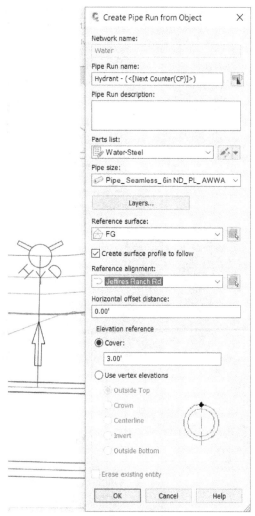

Figure 10–98

7. The connection to the water main is incomplete. To rectify this, select the hydrant waterline. Use the triangular grip at the bottom and pull it upward until you see the see the Broken Pipe glyph (⌐□ □⌐). Release the water main and the fitting is made, as shown in Figure 10–99.

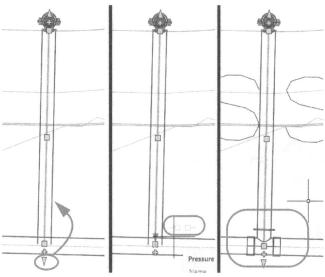

Figure 10–99

8. In the *Pressure Network Plan Layout:Water* contextual tab> Layout panel, select **Hydrant_ 42in_ Bury Depth_ MJ** from the Appurtenance drop-down list.

9. Click on (Add Appurtenance), as shown in Figure 10–100.

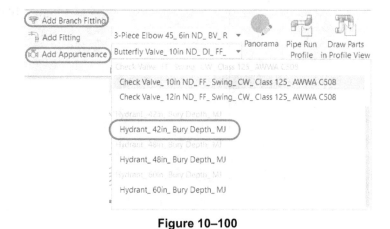

Figure 10–100

10. Select the endpoint of the water line you just created, make sure you get the special yellow glyph, and hit <Enter> to finish. Do not select the blue XREF line, but the end of the pipe.

11. In the *Pressure Network Plan Layout:Water* contextual tab> Layout panel, click on (Add Branch Fitting).

12. For the *First pipe at intersection*, select the Jeffries Ranch Rd Waterline, for the second select the waterline running to the hydrant.

13. Save the drawing.

Task 4 - (Optional) Add more appurtenances.

1. Repeat the steps in Task 3 for the hydrant in the northwest portion of the intersection.

2. Place a 12-inch gate valve near the WV (Water Valve) symbol along Jeffries Ranch Road and move as required. Ensure your Osnap is disabled and you see the Broken Pipe glyph (⊣☐ ☐⊢).

3. Place a 10-inch check valve near the WSO (Water Shutoff Valve) symbol along Ascent Place.

4. Turn off the **Base-Proposed Engineering|C-WATR** layer.

5. Save the drawing.

Task 5 - Draw pressure pipes in the profile view.

1. Continue working with the drawing from the previous task or open **PIP1-E4.dwg**.

2. Select the water line running along Jeffries Ranch Rd. *Pressure Network Plan Layout:Water* contextual tab>Profile panel, click (Pipe Run Profile).

3. In the Pipe Run Profile Settings dialog box, set the following, as shown in Figure 10–101:

- *Offset Style:* **Offset at Fitting**
- *Reference Profile:* **FG Surface (1)**
- *Offset Distance:* **3.00'**
- *Draw Profile in:* **Existing Profile View**

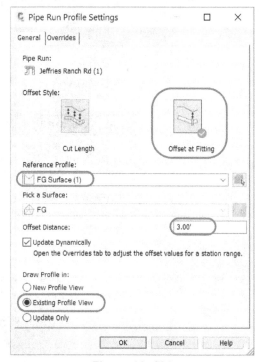

Figure 10–101

4. Click **OK**.

5. When prompted, select the **Jeffries Ranch Rd** profile view.

6. In the **Jeffries Ranch Rd** profile view, select **Pressure Pipe (1)**. Click on the round grip in the center of the pipe and pull it downward to put a downward bend in the pipe, as shown in Figure 10–102. Press <Esc> to finish.

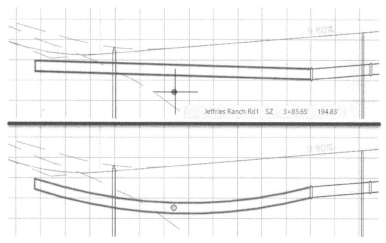

Figure 10–102

7. Save the drawing.

8. (Optional) Save the drawing as **<Your Initials>-Pipe-Complete.dwg** in the *C:\Civil 3D Projects\References\DWG\Proposed* folder.

See the Project Management for how to work with Data Shortcuts.

9. Update the relative paths of the referenced drawings in the alert box.

10. (Optional) Add the **Water** and the **STORM** Sewer networks to the project as Pipe and Pressure Pipe Data Shortcuts.

Chapter Review Questions

1. What does the **Swap Part** command do? (Select all that apply.)

   a. Make a pipe a structure.

   b. Make a structure a pipe.

   c. Change a pipe for another pipe of another size or material.

   d. Change a structure for another structure type or size.

2. What type of structure CANNOT be used in a regular (gravity) pipe network?

   a. Headwall

   b. Manhole

   c. Gate Valve

   d. Catch Basin

3. Pressure pipe networks can contain all of the following except...

   a. Manholes

   b. Appurtenances

   c. Pipes

   d. Fittings

4. To draw gravity pipes and structures in a profile view, you need to...

   a. Manually draw each pipe and structure with the profile creation tools.

   b. Click **Draw Parts in Profile View** on the Network Layout Tools toolbar.

   c. Select the profile view, right-click and select **Draw Parts from Pipe Network**.

   d. Select the pipes and structures in the plan view, click **Draw in Profile View** on the *Pipe Network* contextual tab, and select the profile view in which you want to draw.

5. Pipe Networks can be created from feature lines.

   a. True

   b. False

Command Summary

Button	Command	Location
	Add Branch Fitting	• **Contextual Ribbon:** *Pressure Networks Plan Layout* tab>Layout Panel • **Command Prompt:** AddBranchFitting
	Add Appurtenance	• **Contextual Ribbon:** *Pressure Networks Plan Layout* tab>Layout Panel • **Command Prompt:** AddAppurtenance
	Add Fitting	• **Contextual Ribbon:** *Pressure Networks Plan Layout* tab>Layout Panel • **Command Prompt:** AddFitting
	Create Pipes From Objects	• **Ribbon:** *Home* tab>Create Design panel>Pipe Network • **Command Prompt:** createnetworkfromobject
	Draw Parts in Profile	• **Contextual Ribbon:** *Pipe Networks* tab>Network Tools panel • **Command Prompt:** addnetworkpartstoprofile
	Pipe Run Profile	• **Contextual Ribbon:** *Pressure Networks Plan Layout* tab>Profile Panel • **Command Prompt:** EditPipeRunProfile
	Edit Pipe Network	• **Contextual Ribbon:** *Pipe Networks* tab>Modify panel
	Pipe Network Creation Tools	• **Ribbon:** *Home* tab>Create Design panel>Pipe Network • **Command Prompt:** createnetwork
	Pressure Network Creation Tools	• **Ribbon:** *Home* tab>Create Design panel>Pipe Network • **Command Prompt:** createpressurenetwork

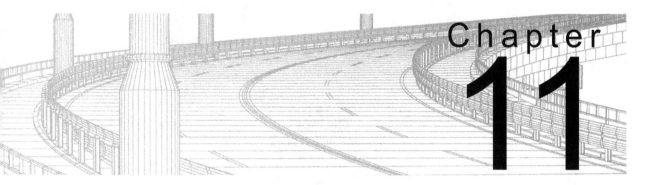

11

Plan Production

The final stage of any project is printing plan sets. Plan sets are sent to contractors for bidding and construction purposes. In this chapter, you will create plan and profile sheets and section sheets for the road design.

Then, you will modify the sheet set properties and title block to make the project information automatically display on every sheet.

Learning Objectives in This Chapter

- List the steps involved in the plan and profile sheets creation workflow.
- Divide the alignment into printable areas using various commands.
- Edit view frames and match lines to better represent your design in plan and profile sheets.
- Create plan and profile sheets using the Plan Production tools and previously created View Frame objects.
- Create section views in draft mode.
- Create multiple section views for plan production.
- Edit sheet and sheet set properties to make annotating sheets easier.

11.1 Final Design

You have now reached the Final Design Stage!

The Conceptual Design has been sketched up in AutoCAD® and referenced into the drawings you have been working on. All of this work has been a part of the Autodesk® Civil 3D® Design Development / Detail Design phase. While there is more work that can be done in that phase, you will now focus on the tasks in the Final Design Phase.

In the Final Design phase, you need to evaluate the project in terms of Quantification, Presentation, and Visualization and Printing.

In this chapter, drawings for Plan/Profile and section sets and a Drawing Index Sheet are created. The next chapter deals with adding sections to the drawing set, performing some Quantity Takeoffs and inspecting the final design.

11.2 Plan Production Tools

In the digital age, although large amount of resources and time are dedicated to creating digital data, printed sets of plans are still necessary for a number of reasons, including:

- Obtaining approval from a Client

- Review and approval from governing agencies

- Bidding

- Construction layout

- Recording as-built conditions

The Autodesk® Civil 3D® software includes a Plan Production system that enables the automated generation of plan, profile, or plan and profile sheet sets, as well as section sheets. The Plan Production tools are found on the *Output* tab and shown in Figure 11–1.

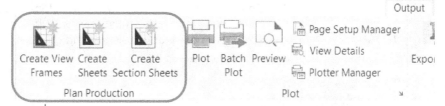

Figure 11–1

Overview for Plan/Profile Sheets

Use the following workflow to create plan and profile sheets:

1. Create title blocks and styles (or configure custom title blocks and styles) or use those provided in the Autodesk templates. This is typically the BIM Manager's responsibility.

2. Create View Frames. The **Create View Frames** command organizes these frames into View Frame Groups and creates interactive Match Lines.

3. Adjust View Frames and Match Lines, as required. This adjustment can be done using object properties or by manipulating the objects directly in Model Space.

4. Create sheets. When you are satisfied with the layout of the frames and Match Lines, plotting layouts can be generated in the current drawing or in new ones.

5. Plot and manage. Sheets generated from this system are automatically included in the Sheet Set Manager for ease of plotting and for organizing with other sheets. (Refer to the Help system for more information on AutoCAD Sheet Sets.)

Overview for Section Sheets

Use the following workflow to create section sheets:

1. Create title blocks and styles as required. This is typically the BIM Manager's responsibility.
2. Create multiple section views with the appropriate production template.
3. Create the section sheets with the Plan Production Section Sheets tools.
4. Arrange the section sets in the Sheet Sets.
5. Use the Sheet Set Manager to plot / archive / publish the sets.

More Information

Describing how to customize a title block and styles can be involved. Due to time limitations, only the fundamentals of this system are covered in this training guide, not its configuration.

11.3 Plan Production Objects

The first step in using the Plan Production tools is to assemble all of the relevant data. This process is the same, whether you use the Autodesk Civil 3D Plan Production tools or not. Some of the steps you might use in assembling base plans and design models involve external referencing of pertinent data into your drawing to give the plan geographic reference (i.e., ROW lines, contours, survey data, aerial photographs, etc.). Autodesk Civil 3D design objects may also be data-referenced into these base plans and design models.

The Autodesk Civil 3D software provides a tool to help automate plan and production sheet creation: the Create View Frames wizard. It is the next step in plan production after the base plan has been created. Using this wizard, you can create View Frames, View Frame Groups, and Match Lines, all of which are plan production objects. The wizard is shown in Figure 11–2.

Figure 11–2

View Frames

View Frames are interactive, rectangular objects that are placed along a selected alignment. These rectangular shapes represent a view for each plan sheet that is created in the Autodesk Civil 3D software. View Frames divide the alignment into segments. These segments are based on the base drawing scale and the viewport proportion, size and settings on the Layout tab from the drawing template that is used to define the views.

View Frame Groups

View Frame Groups are collections of the View Frames along a single alignment. View Frame Groups enable you to manage a group of views, including properties, such as styles and labeling.

Match Lines

A Match Line is a line that designates a location along an alignment that is used as a common reference point for two adjacent plans. If you create plan and profile or profile only sheets, the **Insert Match Lines** option is automatically selected and you cannot edit it.

Match Lines, as with all other Autodesk Civil 3D objects, are style-driven. They include an option for hatching areas which are part of adjacent drawings. Typically, they have labels that can identify both adjacent plans, one plan, or no plans. You can also have these labels displayed at the top, bottom, or middle of the Match Line.

11.4 Plan Production Object Edits

After using the Autodesk Civil 3D wizard to create View Frame Groups, View Frames, and Match Lines, you might need to make some minor adjustments to best present your design. You can access three properties: *Name, Description*, and *Object style*. In addition to adjusting the field properties of the object, you might also want to adjust the geometry properties of the object.

Name

The *Name* is a unique identifier that is appropriate to the object. For example, you might name the View Frame with the alignment name and station, or name the View Frame Group with the alignment name and the starting and ending station that the group encompasses.

Description

The *Description* field provides a detailed description of the View Frame or Match Line.

Object Style

Adjusting the *Object style* impacts the presentation of the object. One application of this property is to ensure that the object conforms to your organization's preferences or standards. The View Frame Properties dialog box is shown in Figure 11–3.

Figure 11–3

View Frame Geometry Properties Edits

You can change the View Frame's location and rotation along the alignment using the object grips, as shown in Figure 11–4.

- The *circle grip* (1) enables you to rotate the View Frame.

- The *diamond grip* (2) enables you to slide the View Frame along the alignment.

- The *square grip* (3) enables you to reposition the View Frame.

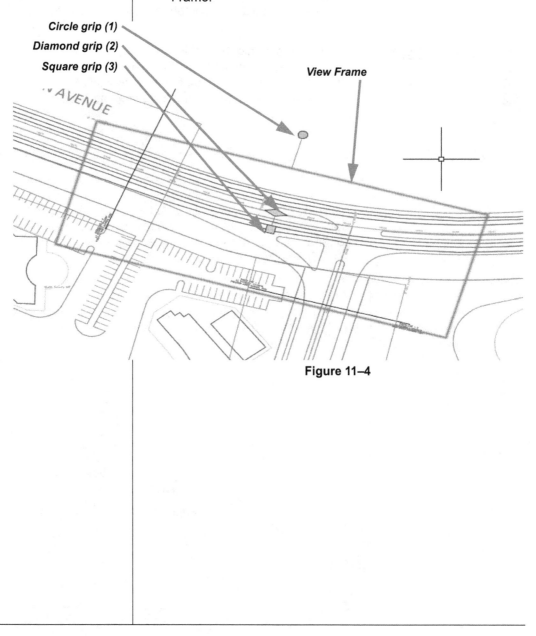

Figure 11–4

Match Line Geometry Properties Edits

Using the object grips, you can change the Match Line's location, rotation, and length, as shown in Figure 11–5. However, you can only move the Match Line in the View Frame overlap area and along the alignment.

- The *triangle grips* (1) enables you to extend the length of the Match Line.

- The *square grip* (4) enables you to move the Match Line label.

- The *diamond grip* (3) enables you to slide the Match Line within the overlap area of the two referenced View Frames.

- The *circle grip* (4) enables you to rotate the Match Line.

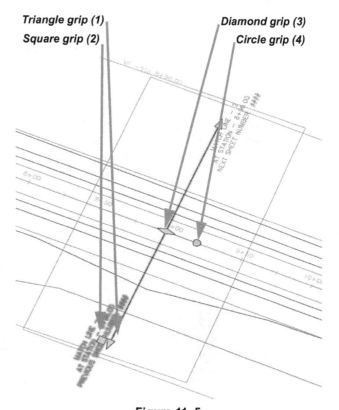

Figure 11–5

Practice 11a

Plan Production Tools - View Frames

Practice Objective

- Create and edit view frames to divide the alignment into printable areas.

For this practice, two alignments from the project have been combined into one alignment and profile to better demonstrate the full power of the plan production tools in the Autodesk Civil 3D software when used with longer corridor projects. Therefore, the dataset is slightly different than for the other chapters.

Combining alignments is not necessary or recommended for real projects.

Task 1 - Create view frames.

1. Open **PPR1-A1.dwg** from the *C:\Civil 3D Projects\Plans* folder.

This reference template has the profile view styles set to 1:5 exaggeration, whereas the Base-styles are set to 1:10.

2. Attach the **ASC-Profile-Styles.dwg** style reference template file from the *C:\Civil 3D Projects\Ascent-Config* folder as done earlier in this course. Ensure it is at the top of the list, as shown Figure 11–6.

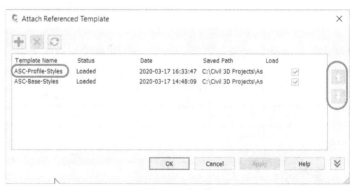

Figure 11–6

3. You will create the plan - profile sheets at a scale of 1"=20'. The sheets will be created more consistently if the Model Space scale matches the final output scale. Set the *Annotation Scale* to **1"=20',** as shown in Figure 11–7.

Figure 11–7

4. In the *Output* tab>Plan Production panel, click  (Create View Frames).

5. In the wizard, in the *Create View Frames - Alignment* page, do the following, as shown in Figure 11–8:

   - In the Alignment drop-down list, select **Michelle Way**.
   - In the *Station Range* area, select the **Automatic** option.
   - Click **Next>**.

Figure 11–8

6. In the *Create View Frames - Sheets* page, do the following:

   - In the sheet settings, select the **Plan and Profile** option.

   - In the *Template for Plan and Profile sheet* area, click .

   - In the *Drawing template file name* field, click  and browse to **ACS-Training Plan and Profile-I.dwt**. This file is located in *C:\Civil 3D Projects\Ascent-Config*.

   - In the *Select a layout to create new sheets* area, expand the drop-down list and select **Arch D Plan and Profile 20 Scale**, as shown in Figure 11–9.

   - Click **OK**.

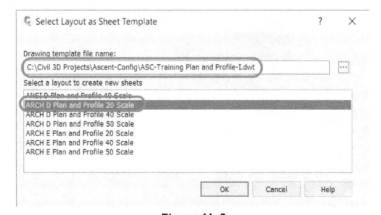

Figure 11–9

- For the *View Frame Placement*, select the **Along alignment** option, as shown in Figure 11–10.
- Click **Next>**.

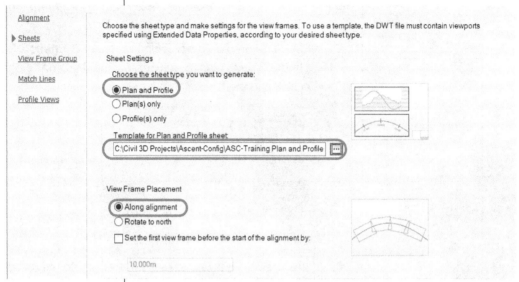

Figure 11–10

This will append the alignment name and a counter to the VFG.

7. In the *Create View Frames - View Frame Group* page, accept the default for the *Name*.

8. To name the View Frame with the starting station, click  (Edit View Frame Name).

If these settings in the name template are standard, you can save them in the Setting tab in the master DWT file.

9. In the Name Template dialog box, shown in Figure 11–11:

   • In the *Name* field, type **VF - Sta**.
   • In the Property fields drop-down list, select **View Frame Start Raw Station**.
   • Click **Insert**.
   • Click **OK** to close the dialog box.

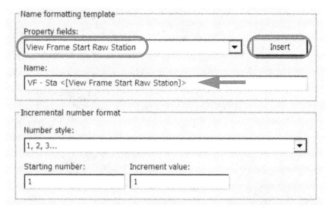

Figure 11–11

10. Accept the Label and Label style. Accept the Label location of **Top left** (as shown in Figure 11–12), and click **Next>**.

Figure 11–12

11. In the *Create View Frames - Match Lines* page, shown in Figure 11–13:

The procedure to do this is similar to Step 8.

- Select **Allow additional distance for repositioning**.
- Change the *Match Line* name to **ML - <[Match Line Raw Station]>**.
- Accept all other defaults and click **Next>**.

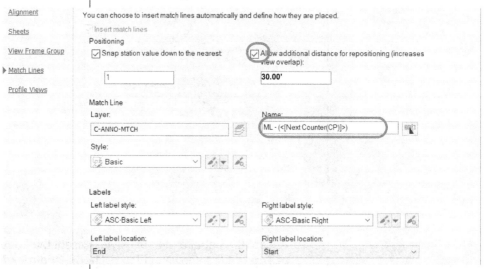

Figure 11–13

12. In the *Create View Frames - Profile Views* page, accept the default values for the *Profile View Style* and the *Band Set*. Click **Create View Frames**, as shown in Figure 11–14.

The following profile view information is required to determine the distances available in viewports.

Alignment

Sheets

View Frame Group

Match Lines

▶ Profile Views

Profile View Style

Select profile view style:

Profile View 1:5

Band Set

Select band set style:

Plan Profile Sheets - Elevations and Stations

< Back   Next >   (Create View Frames)   Cancel   Help

Figure 11–14

13. In the Toolspace, *Prospector* tab, expand the *View Frame Groups* collection, expand the *VFG - Michelle Way View Frame Group*, and then expand the *View Frames* collection and the *Match Lines* collection. Note that the Create View Frame wizard has created eleven Plan Production objects, six View Frames, and five Match Lines, as shown in Figure 11–15.

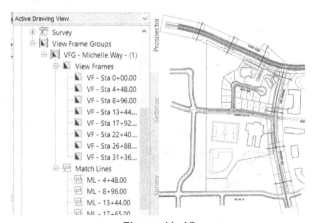

Figure 11–15

14. Save the drawing.

Task 2 - Edit view frames and match lines.

1. Continue working with the drawing from the previous task or open **PPR1-A2.dwg**.

2. Select the preset view **PP-Edit VF**.

3. In Model Space, select the Match Line object for Michelle Way **ML - 17+92.00**, as shown on the right in Figure 11–16. Alternatively, you can select the Match Line in the Toolspace, *Prospector* tab. Expand the *View Frame Groups* collection, expand the *VFG-Michelle Way* collection, expand the *Match Line* collection, select **ML - 17+92.00**, right-click, and select **Select**, as shown on the left in Figure 11–16.

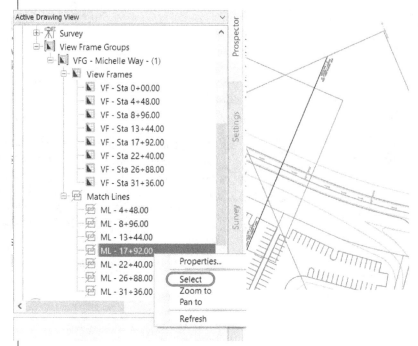

Figure 11–16

If Quick Properties does not display, in the Status bar, click ▦ (Quick Properties) to open it.

4. Select the move grip (the diamond grip), and type **1765**.

5. In the Quick Properties dialog box, also rename it as **ML - 17+65.00**, as shown in Figure 11–17. Press <Esc> to release the Match Line object.

Figure 11–17

6. Now you can adjust the View Frame object corresponding to ML - 17+65.00. Select the View Frame object, select the rotation grip (the circular grip), and graphically rotate the View Frame object so that it is parallel to the Mission Avenue alignment, as shown in Figure 11–18.

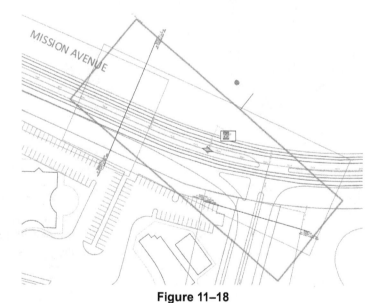

Figure 11–18

7. Press <Esc> to exit the View Frame object selection.

8. Save the drawing.

11.5 Creating Sheets

Once the Match Lines, View Frames, and associated View Frame Groups have been established, you can start the next phase of generating sheet sets.

The Autodesk Civil 3D software includes a wizard that helps you create sheets from the View Frames. The flexibility of this wizard, in addition to the selection of styles, enables you to create sheets that automatically conform to many of your organization's standards. The wizard is shown in Figure 11–19.

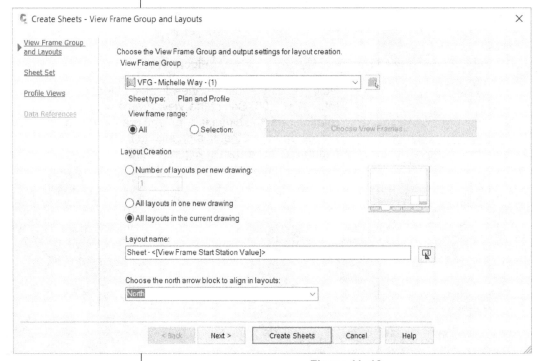

Figure 11–19

Since a dynamic link does not exist between the View Frames and the sheet, it is important that the required View Frames are established before creating the sheets. Changing or editing View Frames after the sheets are created has no effect on the sheets.

* In addition to using the wizard for creating sheets, this workflow also uses the AutoCAD Sheet Set Manager.

Practice 11b

Plan Production Tools - Sheet Generation

Practice Objective

- Create plan and profile sheets using the Plan Production tools and previously created View Frame objects.

1. Continue working with the drawing from the previous task or open **PPR1-B1.dwg** from the *C:\Civil 3D Projects\Plans* folder.

2. In the *Output* tab>Plan Production panel, click (Create Sheets).

3. In the wizard, in the *Create Sheet - View Frame Group and Layouts* page:

   - Ensure that the *View Frame Group* is **VFG - Michelle Way**.
   - Set the *View frame range* to **All**.
   - In the *Layout Creation* area, set the *Layout* creation to **All layouts in the current drawing**.
   - For the *Layout name*, click (Edit Layout Name).

In a production environment, it is recommended NOT to have the layouts in your Design models, but to have them in a separate folder specifically for sheets.

4. In the Name Template dialog box, shown in Figure 11–20:

   - In the *Name* field, delete the current name.
   - Type **Sheet-**.
   - In the Property fields drop-down list, select **View Frame Start Station Value**.
   - Click **Insert**.
   - Click **OK** to close this dialog box.

Figure 11–20

5. Expand the Choose the north arrow block to align in layouts drop-down list and select the **North** block, as shown in Figure 11–21. This North Arrow block is part of the *Template for Plan and Profile sheet* that you chose in the previous exercise. Once this is complete, click **Next>**.

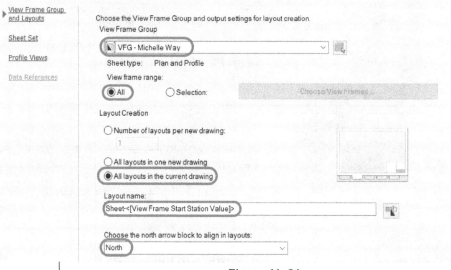

Figure 11–21

6. In the *Create Sheets - Sheet Set* page, set the following:

   • Select the **New sheet set** option and type **Ascent Phase1** in the *Sheet Set name* field. Leave the *Sheet set storage location* field set to the default (*C:\Civil 3D Projects\Plans*), as shown in Figure 11–22. Click **Next>**.

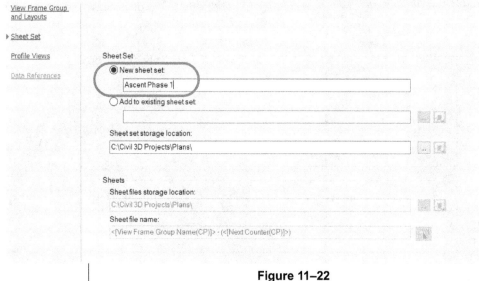

Figure 11–22

7. In the *Create Sheets - Profile Views* page, click on Choose settings for *Other profile views options*. In the Profile View wizard, ensure that the Split profile views are as follows, as shown in Figure 11–23:

These 1:5 profile views belong to the **ASC-Profile-Styles.dwg** *style reference template you attached earlier.*

- *First View 1:5*
- *Intermediate View 1:5*
- *Last View 1:5*

8. Click **Finish** to dismiss the Profile View wizard, then accept the other defaults, and click **Create Sheets**.

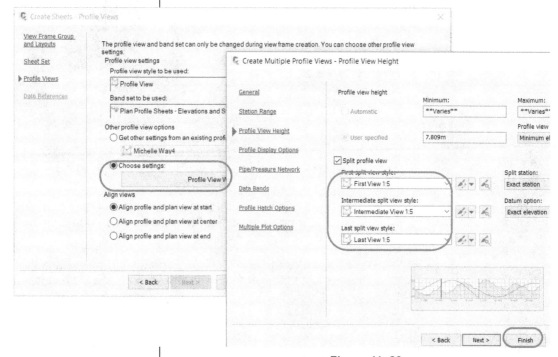

Figure 11–23

9. The wizard prompts you that the drawing will be saved before creating the new sheets. Click **OK** to accept this.

10. When prompted for the location of the profile, select a blank space in your drawing, as shown in Figure 11–24. The Autodesk Civil 3D software will use this location to insert a profile of your alignment. Since the point you pick will be the lower left corner of the profile views to be generated, assure there is nothing to the right and above that can overlap the new profile views.

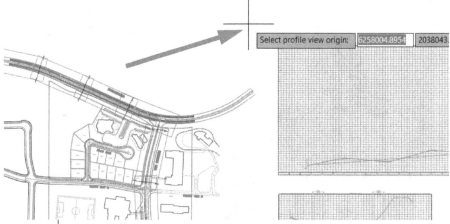

Figure 11–24

You may have to regenerate (command RE) the drawing to update the newly created profile views.

11. The Event Viewer opens to tell you that sheets were created. Expand **Action** and select **Clear All Events**, then click the **X** to close the Event Viewer.

12. The Autodesk Civil 3D software creates the sheets and the Sheet Set Manager files. The Sheet Set Manager opens, as shown in Figure 11–25.

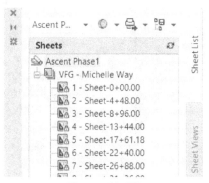

Figure 11–25

13. Hover the cursor over the filename in the Sheet Set Manager to display all of the properties of the sheet, including the name and location of the drawing file, as shown in Figure 11–26.

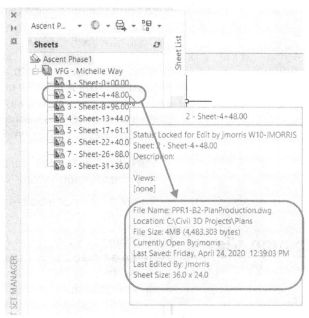

Figure 11–26

14. New profiles were also created, starting with the point you picked previously. You may have to regenerate the drawing for them to display fully.

15. Click on the new layout tabs at the bottom of the drawing area that have been created to study the results. When done, click on the Model layout tab to return to Model Space.

16. Save the drawing.

11.6 Section Views

A section view can display sampled surface sections, corridor assemblies, and pipes or structures where the Sample Lines have been placed. Similar to profiles, sections use a section view to annotate their elevations and center line offsets. Styles affect the look of a section view.

Section views can annotate an assembly's offsets, elevations, and grades. The *All Codes* style assigned to the assembly in the sample line group makes all of the points and links available for labeling. The Section Label styles do not interact with the assembly, only with the corridor surfaces.

- As with profile views, section views can be moved and retain the correct information.
- Section views can be created individually or in groups.

Section View Wizard

In the *Home* tab, the Profile & Section Views panel enables you to create a single section view, multiple sections organized into columns and rows, and project objects to a section view. The **Single** and **Multiple View** commands open the Section View wizard, which guides you through the process of creating section views. There are six parts in the Section View wizard, as shown in Figure 11–27.

Figure 11–27

- **General:** Specifies basic information about the section view, including which alignment to use, the sample group and line, and the view template. If creating multiple views, the Group Plot Style method specifies how to create multiple section views (**All** or **Page**). You can define page styles that define sheet sizes and plottable areas (sheet size minus margins and border).

- **Section Placement:** Only displays when you are creating multiple views. It enables you to set the Group Plot Style to use for setting the row and column settings for placing multiple section views.

- **Offset Range:** Enables you to set the width of the view.

- **Elevation Range:** Enables you to set the height of the view.

- **Section Display Options:** Enables you to select what gets drawn in the view and the section style.

- **Data Bands:** Enables you to specify one or more band set styles for the sections and their positions in the view.

- **Section View Tables:** Enables you to add and modify volume tables calculated using the section view (a material list must be created from the sample line group for this option to be available).

Section View Styles

A Section View style defines the vertical and horizontal grid and its annotation. The horizontal lines represent the elevations and the vertical lines represent the center line offset.

Section View Band Styles

A band style defines the offset and elevation annotation at the bottom of a section view. The style affects the annotation's format and the information that displays in the band. Using the band styles provided in the sample templates, set your existing ground surface as **Surface 1**, and the proposed surface (such as a Corridor Top surface) as **Surface 2**.

Section Styles and Section Label Styles

A section style assigns a layer and other layer properties to a surface section. The section label styles annotate grade breaks, slopes, and offsets.

Code Set Styles

In Multi-Purpose styles, **Code Set Styles** are collections of customized **Link, Point** and **Shape Styles**. The *All Codes* style assigns object and label styles for corridor assemblies. This is the default style for section labeling.

Code Set Styles define object styles for points, links, or shapes for corridors, assemblies, section and section views. It specifies which labels display in a Section view.

- All link styles annotate a grade or slope.

- All point styles annotate an offset and elevation.

Other Code Set Styles are available (or can be created or modified by the BIM Manager) for specific purposes, such as:

- Plotting with or without hatching

- Design development

- No Display

- Visualization

Page Styles

A page style defines the plottable area of a sheet size. The plottable area is what remains after removing the non-printing margins and border from the sheet size. The page style also defines a sheet grid. The Plot Group styles use the grid to space sections on a sheet.

Practice 11c

Plan Production Tools - Sections

Practice Objective

- Show what is happening with existing and proposed surface data at predefined intervals along an alignment using section views.

Task 1 - Review Sample Line data.

1. Do not continue working on the previous drawing. Instead, open **PPR1-C1.dwg** from the *C:\Civil 3D Projects\Plans* folder. In this drawing, the Storm pipe network and a water main are added so they can be added to the section views.

2. In the Toolspace, *Prospector* tab, expand the *Alignments> Centerline Alignments>Jeffries Ranch Rd>Sample Line Groups* collection and select **SL Collection - 1**, as shown in Figure 11–28.

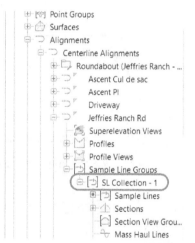

Figure 11–28

3. Right-click and select **Properties**. In the Sample Line Group Properties dialog box, in the *Sections* tab, you can reassign styles and layers and add new data sources.

4. Click **Sample more sources...** in the top right corner.

Note that the Pressure Pipes do not display here.

5. Select **Storm** from the list on the left and click **Add**, then select **Water** from the list on the left and click **Add**, as shown in Figure 11–29. Click **OK** to close the Section Sources dialog box.

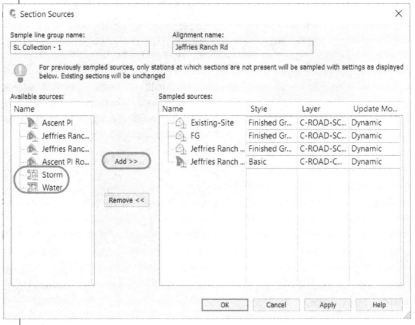

Figure 11–29

6. Click **OK** to close the next dialog box.

7. Save the drawing.

Task 2 - Create a single section view.

1. Ensure that the *Annotation Scale* is set to **1"=40'.**

2. In the *Home* tab>Profile & Section Views panel, expand **Section Views** and click (Create Section View), as shown in Figure 11–30. The Create Section View wizard opens.

Figure 11–30

3. In the *General* page, in the *Sample Line* field, select **4+50.00** as shown in Figure 11–31. Set the *Section view style* to **Road Section** and click **Next>**.

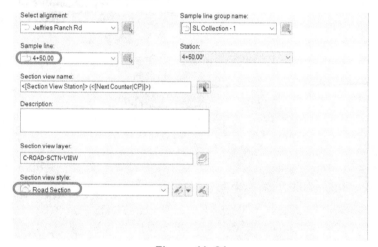

Figure 11–31

4. In the *Offset Range* and *Elevation Range* pages, accept the defaults and click **Next>**.

Note that the quantity take offs only display if the material quantities are calculated before the section views are created.

5. In the *Section Display Options* page, do the following:

- Set the *Style* to **Existing Ground** for *Existing-Site*.
- **ASC-View-Edit with Shading** for the *Jeffries Ranch Rd Corridor* section.
- **Finished Ground** for the *FG* and *Jeffries Ranch Rd Datum*.
- Assign the label options and styles to **_No Labels** for all, as shown in Figure 11–32 and click **Next>**.

Figure 11–32

6. On the left, click **Section View Tables** or click **Next>** to skip setting the Data Bands because **No_Labels** was selected in Step 6.

7. In the *X Offset* field, type **0.50"** and click **Add>>** to add the Total Volume Table to the list. Then expand the Type drop-down list and select **Material**. Click **Add>>** again to include the material table in the section view, as shown in Figure 11–33. Select all of the materials in the **Select Materials** window.

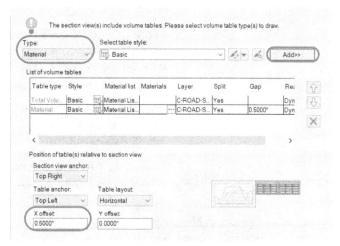

Figure 11–33

8. Click **Create Section View**. At the *Identify section view origin* prompt, click in empty space in Model Space, somewhere northeast of the surface, as shown in Figure 11–34.

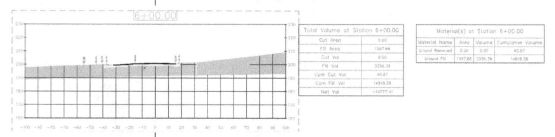

Figure 11–34

Task 3 - Create a multiple section view.

1. Continue working with the drawing from the previous task or open **PPR1-C2.dwg** from the *C:\Civil 3D Projects\Plans* folder.

2. Ensure that the *Annotation Scale* is set to **1"=40'**.

3. In the *Home* tab>Profile & Section Views panel, expand

   Section Views and click 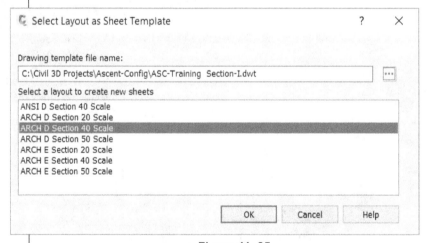 (Create Multiple Section Views).

4. In the Create Multiple Section Views - General dialog box, ensure that Jeffries Ranch Rd is the selected alignment (it should be since that is the only alignment with sample lines), accept all the other defaults, and click **Next>**.

5. In the Create Multiple Section Views - Section Placement dialog box, for *Placement Options,* choose **Production**, then click on the ellipsis (...) to open the Select Layout as Sheet Template window.

6. Click the ellipsis (...) again to choose the proper template. Browse to the *C:\Civil 3D Projects\Ascent-Config* folder and select **ASC-Training Section-I.dwt**. Click **OK**.

7. Select the **ARCH D Section 40 Scale** layout, third in the list, as shown in Figure 11–35.

Select Layout as Sheet Template   ?   X

Drawing template file name:

C:\Civil 3D Projects\Ascent-Config\ASC-Training Section-I.dwt   [...]

Select a layout to create new sheets

ANSI D Section 40 Scale
ARCH D Section 20 Scale
ARCH D Section 40 Scale
ARCH D Section 50 Scale
ARCH E Section 20 Scale
ARCH E Section 40 Scale
ARCH E Section 50 Scale

OK   Cancel   Help

Figure 11–35

8. Accept the defaults for the next four windows by clicking **Next>,** until you come to the last window named Create Multiple Section Views - *Section View Tables.*

9. In the *X Offset* field, type **0.50"** and set *Table layout* to **Vertical**, then click **Add>>** to add the Total Volume Table to the list. Then expand the Type drop-down list and select **Material**. Click **Add>>** again to include the material table in the section view. Select all of the materials in the **Select Materials** window. Change the *Gap* for the Material table to **0.250"**, as shown in Figure 11–36.

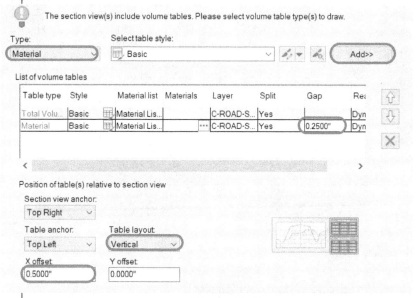

Figure 11–36

10. Click **Create Section View**. At the *Identify section view origin* prompt, click in empty space in Model Space, somewhere north of the previous section.

Task 4 - Create section sheet files and add them to the sheet set.

---

1. Continue working with the drawing from the previous task or open **PPR1-C3.dwg** from the *C:\Civil 3D Projects\Plans* folder.

2. In the *Output* tab>Plan Production panel, click ![icon] (Create Section Sheets).

3. Fill in the following, as shown in Figure 11–37:

- *Alignment*: **Jeffries Ranch Rd**
- *Sample line group*: **SL Collection - 1**
- *Section view group*: **Sample View Group**
- *Layout name*: Select the name template icon and fill in **Section-<[Parent Alignment]>-<[Next Counter]>** in the New Template, as shown in figure Figure 11–37.

4. For *Sheet Set,* select *Add to existing sheet set* and use the ellipses (...) to browse to the *C:\Civil 3D Projects\Plans* folder and select **Ascent Phase1.dst.** If you did not complete the previous practice, select **Ascent Phase1A.dst** instead.

5. Click on **Create Sheets**.

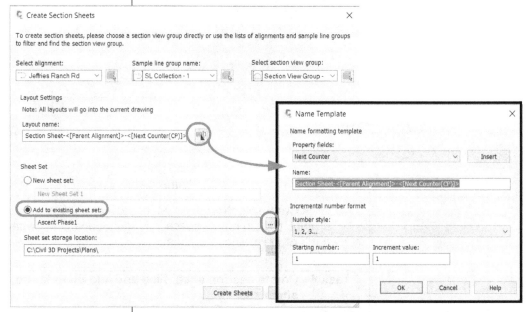

Figure 11–37

6. Click **OK** to dismiss the *Drawing will be saved* message.

7. Note the new layouts that have been created in the drawing.

8. Save the drawing as **<Your Initials>-Sections-Complete.dwg** in the *C:\Civil 3D Projects\References\DWG\Proposed* folder and close it.

9. If prompted, update the relative paths of the referenced drawings.

11.7 Sheet Sets

The sheet set is not exclusive to the Autodesk Civil 3D software, but is used in all AEC products. A sheet set is a collection of sheets that are created from a combination of several different drawings. Sheets listed in the Sheet Set Manger file (DST) refer to layouts in a drawing file. The sheet set can reference any number of layouts from any number of drawings.

For example, you might be working on a commercial site plan or a highway project drawing. Using the Sheet Set Manager, you can create a construction set or tender documents by compiling a sheet set that lists all of the required sheets from the Existing Conditions plans and a variety of Design Models. Additionally, if the project is a multi-disciplined project that includes structural engineers and architects, you can compile a list of sheets from those sources as well. Figure 11–38 outlines the structure of sheet sets in a project.

1. Drawings residing in various folders from various disciplines

2. Layouts in those drawings organized into sheet sets

3. Final documents

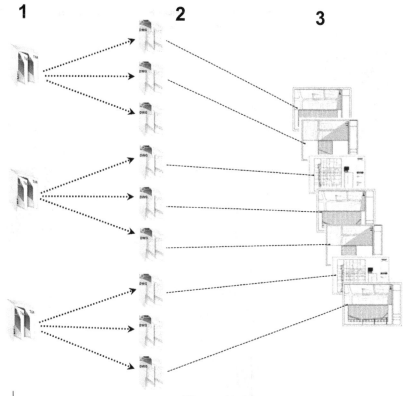

Figure 11–38

Sheet Set Manager Palette

All tools required for managing sheet sets are available through the *Sheet Set Manager*, which is accessible though the *View* tab>Palettes panel. Expand the panel and click (Sheet Set Manager) from the drop-down list, as shown in Figure 11–39.

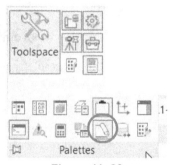

Figure 11–39

The <Ctrl>+<4> keyboard shortcut also invokes the Sheet Set Manager.

You can also access sheet sets from the *Start* tab of Civil 3D, as shown in Figure 11–40.

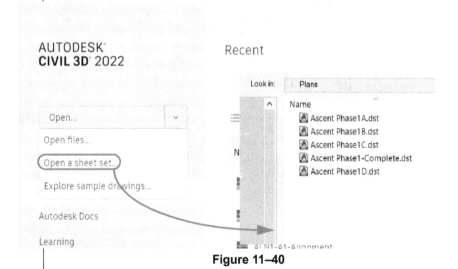

Figure 11–40

Structuring Sheet Sets

Figure 11–41 displays a typical hierarchical structure of the sheet set elements.

- The *Sheet Set Name* (1) identifies the sheet set (i.e., the DST file). This file can reside anywhere on your server.

- The *Sheet* subset (2) is used to organize sheets in a logical manner (e.g., Plan Profiles, Structural, Electrical, etc.).

- The *Individual Sheets* (3) are layouts from drawings imported into the sheet set.

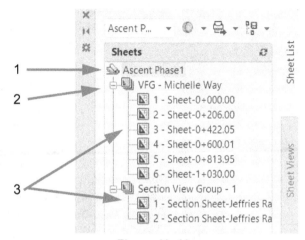

Figure 11–41

Each of the elements represents a core component in a typical sheet set. As with other Autodesk Civil 3D object functionality, right-clicking on any of these elements lists all of the available options for that element.

Editing Sheet Sets

You can modify and re-organize sheet sets in a number of ways. For example, you can reorder the sheets in the set, rename or renumber sheets, create new sheets or subsets, and import new layouts as sheets. To reorder elements in the sheet set, drag the element to a new location. Reordering sheets using this method does not automatically renumber the sheets.

The options to edit sheet sets are shown in Figure 11–42.

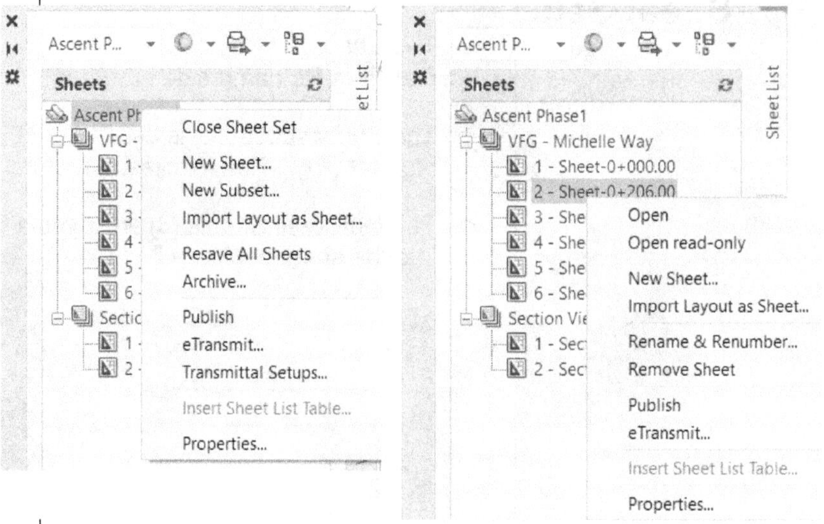

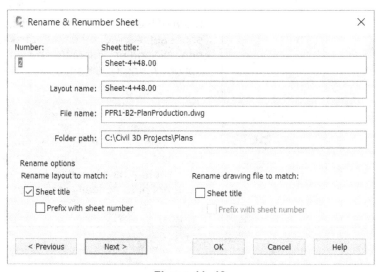

Figure 11–42

To rename and renumber sheets automatically, enter a *Number* and *Sheet title*. To change the associated filename, type a new *File name*. You can also have the associated filename change when you rename the sheet. To enable this feature, select the **Sheet title** option to rename the drawing file to match the sheet title, as shown in Figure 11–43.

Figure 11–43

Sheet Set Manager Properties

In the Sheet Set Properties dialog box, you can change the name, the path of the drawing files or the template associated with the sheet set, and any custom properties associated with the sheet set.

To access the properties, right-click on the Sheet Set Manager name and select Properties. Information specific to the sheet set displays.

The Sheet Set Properties dialog box contains the following, as shown in Figure 11–44:

- Sheet Set properties (1)
- Project Control properties (2)
- Sheet Creation properties (3)

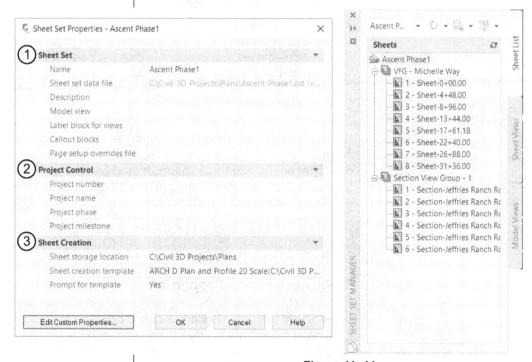

Figure 11–44

1. Sheet Set Properties

The sheet set properties provide access to the following:

- Name of the sheet set.
- Sheet set data file location (read only).
- Description.
- Model view drawing location (the location of the resource drawings).
- Label block for views (the location of the drawing and blocks that contain the block, which can be used for the views).
- Callout blocks (a list of blocks that can be used for callouts), which ensures that drawing references in the various callouts (such as details) are always up-to-date.
- Page setup override file (a drawing template that contains the page setup overrides for the sheet set). The page setup override enables you to override existing page setups for individual drawings in the sheet set.

2. Project Control Properties

You can use four preset project properties: *Project Number, Name, Phase,* and *Milestone*. These properties can also be displayed on the individual sheets. In addition to these four properties, you can create custom properties. There are two types of properties:

- *Sheet Set properties* are applied to all of the sheets in the set.
- *Sheet properties* are only applied to a single sheet.

3. Sheet Creation Properties

In the Sheet Creation Properties dialog box, you can access the location of the folder to store your sheets, and the default template that is used when creating a new sheet. The sheet storage location is where the new drawing sheet that is created is stored. The sheet creation template is the template that is used when creating the new sheet.

Practice 11d

Plan Production Tools - Sheet Sets

Practice Objective

- Edit sheet and sheet set properties to make annotating sheets easier.

Task 1 - Define the Sheet Set Manager properties.

1. Close any drawings you may have open so that only the *Start* tab is open in Civil 3D.

2. If the **Ascent Phase1** sheet set is not listed in the Recent files of the *Start* tab, you will have to open and browse to **Ascent Phase1.dst** in the *C:\Civil 3D Projects\Plans* folder, as shown in Figure 11–45. If you did not complete the previous practice, select **Ascent Phase1B.dst** instead.

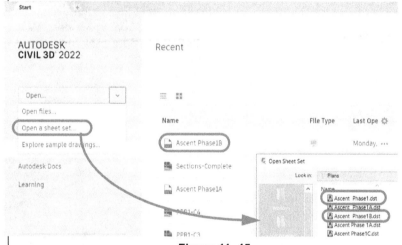

Figure 11–45

3. In the *Sheet Set Manager palette*, double-click on the first sheet listed, as shown in Figure 11–46. Note that the drawing name opens to the "*Sheet-0+000.00*" layout tab, just as it is listed in the Sheet Set Manager.

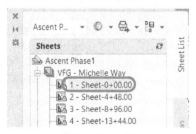

Figure 11–46

---

4. Select **VFG - Michelle Way**, right-click, and select **Rename Subset...**, as shown on the left in Figure 11–47. For the *Subset Name*, type **Plan-Profile - Michelle Way**, as shown on the right. Click **OK** to close the dialog box.

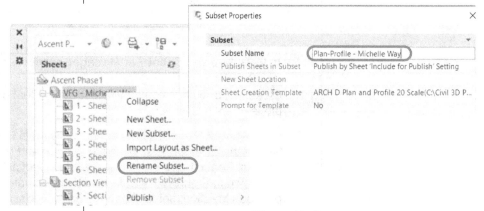

Figure 11–47

5. In the *Plan-Profile - Michelle Way* collection, select **1 - Sheet - 0+000.00**, right-click, and select **Rename & Renumber**, as shown in Figure 11–48.

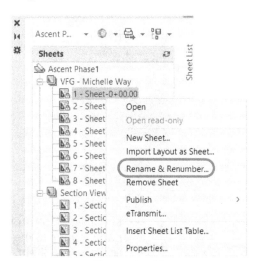

Figure 11–48

6. In the *Rename & Renumber Sheet* dialog box, change the *Number* to **3** to make room to add a title sheet and overall plan sheet later, and select **Sheet title** in the *Rename layout to match* area, as shown in Figure 11–49. Click **Next>**.

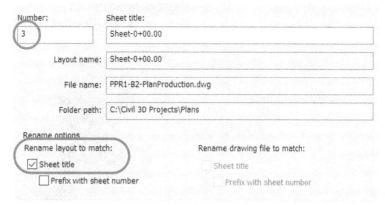

Figure 11–49

7. Change the next sheet number to **4**, and continue to click **Next>** to continue increasing the page number for each sheet until all of the sheets are renumbered, as shown in Figure 11–50. Note the changes to the sheet names. Click **OK** to accept the changes and close the dialog box.

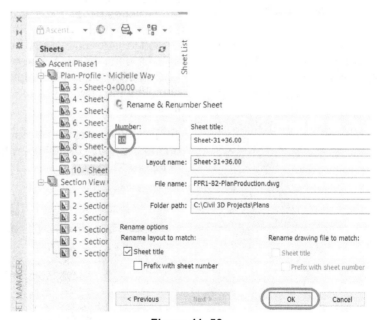

Figure 11–50

8. Repeat the same procedure for the Section View Group - 1 subset as follows:

- Rename the subset to **Sections - Jeffries Ranch**
- Renumber the sheets, starting with 11 and upward.
- Select **Sheet title** in the *Rename layout to match* area.

9. Right-click on the Sheet Set name (*Ascent Phase1)* and select **Resave All Sheets**, as shown in Figure 11–51.

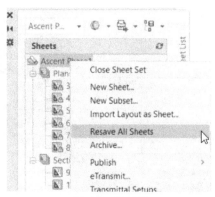

Figure 11–51

Task 2 - Define the Sheet Set properties.

---

1. If the Sheet Set Manager is not displayed, open it in the *View* tab>Palettes panel. Expand the panel and select the **Sheet Set Manager**. Expand the Sheet Set drop-down list at the top of the Manager palette and select the **Ascent Phase 1** sheet set. If it is not in the list, browse to **Ascent Phase1.dst** in the *C:\Civil 3D Projects\Plans* folder and open it. If you did not complete the previous practice, select **Ascent Phase1C.dst** instead.

2. To navigate to one of the drawings, double-click or right-click on the **3-Sheet - 0+000.00** entry and select **Open**, as shown in Figure 11–52.

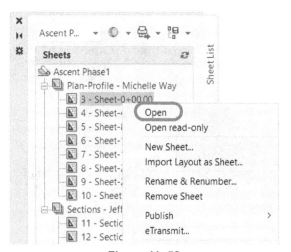

Figure 11–52

---

3. Once the drawing is open, zoom in to the lower right corner of the drawing, as shown in Figure 11–53. Note the title block. The values for the **Project Name** and **Project Number** do not display any values.

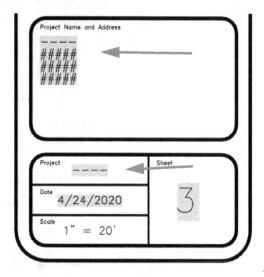

Figure 11–53

4. In the Sheet Set Manager for *Ascent Phase1*, select the sheet set name **Ascent Phase1**, right-click, and select **Properties**, as shown in Figure 11–54.

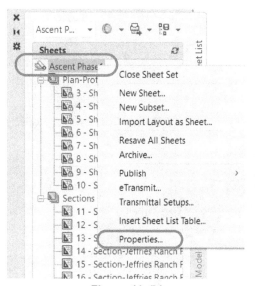

Figure 11–54

5. As shown in Figure 11–55, in the Sheet Set Properties - Ascent Phase1 dialog box, type:

- **30042020** in the *Project Number* field.
- **ASCENT C3D TRAINING** in the *Project Name* field.
- **PRE-TENDER** in the *Project phase* field.
- **66%** in the *Project milestone* field.

6. Click on **Edit Custom Properties**.

7. In the *Custom Properties* dialog box, click on **Add...**

8. In the *Add Custom Property* dialog box, do the following (as shown in Figure 11–55):

- Enter **CIVIC ID** for the *Name*.
- Enter **Z-1234** for the *Default Value.*
- Ensure that *Owner* is set to **Sheet Set**.

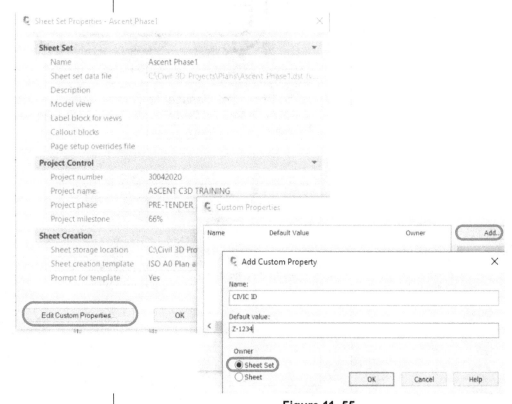

Figure 11–55

9. Click **OK** three times to complete the procedure. You will need to type **regen** and press <Enter> in the Command Line to display the updated fields. The values in your drawing title sheet should now be displayed, as shown in Figure 11–56.

Figure 11–56

10. For the custom properties (such as *CIVIC ID), Project milestone,* and *Project Phase to* appear in the title block, special attributes need to be added. Your CAD Manager is responsible for configuring this.

11. Resave all sheets as you did earlier and exit all of the drawings.

Task 3 - Define Sheet Set properties.

---

1. Open a new drawing session by selecting **File>New**. Then select **_Autodesk Civil 3D (Imperial) NCS.dwt** from the default template location.

2. If the Sheet Set Manager for *Ascent Phase 1* is not active, you can open the sheet set.dst file using one of the following methods:

   • Select the Autodesk Civil 3D file and click **Open**. Select **Sheet Set** and browse to **Ascent Phase1.dst** from the *C:\Civil 3D Projects\Plans* folder, or select **Open the Sheet Set Manager** and select the **Ascent Phase 1** in the drop-down list. If you did not complete the previous practice, select **Ascent Phase1D.dst** instead.

   • In the *View* tab>Palettes panel, select the **Sheet Set Manager** in the drop-down list.

---

3. In the Sheet Set Manager dialog box, select the sheet set **Ascent Phase1**, right-click, and select **New Subset**, as shown on the left in Figure 11–57. Type **Base Plans** for the *Subset Name*, as shown on the right. Set the *Prompt for Template* to **No**, so that all new sheets use the preset template. Click **OK** to exit the dialog box.

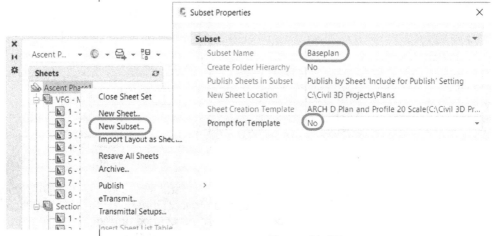

Figure 11–57

4. In the Sheet Set Manager, select the subset **Base Plans** and drag it to the top, as shown in Figure 11–58.

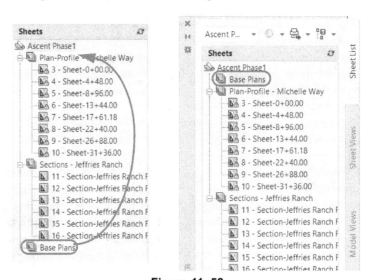

Figure 11–58

5. To create a new sheet, select the subset **Base Plans**, right-click, and select **New Sheet**, as shown in Figure 11–59.

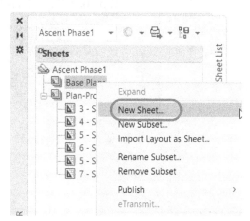

Figure 11–59

6. In the New Sheet dialog box, type **00** in the *Number* field, and type **Index** in the *Sheet title* field, as shown in Figure 11–60. Select the **Open in drawing editor** option to open the drawing when done. The Sheet Set Manager will create a drawing named **00 Index.dwg**.

Figure 11–60

7. The Sheet Set Manager has created a new drawing based on the template and the sheet set properties. Select and delete the two viewports, as well as the North Arrow in the upper right corner, as they are not necessary. Zoom in to display the entire title block.

8. In the Sheet Set Manager, select the sheet set **Ascent Phase1**, right-click, and select **Insert Sheet List Table**, as shown in Figure 11–61.

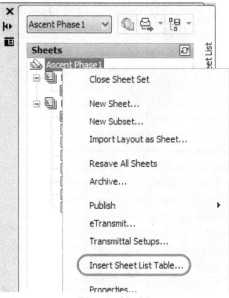

Figure 11–61

9. In the Sheet List Table dialog box, expand the Table Style name drop-down list, and select **Legend**. Select the **Show Subheader** option and click **OK** to close the dialog box, as shown in Figure 11–62.

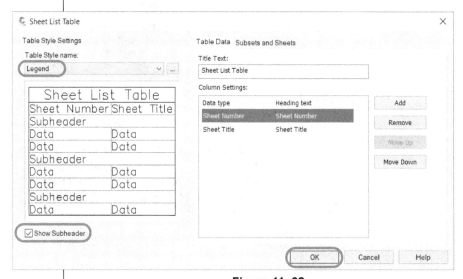

Figure 11–62

10. When prompted for the location of the table, select a point in the middle of the title block, as shown in Figure 11–63. If the table scale is too small, use the AutoCAD **Scale** command to adjust it.

Sheet List Table	
Sheet Number	Sheet Title
Base Plans	
00	Index
Plan–Profile – Michelle Way	
3	Sheet–0+00.00
4	Sheet–4+48.00
5	Sheet–8+96.00
6	Sheet–13+44.00
7	Sheet–17+61.18
8	Sheet–22+40.00
9	Sheet–26+88.00
10	Sheet–31+36.00
Sections – Jeffries Ranch	
11	Section–Jeffries Ranch Rd–1
12	Section–Jeffries Ranch Rd–2
13	Section–Jeffries Ranch Rd–3
14	Section–Jeffries Ranch Rd–4
15	Section–Jeffries Ranch Rd–5
16	Section–Jeffries Ranch Rd–6

Figure 11–63

11. Save the drawing.

Chapter Review Questions

1. What are two of the steps required to create plan and profile sheets using the Plan Production tools?

   a. Create layouts.

   b. Create View Frames.

   c. Create new drawings with references to data.

   d. Generate Sheets.

2. How can you integrate the Autodesk Civil 3D software's Plan Production system layouts into an existing sheet set?

   a. When generating the sheets, select the option to **Add to existing sheet set** on the Sheet Set page in the Create Sheets wizard.

   b. Open the sheet set and manually import the sheets and views one by one.

   c. It is not possible, you have to have a separate sheet set for each alignment and profile.

   d. When generating the view frames, select the option to **Add to the existing sheet set** in the Sheets page.

3. How is the scale of the plan and profile sheet determined?

   a. Using the **Annotation Scale** tool in the Status Bar.

   b. Using the scale in the *Graph* tab in the Profile View Style dialog box.

   c. Using the template and layout selected during the View Frame creation process.

   d. Select the Toolspace, *Setting* tab. Right-click on the current drawing, select **Edit Drawing Settings**, and then in the Drawing Settings dialog box, select the *Units and Zones* tab.

4. How do you ensure that the project name and number display on every sheet automatically?

  a. This cannot be automated.

  b. Set up the sheet template with project name and number fields, and then set the project name and number in the **Sheet Set Manager>Sheet Set Properties**.

  c. Set up the sheet template with project name and number fields, and then set the project name and number during the View Frame Creation process.

  d. When generating the sheets, select the option to add the project name and number to the sheets.

5. After creating the plan and profile sheets, you can easily create additional sheets using the Sheet Set Manager.

  a. True

  b. False

Command Summary

Button	Command	Location
	Create Section Sheets	• **Ribbon:** *Output* tab>Plan Production panel • **Command Prompt:** CreateSectionSheets
	Create Sheets	• **Ribbon:** *Output* tab>Plan Production panel • **Command Prompt:** CreateSheets
	Create View Frames	• **Ribbon:** *Output* tab>Plan Production panel • **Command Prompt:** CreateViewFrames

12

Quantity Takeoff and Visualization

In this chapter, you will inspect your Civil 3D project, both visually and quantitatively.

You will add content to the model to give it more realism so observers can gain a sense of scale and familiarity. You will calculate miscellaneous quantities on non-Civil 3D objects, such as the items you have added, to assist in estimating. Then, you will navigate around the model and save some vantage points.

Learning Objectives in This Chapter

- Insert Civil 3D multi-view blocks.
- Calculate the cost of design by assigning pay items to specific objects.
- Navigate through the model and "drive" along a corridor.

12.1 Civil 3D Multi-view Blocks

Autodesk Civil 3D multi-view blocks are a collection of special blocks which can add a greater degree of detail to your drawing for reference and a sense of familiarity. There are a variety of predefined blocks representing the following:

- Highways:
  - Road Signs
  - Lighting Columns
  - Railings
  - Vehicles
  - etc.
- Landscape:
  - Trees and shrubs
  - For rendering purposes
  - For annotation purposes
- External Works:
  - Amenity lighting
  - Playground
  - Fencing
  - People
  - etc.
- Building Footprints:
  - Apartments
  - Row housing
  - Single family dwellings
  - Sheds

Multi-view Blocks

Multi-view blocks are a type of special AutoCAD blocks that have separate embedded blocks for different view directions. You can create your own multi-view blocks from AutoCAD blocks that represent the different views of the item you want to display.

There are a good collection of multi-view blocks representing different types of objects in Autodesk Civil 3D. For example, the top view of a multi-view block representing a building shows only the building footprint as would be seen in plan view. There are representations for left, right, front, and back views, which are your standard architectural elevation views. Additionally, in 3D you get a three dimensional representation that can be rendered or viewed in wireframe mode, as shown in Figure 12–1.

Elevation view **Rendered 3D view**

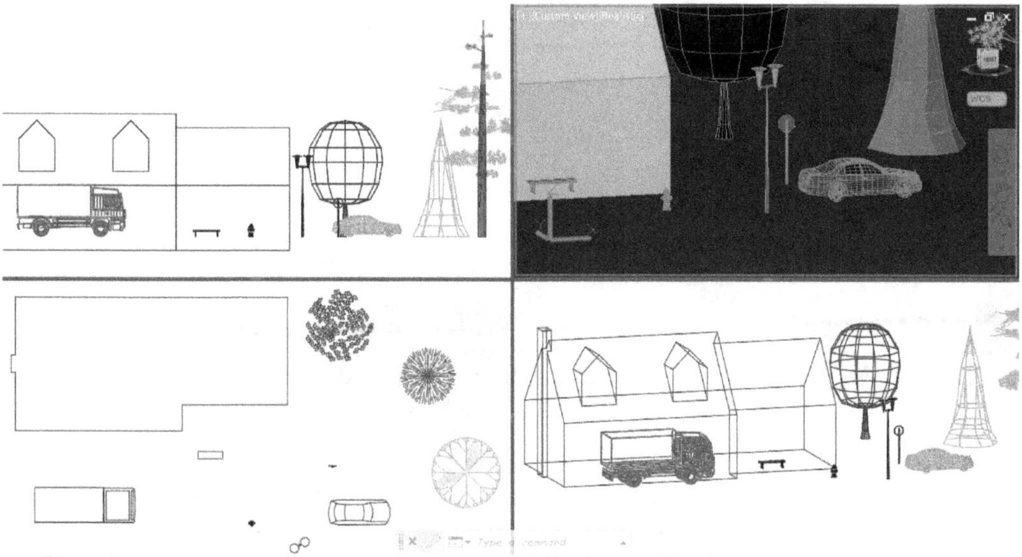

Plan view **Wireframe 3D view**

Figure 12–1

Tool Palettes

The easiest way to add an Autodesk Civil 3D subassembly to an assembly is using the Tool Palettes. You can open the Tool Palettes by clicking 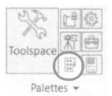 in the *Home* tab>Palettes panel, as shown in Figure 12–2, or in the *View* tab>Palettes panel. You can also use <Ctrl>+<3>.

Figure 12–2

The Autodesk Civil 3D software provides a number of stock multi-view blocks divided into different tabs of the *Civil Multiview Blocks* tool palette, as shown in Figure 12–3.

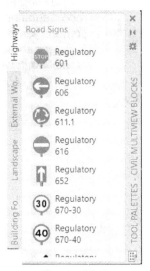

Figure 12–3

To select the correct palette, right-click on the Tool Palette band and select the *Civil Multiview Blocks* tool palette.

You can customize various properties of the block to be inserted, such as its layer, color and linetype, etc. by right-clicking on the block name and selecting Properties, as shown in Figure 12–4.

Figure 12–4

Most of the blocks are created at full scale, therefore you do not need to adjust their size. However for the Landscape blocks you need to provide a scale after you insert them. You can pre-define the scale through the properties of the item in the tool palette, as shown in Figure 12–5.

Figure 12–5

Once the landscape block is inserted, you can change the X, Y and Z scale of the block. If you want a taller, more slender tree, increase the Z scale, conversely for a shorter, broader tree, either increase the X and Y scales, or decrease the Z scale.

To insert a block, you click on the block name and select the insertion point on-screen. Do not click and drag, you need to "click and click". Once you select the insertion point, you give the rotation angle, depending on the type of block.

Do not worry about the elevation value of the insertion point of the inserted blocks. Once all the blocks are inserted, there is a routine in the Surface textual ribbon to move blocks to the surface. You select the blocks from a list (as shown in Figure 12–6), and the routine adjusts the Z value of the insertion point of the block to the surface elevation.

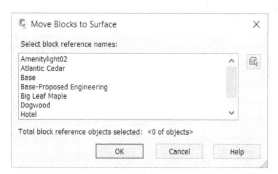

Figure 12–6

Practice 12a | Adding Detail to Drawings

Practice Objective

- Populate the drawing with objects to add contextual references.

Task 1 - Insert Civil 3D multi-view blocks.

For this drawing, a variety of multi-view blocks have already been inserted in the northern portion of the site. You will add some more detail near the Jeffries Rand Rd. and Ascent Place intersection. The XREF models of the hotel, school, and office building have been swapped from 2D building footprint drawings to 3D models.

1. Open **QTO1-A1.dwg** from the *C:\Civil 3D Projects\Working\ QTO-Viz* folder.

2. Select the preset view **Intersection-2D**.

3. Open the Tool Palettes by clicking 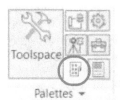 in the *Home* tab> Palettes panel, as shown in Figure 12–7, or use the <Ctrl>+<3> keyboard shortcut.

Figure 12–7

Do not "Click and Drag", rather "Click and Click" by releasing the mouse button after you select the block and clicking again for the insertion point.

4. Right-click on the Tool Palette band and select the *Civil Multiview Blocks* tool palette, as shown in Figure 12–8.

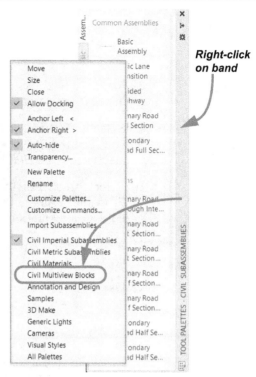

Right-click on band

Figure 12–8

5. If the block does not resize itself properly, you will need to scale it with the AutoCAD Properties palette, setting the X, Y, and Z scale to 0,3048.

6. Click on the Building Footprints tab and select the **Colonial 01**C to select it. It may take a short while for the block to be loaded into the drawing, as shown in Figure 12–9. Move your cursor into the drawing area into the *BLK1-Lot 1* parcel and you see a preview of the building footprint, which may appear to be oversized. Once you pick an insertion point it will adjust itself to the proper units (metric or imperial).

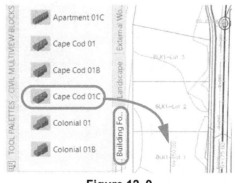

Figure 12–9

7. Use the AutoCAD Rotate command or the AutoCAD Properties palette to rotate the block. Do not worry about the elevation, you will take care of that once all the blocks are inserted.

8. Repeat the process to insert the **Farm House 01** block into the *BLK2-Lot 6* parcel and adjust its rotation angle.

9. Select the *Landscaping* tab and scroll down to the LandScape MV Blocks section. Select the **Apple** tree and insert it into the *BLK1-Lot 1* parcel.

10. Select the block in the drawing and go to the AutoCAD Properties (either through the contextual ribbon, the right-click menu or the <Ctrl>+<1> keyboard shortcut).

11. Adjust the Scale X, Scale Y, and Scale Z factors by setting them all to 5.

12. Insert some more trees around the 2 lots, adjust their scales. experiment with providing a different Scale Z.

13. Select the *Highways* tab and pick the Stop sign at the top of the list. Select a point at the intersection of the two corridors for the insertion. Now you give it the rotation angle, so insure it is parallel to the curb.

14. Continue to populate the area with a variety of multi-view blocks, adjusting their scales and rotation angles as required.

15. Save the drawing.

Task 2 - Adjusting the elevations of the multi-view blocks.

---

1. Continue with the drawing from the previous task or pen **QTO1-A2.dwg** from the *C:\Civil 3D Projects\Working\ QTO-Viz* folder.

2. Select the Final surface in the drawing (select one of the contour lines).

3. In the **Final** *surface* contextual tab, in the Surface Tools panel, expand the Move to Surface drop-down list and select (Move Blocks to Surface), as shown in Figure 12–10.

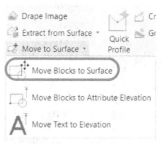

Figure 12–10

Select the first item, hold the <Shift> key when selecting the last item and then hold the <Ctrl> key to de-select the blocks you do not want.

4. In the Move Blocks to Surface selecting window, select all multi-view blocks you had previously inserted. Do NOT select the following (for they are the existing XREFs):

   - Base
   - Base-Proposed Engineering
   - Hotel
   - Office
   - School
   - Residentialpu

5. Click the **OK** button when done and the multi-view blocks are adjusted so the Z value of the insertion point matches the elevation of the surface.

6. Select the preset view **Intersection-3D** to ensure the blocks have moved properly. (Later you will learn how to change the visual style of this view).

7. Also note the hydrants at the intersection. These are not multi-view blocks but actual components of the Pressure Pipe appurtenance parts list created in the Pipe Network practices.

8. Select the preset view **Intersection-2D**.

9. Save the drawing.

12.2 Pay Items

An important element in any design is the cost of the design. The cost of a design can be determined by putting a price on a specific unit of work. To do this in the Autodesk Civil 3D software you assign a pay item to specific objects. Using the QTO Manager helps to automate this task and reduce errors and eliminate disputes with contractors.

There are three commonly used pay item properties:

- **Item number:** A unique number for each item in a plan.

- **Specification:** Determines how the work is measured and paid for, the material to use, and the method for incorporating the material.

- **Cost estimate:** Ensures that the design falls in the available project budget.

Pay Item File

Civil 3D ships with a default Pay Item file in comma delimited text file **Payitems-BidItems.csv**. It can be copied into your organization's standards folder, opened up in MS Excel and edited to suit your standards. It has the following columns:

- Name
- Item Description
- Units
- Bid Description
- Pay Item Type
- Year
- Date added / modified
- Division
- Comments

Assigning Pay Items

Pay items can be manually assigned to any of the following items once they have been created in the drawing file: AutoCAD lines, polylines, blocks, and Autodesk Civil 3D entities. They can be assigned to individual items, linear objects or within enclosed areas.

You can also assign pay items to Autodesk Civil 3D code set styles, pipe network and pressure pipe network parts lists so that corridor objects and pipes/structures are automatically tagged with the correct pay items, as shown in Figure 12–11.

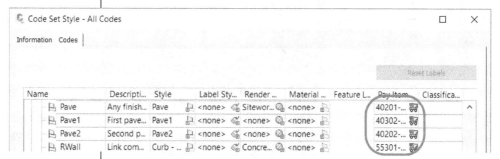

Figure 12–11

How To: Assign a Pay Item

1. In the *Analyze* tab>QTO panel, click 🚚 (QTO Manager).
2. Open the pay item file required for the project.
3. Assign a pay item to an object:
   - Individual items, such as blocks
   - Linear objects, such as lines and plines.
   - Areas
4. Run a report. The report can be limited to an alignment, and it is for this reason that you can associate a Pipe-Run to an alignment.

Practice 12b | Integrated Quantity Takeoff

Practice Objective

- Calculate the cost of design by assigning pay items to specific objects and then running a report.

Task 1 - Assign Pay Item ID.

A tool available in the Autodesk Civil 3D software enables you to automate the process of quantity takeoff. The traditional method involves a manual process of counting pay items individually (e.g., street lights) or performing linear measurements to obtain quantities of items, such as curb and gutter.

1. Open **QTO1-B1.dwg** from the *C:\Civil 3D Projects\Working\QTO-Viz* folder.

2. Select the preset view **Trees-2D**.

3. In the *Analyze* tab>QTO panel, click ⛃ (QTO Manager), as shown in Figure 12–12.

Figure 12–12

4. In the Panorama, expand 📂▼ and select **Open pay item file** as shown in Figure 12–13.

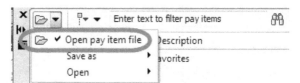

Figure 12–13

5. In the Open Pay Item File dialog box, shown in Figure 12–14:

- In the Pay item file format drop-down list, select **CSV (Comma delimited)**.
- Next to the Pay item file drop-down list, click 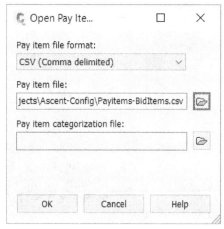.
- From the *C:\Civil 3D Projects\Ascent-Config* folder, select **ASC-Payitems-BidItems.csv**.
- Click **OK** to accept the changes and close the dialog box.

Figure 12–14

6. The *Pay Item ID* list will be populated with pay item numbers from the CSV file. To display only the required pay items, type **shrubs** in the *Filter* field at the top and press <Enter>. Only the shrubs pay items will be listed.

7. Right click on the **Pay Item ID** and select *Add to favorites list* so you can find it more easily next time you need it. It will now be part of your Favorites shown in Figure 12–15.

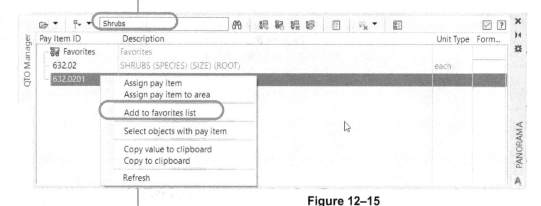

Figure 12–15

8. Assign a **Pay Item ID** to the object in the drawing. In Model Space, select a shrub, right-click, and select **Select Similar**, as shown in Figure 12–16.

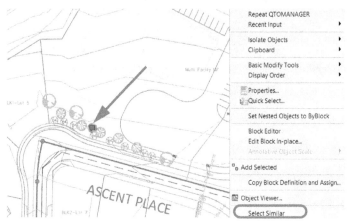

Figure 12–16

At the Command Line, a message prompts you that pay items are assigned to objects.

9. With all similar objects selected, select pay item **632.02** in the Panorama, right-click, and select **Assign pay item**, as shown in Figure 12–17. Press <Esc> to clear the current selection.

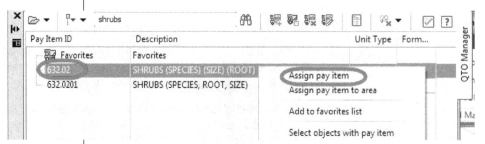

Figure 12–17

10. Next, apply Pay items to street light objects. Type **light** in the *Filter* field at the top and press <Enter>. Only pay items with the word *lighting* will be listed, as shown in Figure 12–18.

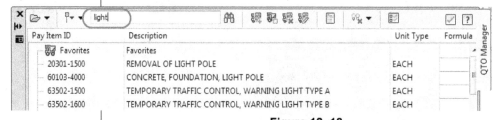

Figure 12–18

11. To assign a Pay Item ID to the object in the drawing, ensure that the previous selection set has been cleared by pressing <Esc>. In Model Space, select a street light, as shown in Figure 12–19, right-click, and select **Select Similar**.

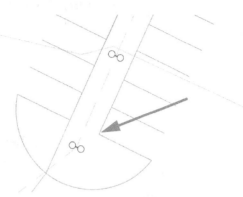

Figure 12–19

12. With all similar objects selected, select pay item **60103-4000 CONCRETE, FOUNDATION, LIGHT POLE** in the Panorama, as shown in Figure 12–20. Right-click and select **Assign pay item**. In the Command Line, a message prompts you that pay items have been assigned to objects. Press <Esc> to clear the current object selection.

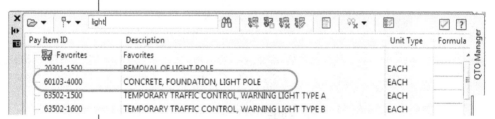

Figure 12–20

13. As these objects are now linked to QTO pay items, using the AutoCAD **Copy** command will also copy the reference to the pay item list. Press <Esc> to clear the selection set. Launch the AutoCAD **Copy** command, select any of the street lights, and copy to the far west end of the parking lot, as shown in Figure 12–21.

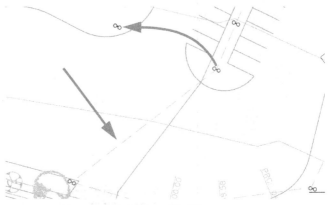

Figure 12–21

14. Search for Conduit, assign **63610-0500 Conduit, 1 INCH, RIGID GALVANIZED STEEL,** and add it to your Favorites List. Then, assign it to the orange dashed pline, as shown in Figure 12–21. Also assign **655.061 ELECTRICAL WIRE LIGHTING 12 AWG** to the same pline (search for *Wire*). Add it to your Favorites List.

15. Search for Sod, and select **62701-0000 SOD, SOLID.** Add it to your Favorites List.

16. Either right-click on the item or click ![icon] (Assign pay item(s) to a closed area) as shown in Figure 12–22.

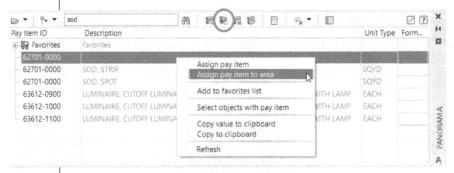

Figure 12–22

17. Type *O* for **[select Object]** and then 2 green plines, as shown in Figure 12–23. When you pick them, they turn black. This is because QTO adds a hatch pattern, by default Solid, on the current layer. Press <Esc>.

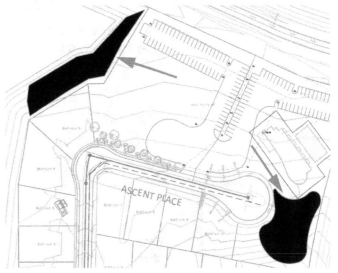

Figure 12–23

18. Select the two hatches created. In the *Hatch Editor* contextual ribbon, select the *GRASS* pattern and set the Scale to *12.0,* as shown in Figure 12–24. Also, change the layer to *L-PLNT-TURF* and the color to *BYLAYER* (through the AutoCAD Properties palette).

Figure 12–24

19. (Optional) Add another conduit line to the new (copied) light and assign the proper *Payitems*. (That is why you added them to the favorites list.) Add your choice of *Payitems* to the remaining tress (2 types).

20. Save the drawing.

Task 2 - Compute Quantity Takeoff.

Once pay items have been assigned to Autodesk Civil 3D or AutoCAD objects in the model, you will be able to compute quantities and generate a report.

1. Continue working with the drawing from the previous task or open **QTO1-B2.dwg**.

2. View the objects that have been tagged with Pay Item IDs. In the **Analyze** tab>QTO panel, click 🚚 (QTO Manager).

3. Type **light** in the **Filter** field at the top, and press <Enter>. Only the lighting pay items will be listed, as shown in Figure 12–25.

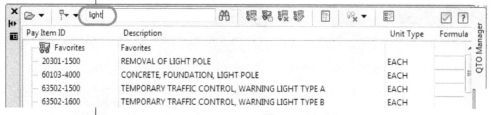

Figure 12–25

4. In the QTO Manager Panorama, select pay item **60103-4000**, right-click, and select **Select objects with pay item**, as shown in Figure 12–26. All tagged pay items in the drawing with its unique Pay Item ID will be highlighted. Review your selection and press <Esc> to clear the current object selection.

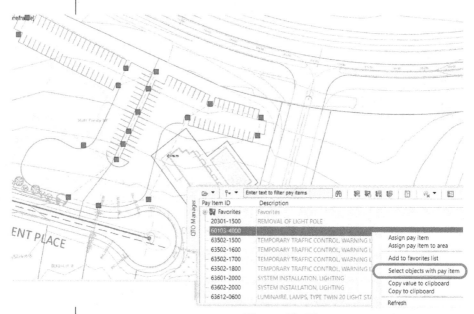

Figure 12–26

5. To generate a Quantity report, in the *Analyze* tab>QTO panel, click  (Takeoff), as shown in Figure 12–27.

Figure 12–27

6. In the Compute Quantity Takeoff dialog box, shown in Figure 12–28:

   - In the *Report type* area, select **Summary**.
   - In the Report extents drop-down list, select **Drawing**.
   - Accept all other default values.
   - Click **Compute** to accept the changes and calculate the quantities.

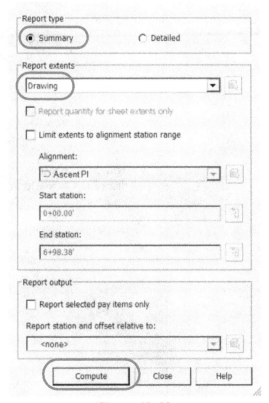

Figure 12–28

7. In the Quantity Takeoff report, select **Summary (HTML).xsl** as the output type, as shown in Figure 12–29.

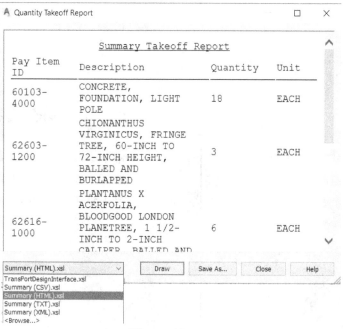

Figure 12–29

8. A number of different output formats will enable you to import the results into other software. You can also tag Autodesk Civil 3D objects (such as corridor materials with Pay Item ID).

9. You can save this report or draw a table in your CAD drawing. Click **Close** to close the dialog box, and click **Close** again to close the Compute Quantity Takeoff dialog box.

10. Save the drawing.

12.3 Visualization

For this phase, more Data shortcuts are being used. The Storm Pipe Network and Corridors (and their surfaces) have been referenced, while the grading surfaces have been combined into a Final (Final Ground for Visualization) surface and referenced as well.

From the architect, both 2D and 3D drawings were received and have been incorporated. Some landscaping features (vegetation, sod, lighting, and wiring) have been added, as shown in Figure 12–30.

Figure 12–30

Some tricks have been used to easily move from 2D to 3D elements, such as using provided multi-view blocks from Tool Palettes and switching 2D and 3D drawings through the Xref Manager, as shown in Figure 12–31.

Figure 12–31

12.4 3D Navigation Tools

The AutoCAD software includes two additional tools to help you navigate 3D drawings: the ViewCube and the SteeringWheel (located in the Navigation Bar), as shown in Figure 12–32.

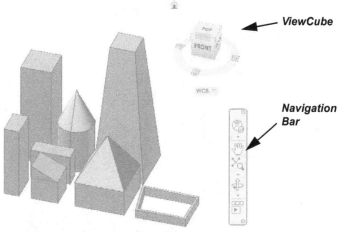

ViewCube

Navigation Bar

Figure 12–32

ViewCube

The ViewCube provides visual clues as to where you are in a 3D drawing and makes it easier to navigate to standard views, such as top, front, right, corner and directional views. Move the cursor over one of the highlighted options and select it. You can also click and drag on the ViewCube to rotate the box, which rotates the model. The ViewCube is shown in Figure 12–33.

*To change the Home view, set the view you want, right-click on the ViewCube, and select **Set Current View as Home**.*

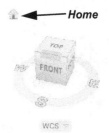

Home

Figure 12–33

- 🏠 (Home) displays when you move the cursor over the ViewCube. Click it to return to the view defined as **Home**.

- To toggle the ViewCube on and off, expand 🔲 (User Interface) in the *View* tab>User Interface panel and select **ViewCube**.

Hint: Parallel and Perspective Views

Traditional 2D drawings display objects in orthographic (parallel) views, where parallel edges on the object seem to be parallel in the drawing. Perspective views display as the eye sees and parallel edges seem to converge at a vanishing point on the horizon. You can view the model in either Parallel or Perspective projection, as shown in Figure 12–34.

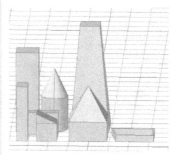 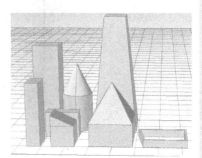

Figure 12–34

A parallel view helps you to evaluate the object's shape and size proportions without any distortion, while a perspective view gives you a better sense of space and depth, especially with large objects (such as buildings).

- You can draw, select, and modify objects while you are in a perspective view.

- You can switch between **Parallel**, **Perspective**, and **Perspective with Ortho Faces** when you right-click on the ViewCube or while you are in a **3D Orbit** command.

- You can also switch between **Parallel** and **Perspective** in the **View Controls** label list of the drawing window.

- Perspective mode is not available in the 2D wireframe visual style.

- If you save a drawing as a version earlier than the AutoCAD 2007 software, the Perspective view is automatically toggled off.

ViewCube Settings

ViewCube settings control the display of the ViewCube, how it works when you are dragging or clicking, and several other settings. Right-click on the ViewCube and select **ViewCube Settings...** to open the ViewCube Settings dialog box, as shown in Figure 12–35.

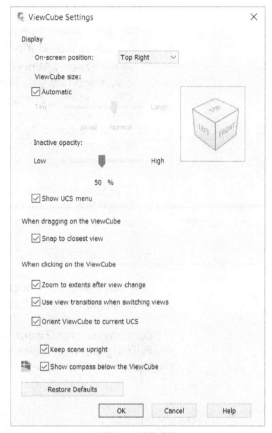

Figure 12–35

Steering Wheel

The SteeringWheel provides access to navigation commands such as **Zoom**, **Pan**, **Orbit**, and **Rewind**. The **Rewind** command navigates through all previous views of the model.

How To: Use the SteeringWheel

1. In the Navigation Bar, expand ⊚ (Full Navigation Wheel) and select a SteeringWheel.

   - Alternatively, you can expand ⊚ (Steering Wheel) in the Navigation Bar or type **navswheel** in the command line.

2. In the SteeringWheel, hover the cursor over the navigation command that you want to use.
3. Click and hold the mouse button to start the navigation command.
4. Move the cursor to change the view as required.
5. Release the mouse button to end the navigation command.
6. Close the SteeringWheel.

   - The SteeringWheel follows the cursor in the drawing window. Verify that the cursor is positioned correctly before launching a navigation command.

Full SteeringWheels

You can select from three different full wheels: Full Navigation, View Object, and Tour Building. The Full Navigation wheel includes all of the navigation tools, the Basic View Object wheel contains **Center**, **Zoom**, **Rewind**, and **Orbit**, and the Basic Tour Building wheel contains **Forward**, **Look**, **Rewind**, and **Up/Down**. The full wheels are shown in Figure 12–36.

*To close the SteeringWheel, press <Esc> or <Enter> or click the **X** in the SteeringWheel.*

Full Navigation

Basic View Object

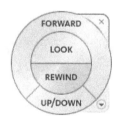

Basic Tour Building

Figure 12–36

Rewind Command

Use the **Rewind** command to navigate to previously displayed views of the model, as shown in Figure 12–37.

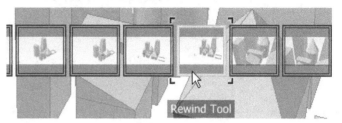

Figure 12–37

How To: Use the Rewind Command

1. Start the **SteeringWheel** command.
2. Hover the cursor over the **Rewind** option.
3. Click and hold the mouse button to start the **Rewind** command. A series of thumbnails display.
4. Move the cursor over the thumbnails to navigate to the highlighted view. The model updates as you move over the thumbnails.
5. Release the mouse button to make the highlighted view active.

SteeringWheel Settings

The SteeringWheels Settings dialog box controls the appearance of the SteeringWheels. With a SteeringWheel active, right-click and select **SteeringWheels Settings...** to open the dialog box, as shown in Figure 12–38.

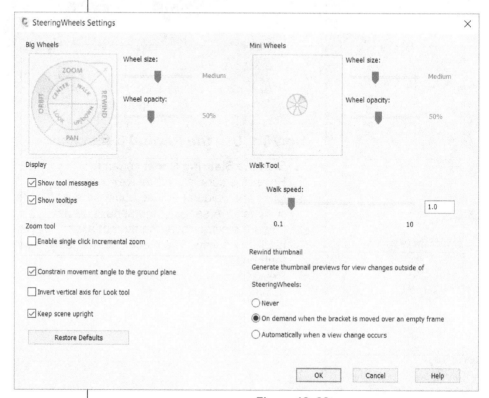

Figure 12–38

12.5 Managing Views in 3D

Named views capture your current vantage point of a drawing under specified names that can easily be restored in the drawing window.

Existing named views are available in the *View* tab>Named Views panel, or through the Viewport Control in the top left corner of your drawing area, as shown in Figure 12–39.

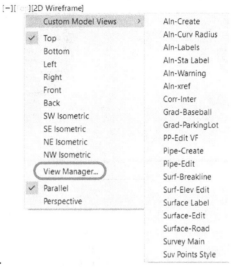

Figure 12–39

- Named views can be used in Model Space or in an active layout viewport.

- The View Manager dialog box sets, creates, deletes, modifies, and renames named views. It also manages model views, layout views, preset views, and camera views. You can select a named view and click **Set Current** to make it the current view.

- To open the View Manager dialog box, click 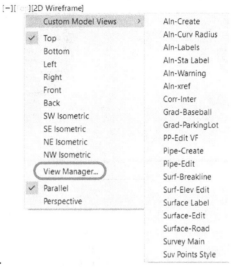 (View Manager) in the *Visualize* tab> Named Views panel or through the Viewport Control, as shown above in Figure 12–39.

How To: Create a New Named View

1. Set up the view as you want it to be saved.
2. In the *Home* tab>View panel, expand the 3D Navigation Control and select **View Manager...**.
3. In the View Manager, click **New**, as shown in Figure 12–40.

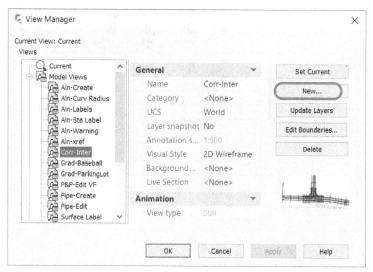

Figure 12–40

4. Fill out the New View/Shot Properties dialog box, as shown in Figure 12–41, including the *View name*, *Boundary*, *Settings*, and *Background* areas.

*The **View category** option refers to views that are used in sheet sets, such as plans and elevations. The categories are created in the Sheet Set Manager.*

Figure 12–41

5. Click **OK**.

New View Options

Save layer snapshot with view	Enables the view to retain the layer states that are set when the view is saved. Use this with caution, for it may change your layers whenever you restore a view.
UCS	Sets a UCS to be saved with the view.
Live section	Enables you to activate a section plane, if one is available in the drawing. Once a Live Section is on, it stays on until you deactivate it through the **Section Plane** shortcut menu option.
Visual style	Sets a visual style to be saved with the view.

Adding Backgrounds to Views

To add more realism or to highlight your design in the drawing window, you can add backgrounds to views. These backgrounds can be a solid, gradient, image, or Sun & Sky, as shown in Figure 12–42.

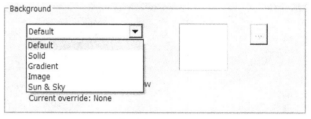

Figure 12–42

- Solid backgrounds can be any single color, while gradient backgrounds can be a mix of two or three colors.

- Images can be any of the standard image files that the Civil 3D software can view. In the Background dialog box shown in Figure 12–43, click **Browse** to select an image and then click **Adjust Image** to modify the image as required.

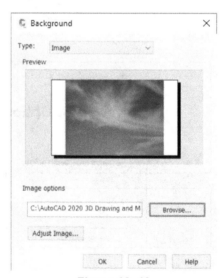

Figure 12–43

- The Sun & Sky setting mimics the effects of sunlight in your drawing. The position of the sun is determined by the geographic location and the time settings. To remove a background, select a view in which a background has not been set. Preset views do not remove a background.

12.6 Corridor Visualization

Visualizing corridors in a 3D view can be very helpful to ensure that the true design intent has been followed. Displaying the corridor along with the existing ground surface around it also helps to ensure that there are good sight distances as you drive down the corridor. Unfortunately, if there is a large cut area, the existing ground surface might obstruct the corridor from view, as shown on the left of Figure 12–44.

In these cases, it might be necessary to create a hide boundary in the existing ground surface using the outer boundary of the corridor surface. Doing so cuts a hole in the existing ground surface only where the corridor surface resides, as shown on the right of Figure 12–44. In addition, the interior boundary is updated if the corridor changes.

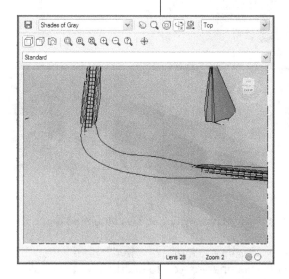 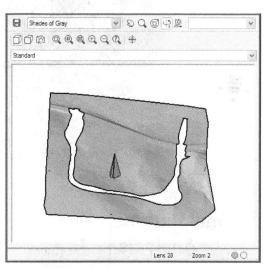

Figure 12–44

To make this work correctly, you need to copy the existing ground surface before adding the corridor surface as a hide boundary. This is because the corridor daylight lines reference the existing ground. If a hide boundary is then created from a surface that is referencing the surface into which it is being placed, a circular reference is created. To avoid this, create a new surface, paste the existing ground surface into it, and then create the hide boundary for the existing ground from the corridor surface. This ensures that the boundary is updated as the corridor changes without creating a circular reference.

Once the circular reference issue has been corrected, you can

use ⊙ (Drive) in the *Alignment* tab>Analyze panel. You can

then click ▷◫ (play/pause) in the *Drive* contextual tab to
preview the finished design in relation to the existing ground
surface as you drive down the corridor, as shown in
Figure 12–45. While in the **Drive** command, you can change the
drive path to another linear object if you have a network of road
alignments, such as a subdivision, that you want to simulate
driving through.

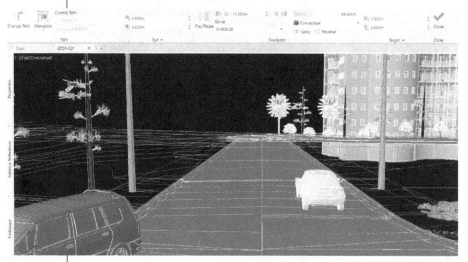

Figure 12–45

Line of Sight Analysis

The sight distances along a roadway can be calculated using the

⊙ (Sight Distance) command found on the *Corridor* contextual
tab>Analysis panel. This enables you to ensure that the design
meets the minimum sight distances at specified intervals along a
corridor. You can set the minimum sight distance.

How To: Check Sight Distance Along a Roadway

1. On the *Corridor* contextual tab>Analyze panel, click

   ⊙ (Sight Distance).

2. In the Sight Distance Check dialog box, in the *General* tab,
   select the **Alignment** and **Profile** to analyze. Set the **From
   station, To station**, **Check interval**, and **Select surface to
   check against** fields, as shown in Figure 12–46. Click
   Next>.

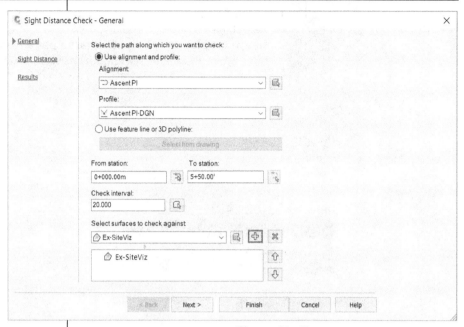

Figure 12–46

3. In the Sight Distance Check dialog box, in the *Sight Distance* tab, set the **Minimum sight distance**, **Eye height**, **Eye Offset**, **Target height**, and **Target offset**, as shown in Figure 12–47. Click **Next>**.

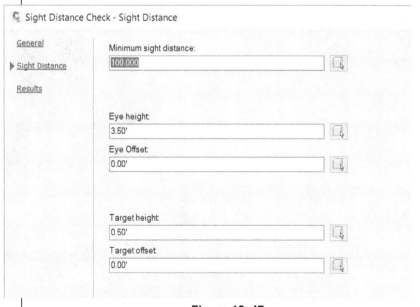

Figure 12–47

4. In the Sight Distance Check dialog box, in the *Results* tab, select the components to display in the model. Set the **Select hatch display for obstructed area** pattern, and select the file format and save location for the report, as shown in Figure 12–48. Click **Finish**.

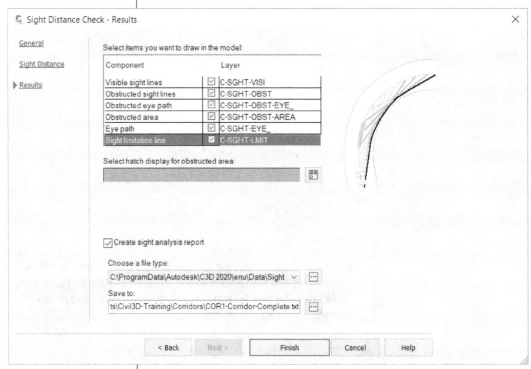

Figure 12–48

12.7 Share

Share your current drawing by using the 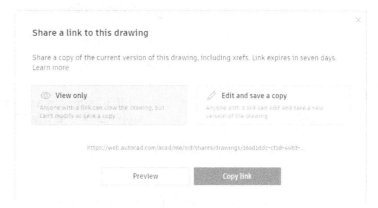 (Share) command in the Quick Access Toolbar. It opens a dialog box to create a copy of the current drawing for viewing only or for editing and saving, as shown in Figure 12–49.

Figure 12–49

Click on **Copy link** to create a link of the copy you can send. Anybody with the link can open the drawing in the AutoCAD web app. This copy of the drawing contains all the XREFs, layers, blocks, and properties.

The AutoCAD web app (shown in Figure 12–50) allows users to navigate through drawings and their settings in a similar manner to using the AutoCAD program.

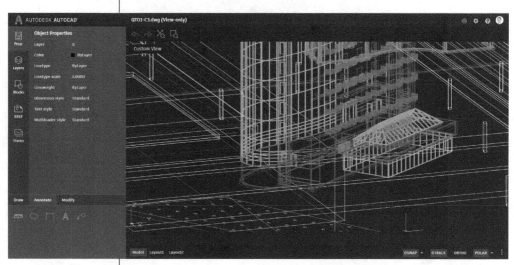

Figure 12–50

In the AutoCAD web app, you can:

- Navigate around the drawing.

- Draw, annotate, and modify the drawing.

- Control the layer visibility.

- Explore drawing element properties.

- Toggle drawing aids (Otrack, Ortho, etc.).

- Explore blocks and XREFs.

Hint: The Civil 3D objects are not properly displayed in the AutoCAD web app if the Civil 3D Object Enablers are not present.

Practice 12c | Visualizing Corridors

Practice Objectives

- Display the corridor in 3D along with the interim ground surface to visualize what it is like to drive on the road.
- Check for any sight obstructions along a corridor.
- Share the drawing with others via the AutoCAD web app.

Task 1 - Analyze the site visually using the Drive command.

In this task, you will create a new surface for visualization using an interim design surface with the Ascent Place Top surface cut into it. Then, you will use that surface for checking site distances.

1. Open **QTO1-C1.dwg** from the *C:\Civil 3D Projects\Working\ QTO-Viz* folder. Do not continue from the last drawing, for this drawing has the interim design surface in it.

2. In the *Home* tab>Create Ground Data panel, click ⌂ (Create Surface). Proceed as follows:

    - Type **SiteViz** for the name.
    - For the description, type **Design & Road Surface for visualization purposes**.
    - Select **ASC-Contours 2' and 10' (Design)** for the style.
    - Select **Sitework.Planting.Grass.Thick** for the render material.
    - Click **OK**.

3. In the Toolspace, *Prospector* tab, expand the definition of the new **SiteViz** surface. Right-click on **Edits** and select **Paste Surface**. Select **IDG** and click **OK**.

4. Right-click on **Boundaries** and select **Add**.

5. In the Add Boundaries dialog box, name it **Ascent PI**, and select **Hide** in the list of boundary types. Verify that **Non-Destructive** is selected and click **OK**.

6. Type **S** for surface, select the **Ascent PI Top** corridor surface, and press <Enter>.

7. In the *Modify* tab, select **Alignments**. In the *Alignments* contextual tab, click 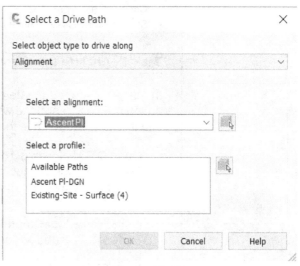 (Drive). When prompted to select an alignment, press <Enter> to select **Ascent PI** from the alignment list and **Ascent PI-DGN1** from the profile list, as shown in Figure 12–51.

Figure 12–51

8. Click **OK**.

9. In the *Drive* contextual tab, click ▷❙❙ (Play/Pause).

10. When you've arrived at the end, in the Navigate panel, use the *Go to:* drop-down list and select station 3+34.98.

11. Click and drag on the *ViewCube* to orbit around the drawing.

12. From the Navigation Bar, invoke the **Full Navigation Wheel**.

13. Experiment with the **Walk**, **Look**, **Orbit**, **Up/Down**, and **Rewind** buttons.

14. When you have an interesting vantage point you want to save, close the *Navigation Wheel* through the **X** in the upper right corner.

15. Go to the *View Manager*, click on **New...** to save this view, giving it a meaningful name.

16. Select the blue Drive tab and click ✔ (Close) to close the *Drive* contextual tab.

If the Navigation Bar is not visible on the screen, go to the View tab>Viewport Tools panel to display it.

Task 2 - Analyze the sight distance.

In this task, you will use the **Sight Distance** command to ensure that the design meets the minimum required sight distances.

1. Continue working in the same file from the last task, or open **QTO1-C2.dwg** from the *C:\Civil 3D Projects\Working\QTO-Viz* folder.

2. On the *Modify* tab>Design panel, click 🔌 (Corridor).

3. On the *Corridor* contextual tab>Analyze panel, click

   🔍 (Sight Distance).

4. In the Sight Distance Check dialog box, in the *General* tab, (shown in Figure 12–52), proceed as follows:

   - Select **Use alignment and profile**.
   - For *Alignment*, select **Ascent PI**.
   - For *Profile*, select **Ascent PI-DGN1**.
   - In the *To station* field, type **550**.
   - In the *Select surfaces to check against* field, select **SiteViz** and the **+** symbol.
   - Click **Next>**.

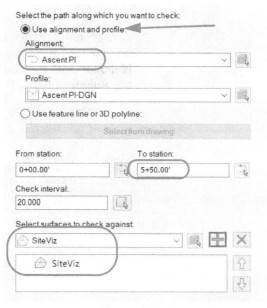

Figure 12–52

5. In the Sight Distance Check dialog box, in the *Sight Distance* tab, do the following, as shown in Figure 12–53:

- In the *Minimum sight distance* field, type **100**.
- If need be, set the other values as shown.
- Click **Next>**.

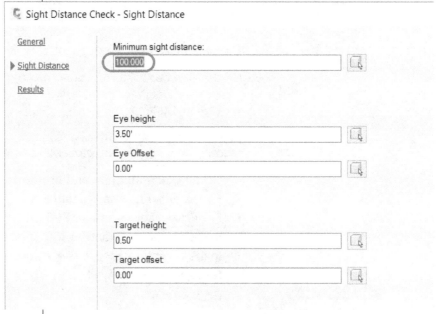

Figure 12–53

6. In the Sight Distance Check dialog box, in the *Results* tab, change the layers, as shown in Figure 12–54. These are the National CAD Standards Layers (which are not included in the Autodesk Civil 3D templates).

Component		Layer
Visible sight lines	☑	C-SGHT-VISI
Obstructed sight lines	☑	C-SGHT-OBST
Obstructed eye path	☑	C-SGHT-OBST-EYE_
Obstructed area	☑	C-SGHT-OBST-AREA
Eye path	☑	C-SGHT-EYE_
Sight limitation line	☑	C-SGHT-LMIT

Figure 12–54

7. Click **Finish**.

8. In the model, note that the obstruction lines go right to the South-Eastern property line, as shown in Figure 12–55.

9. Save the drawing.

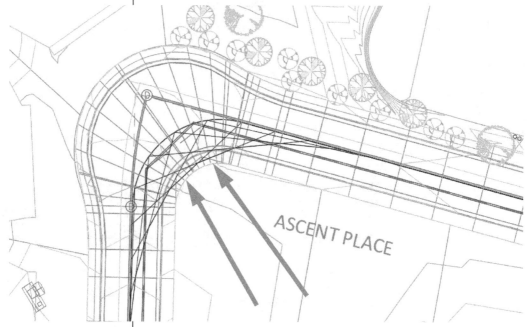

Figure 12–55

Task 3 - (Optional) Create a Share link.

In this task, you will use the **Share** command.

1. Select the preset view **Hotel-3D**.

2. Launch the ⫴ Share (Share) command in the Quick Access Toolbar.

3. In the Share a link to this drawing dialog box, note that you can decide to share this drawing as **View only** or to be able to **Edit and save a copy**. For now, select **Preview**, as shown in Figure 12–56.

Figure 12–56

4. You are prompted to sign in to your Autodesk Account. Then, your drawing is uploaded and prepared for the AutoCAD web app. This can take some time.

5. Navigate around the drawing. Note that the Civil 3D objects are only represented as boxes. This indicates that the Civil 3D Object Enablers are not present.

6. Return to Civil 3D and close the Share a link to this drawing dialog box, which is still open.

7. Save and close the drawing.

Chapter Review Questions

1. What does the Create Section View dialog box do?

   a. Creates a Model Space viewport for viewing sections.

   b. Creates grid(s) with a cross-section and labeling of a corridor model inside it at specified stations.

   c. Creates a Paper Space viewport for viewing sections.

   d. Enables you to review and edit sections interactively using the appropriate panels.

2. Where do you assign Pay Items?

   a. In the Grading Volume Tools.

   b. In the Volumes Dashboard.

   c. In the QTO Manager.

   d. In the Volume Reports.

3. What is the most efficient way to assign elevations to multi-view blocks?

   a. You switch to a side view and move the blocks up.

   b. You find the elevation of the surface and change the block Z value in the Properties palette.

   c. You use the Move Blocks to Surface routine.

   d. Multi-view blocks automatically are inserted at the proper elevation.

Command Summary

Button	Command	Location
	Full Navigation Wheel	• Navigation Sidebar • Command Prompt: Navswheel
	Move Blocks to Surface	• **Surface Textual Ribbon**>Surface Tools panel. • **Command**: AeccMoveBlocksToSurface:
	QTO Manager	• **Ribbon:** *Analyze* tab>QTO panel • **Command Prompt:** QTOManager
	Takeoff	• **Ribbon:** *Analyze* tab>QTO panel • **Command Prompt:** Takeoff
	View Manager	• **Ribbon:** *View* tab>Named Views • View Control bar • **Command Prompt:** View
▷❙❙	**Play/Pause Drive**	• **Contextual Ribbon:** *Drive* tab> Navigate panel
	Sight Distance	• **Contextual Ribbon:** *Alignment* tab> Analyze panel • **Contextual Ribbon:** *Corridor* tab> Analyze panel • **Contextual Ribbon:** *Profile* tab> Analyze panel • **Command Prompt:** SightDistanceCheck
	ViewCube	• Upper right corner of drawing area.

Additional Information

It is important to remember how to open an existing survey database and take advantage of the points and figures within it. Here, you will learn how to open a survey database for editing and review purposes. Point cloud data is becoming more widely available, hence you will learn how to deal with point clouds in Civil 3D and create a surface from point cloud data.

Additional design requirements are also listed for the project. Use this information to create additional practices for learning and reinforcing commands taught in this training guide.

Learning Objectives in This Appendix

- Open a survey database for editing or as read-only.
- Create Autodesk Civil 3D surfaces from point cloud data files.
- Review the design requirements for the project.

A.1 Opening a Survey Database

1. To set the working folder for the Survey Database, in the Toolspace, *Survey* tab, select **Survey Databases**, right-click, and select **Set working folder...**, as shown in Figure A–1. Browse to *C:\Civil 3D Projects\Survey Databases* and click **Select Folder**. When done, click **Select Folder** to close the dialog box.

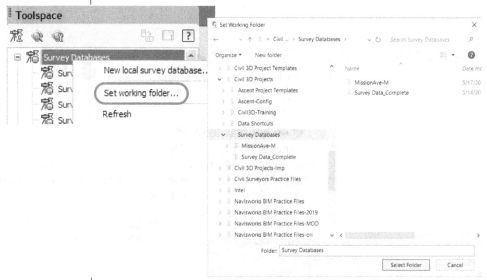

Figure A–1

2. To open a survey database, expand the survey database branch, select the survey database that you want to open, right-click and select **Open for edit** or **Open for read-only**, depending your requirements, as shown in Figure A–2.

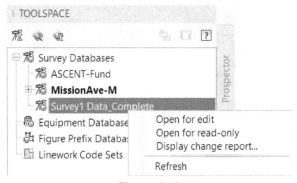

Figure A–2

A.2 Point Cloud Surface Extraction

Point Clouds are dense groupings of points created by 3D scanners. The AutoCAD software has been capable of working with point clouds. The accepted point cloud file formats are .RCP and .RCS. They are faster and more efficient than the previous file formats and are created using the Autodesk Recap software.

- As with XREFs, images, and other externally referenced files, you can attach and manage point clouds using the External References Manager.

- Point cloud object snaps have been added to the *3D Object Snap* tab in the Drafting Settings dialog box and the 3D Object Snap options in the Status Bar.

- In a point cloud, you can use the **Object** option in the **UCS** command to align the active UCS to a plane.

- Dynamic UCS now aligns to a point cloud plane according to point density and alignment.

Attach Point Cloud

In the Attach Point Cloud dialog box, you can preview a point cloud and its detailed information (such as its classification and segmentation data) before attaching it, as shown in Figure A–3. You can also use a geographic location for the attachment location (if the option is available).

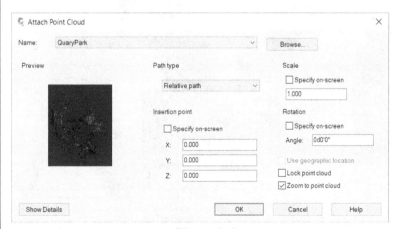

Figure A–3

How To: Attach a Point Cloud

1. In the *Insert* tab>Point Cloud panel, click ⬚ (Attach).
2. In the Select Point Cloud File dialog box, expand the Files of type drop-down list and select a file type. In the *Name* area, select a file and click **Open**.

   • The AutoCAD software can attach Point Cloud Project (RCP) and Scan (RCS) files (which are produced by the Autodesk ReCap software).

   • The Autodesk ReCap software enables the creation of a point cloud project file (RCP) that references multiple indexed scan files (RCS). It converts scan file data into a point cloud format that can then be viewed and modified in other products.

3. In the Attach Point Cloud dialog box, click **Show Details** to display the point cloud information
4. In the Path type, Insertion point, Scale, and Rotation areas, set the options that you want to use to attach the point cloud, as shown in Figure A–4. Click **OK**.

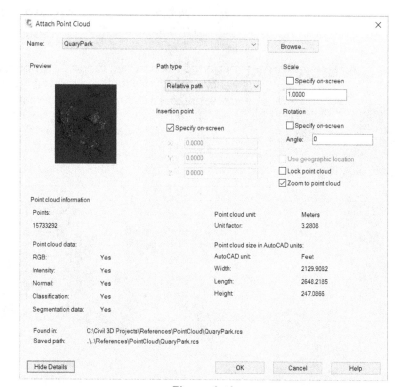

Figure A–4

5. At the *Specify insertion point* prompt, click in the drawing to locate the point cloud.

Point Cloud Transparency

When point clouds exist in a drawing with other geometry, it can be difficult to see anything behind the point cloud. A tool in the *Point Cloud* contextual tab>Visualization panel enables you to adjusts the transparency of the point cloud, as shown in Figure A–5. Alternatively, you can adjust the point cloud transparency in the Properties palette, as shown in Figure A–5.

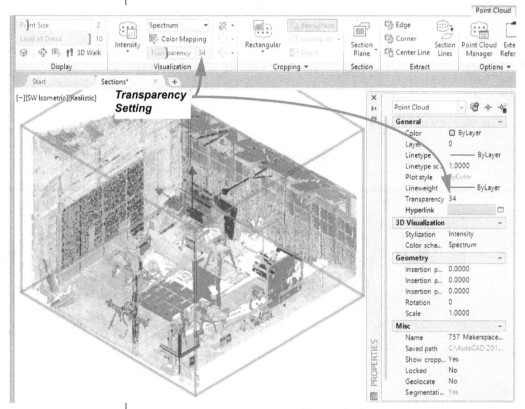

Figure A–5

Cropping Point Clouds

Displaying the bounding box around the point cloud data enables you to determine its position in 3D space relative to the other objects in the drawing. The cropping tools in the Cropping panel enable you to display only the information that is required for your project, as shown in Figure A–6. The cropping boundary can be rectangular, circular, or polygonal and is normal to the

screen. You can use  (Invert) to reverse the displayed points from inside to outside the boundary.

Figure A–6

A tool in the Cropping panel (displayed by expanding the panel) enables you to save and restore named cropping states. Both the visibility of the scans and regions as they are displayed and the cropping boundary are maintained in named cropping states, as shown in Figure A–7.

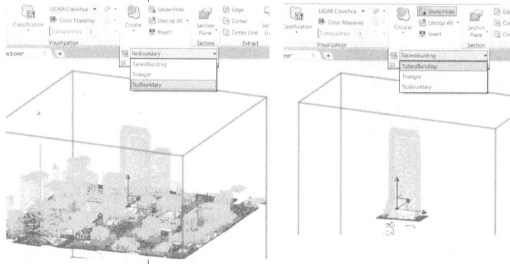

Figure A–7

Hint: List Crop States

The **POINTCLOUDCROPSTATE** command can be used to Save, Restore, and Delete crop states, as shown in Figure A–8. Using the **?** option will list all of the available crop states.

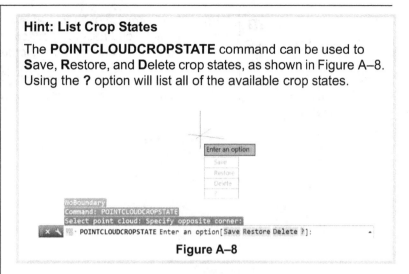

Figure A–8

How To: Save a Named Crop State

1. Once a point cloud has been attached, select it in the model.
2. In the *Point Cloud* contextual tab>Cropping panel, select an appropriate crop boundary, as shown in Figure A–9.

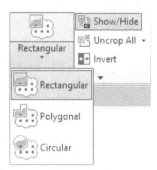

Figure A–9

3. In the model, pick points to draw the boundary. If a Polygonal boundary was selected, press <Enter> when done.
4. At the cursor, select either **Inside** or **Outside** to indicate which points to keep.
5. Expand the *Point Cloud* contextual tab>Cropping panel, click (New Crop State).
6. Enter a name for the new crop state.

Surfaces from Point Clouds

Point clouds can be used to create Autodesk Civil 3D surfaces. Once a point cloud has been attached to the drawing, it can be used to create a surface. In the *Home* tab>Create Ground Data panel, expand Surfaces and select (Create Surface from Point Cloud), as shown in Figure A–10.

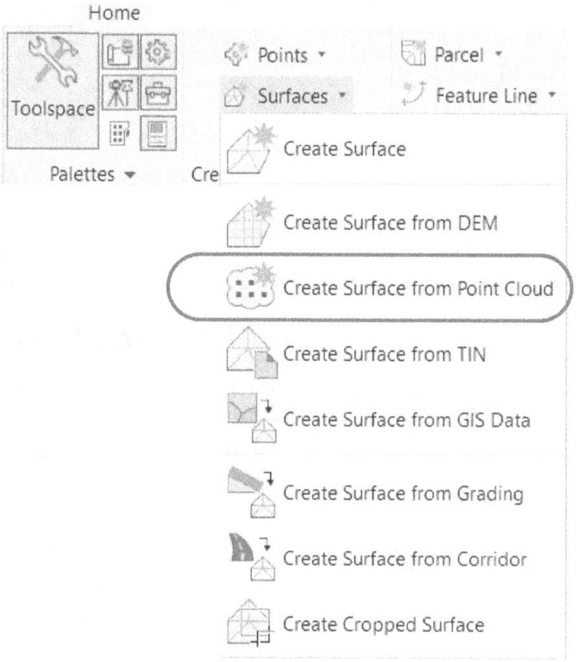

Figure A–10

(Create Surface from Point Cloud) extracts point data from the point cloud to create a TIN surface. During the surface creation process, you can:

- Name the surface.
- Select a style for the surface.
- Select a render material.
- Select part or all of a point cloud.
- Select a filter method for Non-Ground points.

Point Cloud Selection

If there are one or more point clouds in the model, it is important to communicate to the software which points from the point clouds to use in the surface. The three available options for this are described as follows:

Button	Description
	Add an entire point cloud
	Remove a selection from the list
	Add a selected area of a point cloud

Non-Ground Point Filtering

When point clouds are created, they create points on any and every object visible in the scan area. This means that points can fall at the tops of buildings, trees and other structures. In order to create a surface that represents the ground terrain, the points that are not on the ground must be filtered out. Three filter methods exist when creating a surface from point clouds:

1. Planar average: Predicts the elevation of a surface by finding the average elevation of a plane of points. An example is shown in Figure A–11.

Figure A–11

2. Kriging interpolation: Predicts the elevation of a surface by computing a weighted average of the elevations of neighboring points. An example is shown in Figure A–12. This is usually the most accurate option.

Figure A–12

3. No filter: Uses the point cloud point elevations for the surface elevations. An example is shown in Figure A–13.

Figure A–13

How To: Create a Surface from Point Clouds.

1. In the *Home* tab>Create Ground Data panel, expand

   Surfaces and select 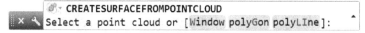 (Create Surface from Point Cloud).
2. In the model, select the point cloud or select any of the following options in the command line, as shown in Figure A–14.
   - **Window**
   - **polyGon**
   - **polyLIne**

```
⚙ ▾ CREATESURFACEFROMPOINTCLOUD
× �’ Select a point cloud or [Window polyGon polyLIne]:
```

Figure A–14

3. In the Create TIN Surface from Point Cloud dialog box - General page, type a surface name, set the surface style, and render material, as shown in Figure A–15. Click **Next>**.

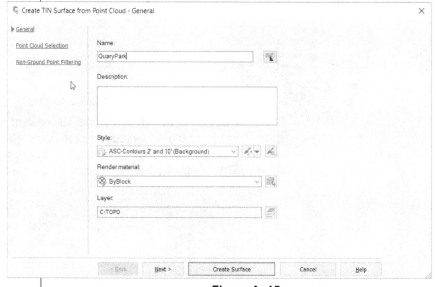

Figure A–15

4. In the Create TIN Surface from Point Cloud dialog box - Point Cloud Selection page, select the Point clouds or parts of the Point clouds, as shown in Figure A–16. Click **Next>**.

Figure A–16

5. In the Create TIN Surface from Point Cloud dialog box - Non-Ground Point Filtering page, select a filter method and click **Create Surface**, as shown in Figure A–17.

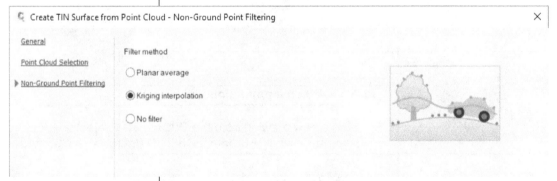

Figure A–17

6. In the Point Cloud Processing in Background message box, click **Close**.

Practice A1 | Create a Point Cloud Surface

Practice Objective

- Gaining familiarity with point clouds.
- Making a Civil 3D surface from point cloud data.

In this practice, you will attach a point cloud to a new drawing file, as shown in Figure A–18. You will then create a surface from the point cloud.

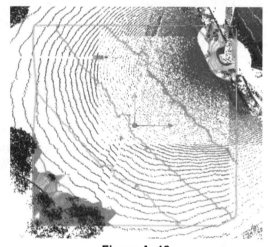

Figure A–18

Task 1 - Attach a point cloud.

1. Start a new drawing from the **C:\Civil 3D Projects\ Ascent-Config_Autodesk Civil 3D (Imperial) NCS.dwt**.

2. In the *Insert* tab>Point Cloud panel, click ⬚ (Attach).

3. In the Select Point Cloud File dialog box, navigate to the C:*Civil 3D Projects\References\PointCloud* folder. In the *Name* area, select **Quarry Park.rcs** and click **Open**.

4. Accept the default options in the Attach Point Cloud dialog box, click **OK**, and use an insertion point of **0,0**.

5. Save the file.

Task 2 - Analyze the point cloud.

1. In the *Home* tab>Create Ground Data panel, expand **Surfaces** and select  (Create Surface from Point Cloud).

2. In the model, select the point cloud.

3. In the Create TIN Surface from Point Cloud dialog box General page, type **Quarry Park** for the surface name. Leave all other defaults and click **Next>**.

4. In the Create TIN Surface from Point Cloud dialog box Point Cloud Selection page, select Point cloud and then click (Remove a selection from the list).

5. In the same page, click (Add a selected area of a point cloud). In the model, draw a window around the area indicated in Figure A–19, and click **Next>**.

Figure A–19

6. In the Create TIN Surface from Point Cloud dialog box Non-Ground Point Filtering page, select **Kriging interpolation** and click **Create Surface**.

7. In the Point Cloud Processing in Background message box, click **Close**. It may take a few minutes to process the points.

8. Close the file without saving.

A.3 3D Solid Surface from TIN Surface

Autodesk Civil 3D software has the capability to extract an AutoCAD3D solid surface from any TIN surface. During the extraction process, you can define the vertical properties, the output properties, and which surface to extract.

Vertical Definition

Three options are available for setting the vertical definition of a 3D solid from a TIN surface, as shown in Figure A–20.

1. The first option creates a solid with a consistent depth across the entire surface. This may be used to quickly calculate the volume of top soil to be removed.
2. The second option creates a solid with a fixed elevation. This option may be used to quickly calculate the water volume of a pond, which will have a consistent water elevation.
3. The last option creates a solid between two surfaces. This could be used to create various solids from soil report point. Doing so provides a solid for each type of material.

Depth *Fixed Elevation* *Surface*

Figure A–20

Output Properties

Multiple output settings enable you to define where the solid is created during the extraction process. The layer and color for the solid can also be set. Then, you can create the solid in the current drawing or in a new drawing. If you select a new drawing, you can set the file path and name of the new drawing by clicking

 (Browse).

How To: Create a 3D Solid Surface

1. In the model, select a TIN surface.
2. In the *Surface* contextual tab>Surface Tools panel, expand

   (Extract from Surface) and select   (Extract Solids from Surface).
3. In the Extract Solid from Surface dialog box, shown in Figure A–21, set the vertical definition and the required drawing output.

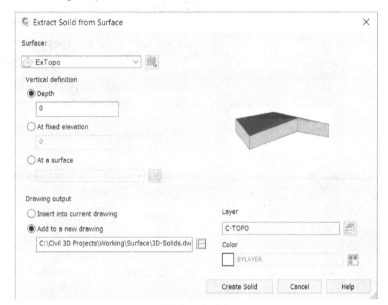

Figure A–21

4. Click **Create Solid**.

Practice A2

3D Surface Solids and Label Adjustments

Practice Objectives

- Output the surface as a solid object.
- Adjust contour labels readability.

Task 1 - Create a 3D solid.

1. Open **SUF1-D2-Surface.dwg** from the
   C:\Civil 3D Projects\Working\Surface folder.

2. Select the **Existing-Site** surface in Model Space. In the
   Surface contextual tab>Surface Tools panel, expand
   (Extract from Surface) and select (Extract Solids
   from Surface).

3. In the Extract Solid from Surface dialog box, shown in
   Figure A–22, set the following:

   - Surface: *Existing-Site*
   - Vertical definition: *At fixed elevation* = **30**
   - Drawing output: *Add to a new drawing* and save it to
     *C:\Civil 3D Projects\Working**Surface\3D-Solid.dwg***.

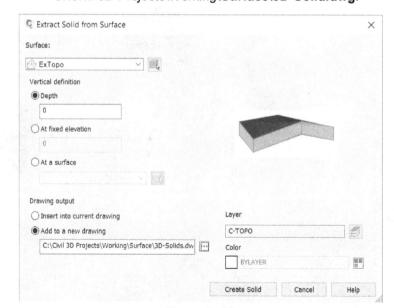

Figure A–22

4. Click **Create Solid** and click **OK** when prompted.

5. Open the *C:\Civil 3D Projects\Working***Surface\
    3D-Solid.dwg**, orbit the model, and verify that the bottom of
    the solid surface is at elevation 100, as shown in
    Figure A–23.

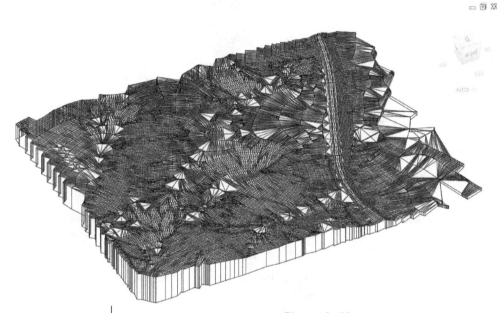

Figure A–23

Task 2 - Work with a label style.

1. Browse to the *C:\Civil 3D Projects\References\DWG* folder.

2. Select **Introduction.dwg** and then select **Open.**

3. Verify that the Toolspace, *Settings* tab is still active.

4. View the label style default. In the *View* tab>Views panel, expand the Named Views drop-down list and select **Contour label**. It will zoom to a preset view of the contour labels, as shown in Figure A–24.

Figure A–24

Note that the labels are not rotated to the correct drafting standards. The contour label style being used is rotating the text so that it remains plan readable (so they do not display upside down). The highlighted labels are rotated more than 90 degrees from horizontal. This is caused by the *Readability Bias* setting being larger than 90 degrees. This setting controls the viewing angle at which the contour text should be flipped.

5. If required, you can change the setting in this specific contour label style only. To assign this new value to all of the surface label styles, in the Toolspace, *Settings* tab, right-click on the *Surface* collection and select **Edit Label Style Defaults**.

6. Under the Plan Readability property, change the *Readability Bias* (shown in Figure A–25) to **110°** and click **OK**.

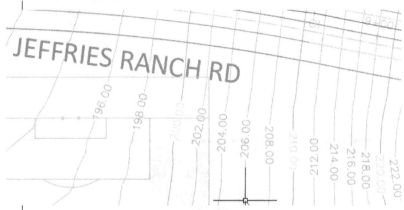

Property	Value	Override	Child Override	Lock
⊞ **Label**				
⊞ **Behavior**				
⊟ **Plan Readability**				
Plan Readable	True		⇩	🔒
Readability Bias	91.0000 (d)		⇩	🔒
Flip Anchors with Text	False		⇩	🔒
⊞ **Components**				
⊞ **Leader**				
⊞ **Dragged State Compone...**				

JEFFRIES RANCH RD

Figure A–25

7. In the Toolspace, *Settings* tab, click **+** next to Surface, and then click **+** next to Label Styles and Contour. Right-click on Existing Major Labels and select **Edit**.

8. In the *Layout* tab, click ⊡ (Browse) next to Contents to open the Text Component Editor. Delete all of the information in the content area to the right.

9. In the Properties drop-down list, select **Surface Elevation**, change the *Precision* to **1**, and click 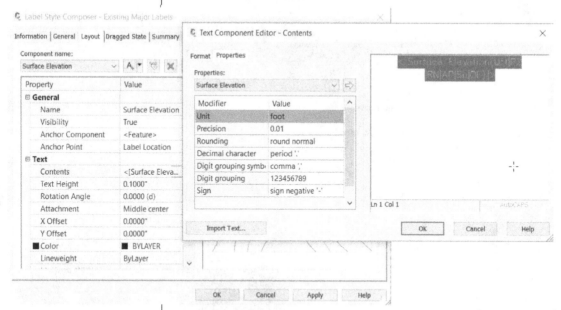 to place it in the content area, as shown in Figure A–26.

Figure A–26

10. Click **OK** to exit the Text Component Editor dialog box. Click **OK** again to exit the Label Style Composer dialog box.

11. Repeat Steps 7 to 9 to change the **Existing Minor Labels** style in the same way.

12. Save the drawing.

A.4 Design Data

Parcel Size

The following data, shown in Figure A–27, describes the parcel size used in the training dataset:

- *Minimum Area:* **10225 Sq. Ft.**

- *Minimum Frontage:* **65'**

- *Frontage Offset:* **20'**

- *Minimum Width:* **65'**

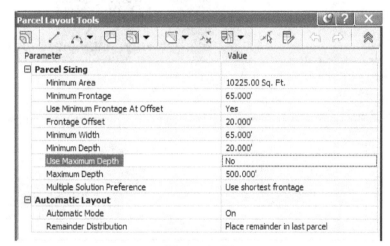

Figure A–27

The following table contains a listing of pipe size conversions between metric and imperial.

Metric Size (mm)	Imperial Size (inches)	Metric Size (mm)	Imperial Size (inches)
-	-	1050	42
150	6	1200	48
200	8	1350	54
250	10	1500	60
300	12	1650	66
375	15	1800	72
450	18	1950	78
525	21	2100	84

600	24	2250	90
675	27	2400	96
750	30	2700	108
825	33	3000	120
900	36		

Road Design Criteria

Figure A–28, Figure A–29, Figure A–30, and Figure A–31, as well as the corresponding tables, specify the design criteria for the expressway design on Mission Avenue, the grand boulevard on Ascent Blvd., the collector streets at Jeffries Ranch Rd., and the residential street design for Ascent Place.

Expressway: Mission Avenue

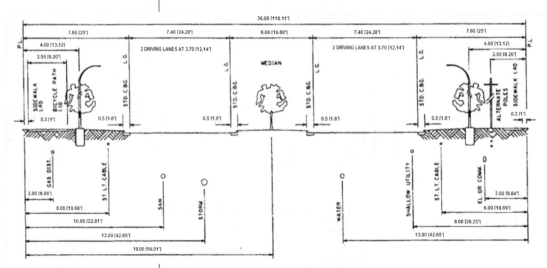

Figure A–28

Daily Traffic Volume (vehicles/day)	# of Lanes	Right-of-way Requirement	Minimum Intersection Spacing
30,000 - 90,000	4, 6, or 8	195' (min.)	2600'

Function
- To permit relatively unimpeded flow for through traffic between major elements.
- To function as part of the Truck Route System.

Access Conditions
- Intersections are grade separated where warranted.
- Divided roadways with full control of access.
- Direct access to abutting property is prohibited.
- Only roadways of Major category or higher can intersection with Expressways.
- Intersections should be half a mile apart but in special circumstances can be a minimum of a quarter of a mile apart.
- At-grade intersections should be signalized.

Traffic Features

Posted Speed (mph)	40-50	On-street Bikeway	No
Parking	None	Bus Route	No
Sidewalk	None	Truck Route	Yes
Traffic Signals	For interim condition only	Sound Attenuation	Yes
Pedestrian Crossing	Grade-separated, at-grade for interim condition		

Note
- Interchange spacing is generally similar to that of Freeways. However, closer spacing might be considered under special circumstances.
- Expressways are designed in accordance with TAG standards and for capacity conditions based on Level of Service D'.
- Pedestrian crosswalks are permitted at intersections. However, grade separated walkways are used where warranted.
- The right-of-way varies from a minimum of 195' depending on the number of lanes, sloping requirements, road grades, and noise attenuation requirements.
- A noise attenuation study is required at the Outline Plan application stage for residential lots adjacent to interchange areas, including the Transportation Utility Corridors (TUG) areas, to determine noise attenuation and right-of-way requirements.

Daily Traffic Volume (vehicles/day)	# of Lanes	Right-of-way Requirement	Minimum Intersection Spacing
30,000 - 90,000	4, 6, or 8	195' (min.)	2600'

Function
- To permit relatively unimpeded flow for through traffic between major elements.
- To function as part of the Truck Route System.

Access Conditions
- Intersections are grade separated where warranted.
- Divided roadways with full control of access.
- Direct access to abutting property is prohibited.
- Only roadways of Major category or higher can intersection with Expressways.
- Intersections should be half a mile apart but in special circumstances can be a minimum of a quarter of a mile apart.
- At-grade intersections should be signalized.

Traffic Features

Posted Speed (mph)	40-50	On-street Bikeway	No
Parking	None	Bus Route	No
Sidewalk	None	Truck Route	Yes
Traffic Signals	For interim condition only	Sound Attenuation	Yes
Pedestrian Crossing	Grade-separated, at-grade for interim condition		

Note
- Interchange spacing is generally similar to that of Freeways. However, closer spacing might be considered under special circumstances.
- Expressways are designed in accordance with TAG standards and for capacity conditions based on Level of Service D'.
- Pedestrian crosswalks are permitted at intersections. However, grade separated walkways are used where warranted.
- The right-of-way varies from a minimum of 195' depending on the number of lanes, sloping requirements, road grades, and noise attenuation requirements.
- A noise attenuation study is required at the Outline Plan application stage for residential lots adjacent to interchange areas, including the Transportation Utility Corridors (TUG) areas, to determine noise attenuation and right-of-way requirements.

Typical Cross Section	See TAC Standards	
Classification	**Design Speed**	**Intersection Design**
Urban Arterial Divided (UAD) 50 Urban Arterial Divided (UAD) 60 Urban Arterial Divided (UAD) 70	30-45 mph	See Appendix II-A Sheets/ -9

Horizontal Alignment	
Minimum Stopping Sight Distance	**Minimum Radius of Curvature**
• Major UAD 50 = 30' • Major UAD 60 = 40' • Major UAD 70 = 45'	• Major UAD 50 = 295', 425' - 20,000' (desirable) • Major UAD 60 = 395', 850' - 20,000' (desirable) • Major UAD 50 = 560', 1300' - 20,000' (desirable)

Median and Left Turn Bay
- The minimum median width on a Major street is 20' for a parallel left turn lane and 30' for parallel dual left turn lanes.
- The introduced median is used to transit an undivided road to a divided road with a left turn median.
- Slot left turn bays are required as an interim design on wide medians, such as those reserved for future LRT or future widening in the median.
- No left turn bays are permitted on curves with a center line radius of less than 1300' nor in 195' of the end of a center line transition curve (spiral) if the radius is less than 1300'.
- Standard left turn bays shall be provided on Major streets at all intersections. For left turn bay designs.
- The minimum storage length for a left turn bay is 195' with a 12' wide left turn lane.
- Dual left turn bays and slot turn bays are to be designed to TAC standards.

Note
- Major streets are classified as Urban Arterial Divided (UAD) roadways and are designed for speeds of 30, 40, and 45 miles per hour. Most Major streets fall in the 40 mph category. However, developers must be informed by the approving authority of Land Use and Mobility of the applicable design speed.
- A standard curb with a 1.5' gutter is to be used on the median and on the outside edges.
- A reverse gutter is used where necessary.
- Street light poles, power poles, and traffic signal poles are to be located a minimum of 12' from the lip of gutter.

Vertical Alignment

Minimum and Maximum Grades
• Maximum grade:
  • Major UAD 50 = 7.0%
  • Major UAD 60 = 6.0%
  • Major UAD 70 = 5.0%
• Minimum grade: 0.6%
The maximum and minimum grades also apply to the development of superelevation.

Grade at Intersections • The grade line of the approaching street (maximum approach grade of 4%) shall tie to the lane line of the Major street with a vertical curve of a minimum length of 100' (i.e., the crossfall of the Major street shall be extended and intersects the grade of the approaching street). The resulting vertical curve ends at the lane line of the Major street. • The maximum profile grade on a Major street at an intersection shall be 4% for a minimum distance of 330' measured from the Vertical Point of Intersection (VPI) to the center line of the intersecting street on both sides of the intersection.
Vertical Curves and Superelevation • The length of a vertical curve is calculated based on the stopping sight distance. • For Major streets, crest vertical curves are to be designed using the "K" values for 14 mph higher than the design speed. • Superelevation shall be developed through the transition spiral by using the following superelevation tables: • Major UAD 50 emax = 0.06 • Major UAD 60 emax = 0.08 • Major UAD 70 emax = 0.08 • The superelevation through all Major street intersections shall not exceed 4%. • A right turn ramp on a Major street shall have a minimum of 4% crossfall within the length of the island.

Grand Boulevard: Ascent Boulevard

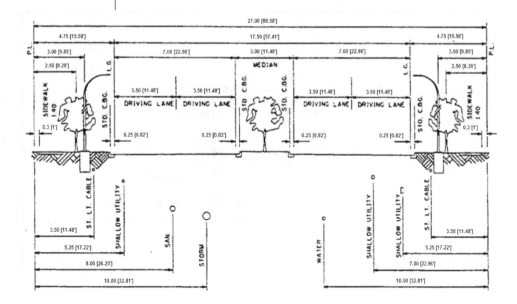

Figure A–29

Daily Traffic Volume (vehicles/day)	# of Lanes	Right-of-way Requirement	Minimum Intersection Spacing
5,000 - 10,000	2	85.3' (min.)	393.7'/196.85'

Function
- Functions are similar to Primary Collector and Collector streets.
- To serve as secondary traffic generators.
- To serve as a min route within the community to accommodate substantial traffic volumes.
- Might be used as bus routes and are designed to accommodate Frequent Transit Service.

Access Conditions
- A minimum intersection spacing of 393.7' shall be provided between a Major Street and the first intersection on the Grand Boulevard from the Major Street.
- Intersection spacing for those subsequent to the above condition shall be a minimum 196.85' spacing.
- No access to abutting commercial properties.
- Access to abutting multi-family residential properties is permitted and is generally restricted to right turns in and out.
- Residential frontage of single and multi-family development is permitted.
- Single family, semi-detached, and duplex style homes must access from a rear alley.

Traffic Features			
Posted Speed (mph)	30	On-street Bikeway	Signed Bicycle Route
Parking	Yes	Bus Route	Yes
Sidewalk	4.59' separate walk on both sides	Truck Route	Yes
Traffic Signals	As warranted	Sound Attenuation	Yes
Pedestrian Crossing	At Grade		

Note
- Undivided roadway with intersections controlled by signage.
- Parking is permitted on both sides but might be restricted under special circumstances.
- Sidewalk is normally only required on one side, but is preferable on both sides. Refer to Section E - Sidewalks and Walkways for more details.

Typical Cross Section	

Collector Streets: Jeffries Ranch Road

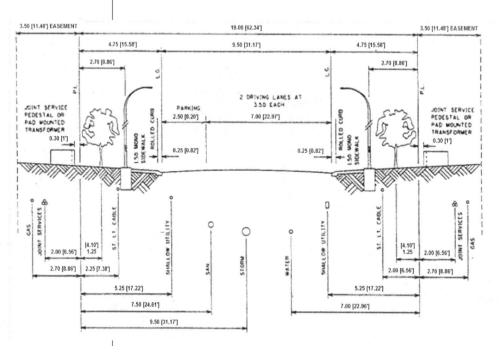

Figure A–30

Daily Traffic Volume (vehicles/day)	# of Lanes	Right-of-way Requirement	Minimum Intersection Spacing
1,000 - 5,000	2	59.06' and 68.90'	19.69'

Function
- To be used where the Daily Traffic Volumes exceed the volumes for a Residential Road but are less than 5,000 vehicles/day.
- To collect and distribute traffic from Major streets to lesser standard streets.
- To serve as secondary traffic generators, such as neighborhood commercial centers, parks, and golf courses, and from neighborhood to neighborhood.
- All Collector streets designated as bus routes must use the 68.90' right-of-way cross-section.
- Might be used as bus routes.

Access Conditions
- Direct access is permitted to abutting properties.
- Minimum intersection spacing is 19.69'. Wherever possible, a desirable intersection spacing of 262.5' should be used.
- Collector streets might intersect with Residential streets, Residential Entrance streets, other Collector streets, Primary Collector streets, Local Major streets, and Major streets.

Traffic Features

Posted Speed (mph)	30	On-street Bikeway	Signed Bicycle Route
Parking	Except at bus zones	Bus Route	Yes
Sidewalk	4.59' separate walk or 4.92' mono walk on both sides	Truck Route	No
Traffic Signals	As warranted	Sound Attenuation	No
Pedestrian Crossing	At grade		

Note

- Collector Streets are undivided roadways.
- There are two types of Collector Streets:
  - 68.89' R.O.W.: 2 driving lane of 11.48' wide and 2 parking lane of 7.38' wide.
  - 62.34' R.O.W.*: 2 driving lanes of 11.48' wide and 1 parking lane of 8.20' wide.
- This standard can only be used where residential and/or commercial frontage occurs on one side of the road and where no bus route is planned.

Typical Cross Section	

Classification	Design Speed	Intersection Design
Urban Collector Undivided (UCU) 50	30 mph	

Horizontal Alignment

Minimum Stopping Sight Distance	Minimum Radius of Curvature
Collect UCU 50 = 213'	Collector UCU 50 = 295'

Median and Left Turn Bay

- Medians, left turn bays, and intersection channelization are not normally required.
- A tear-drop median is required on a Collector street when the Collector street is designated as a bus route and intersecting with a Major street.

Note

- The cumulative length of Collector streets before feeding onto Major streets shall not be excessive. The maximum number of dwelling units serviced shall not exceed 500.
- Low profile rolled curb with 0.82' gutter is to be used except in areas identified as bus zones and adjacent to parcels which that do not contain residential development (e.g., commercial sites, parks, school reserves, etc.) where a standard curb is to be used.
- Standard curb is to be used on Collector streets if the grade is greater than 6%.
- Reverse gutter is used where necessary.

Vertical Alignment

Minimum and Maximum Grades
- Maximum grade: 8.0%
- Minimum grade: 0.6%

Grade at Intersections
- The grade line of the approaching street (maximum approach grade of 4%) shall tie to the Collector street in the following manner:
  - Tie to the property line grade if the approaching street is undivided.
  - Tie to the lane line of the Collector street with a vertical curve of a minimum length of 98.43' if the approaching street is divided (i.e., the crossfall (or 2% if the road is crowned) of the Collector street shall be extended and intersects the grade of the approaching street and the resulting vertical curve ends at the lane line of the Collector street).
- It is desirable to ensure that the grade on the Collector streets is less than the permitted maximum of 8% at intersections to improve operational aspects, such as stopping and starting in winter conditions.

Vertical Curves and Superelevation
- The length of vertical curve is calculated based on the stopping sight distance.
- The maximum superelevation rate for a Collector street shall not exceed emax = 4%.

Residential Street: Ascent Place

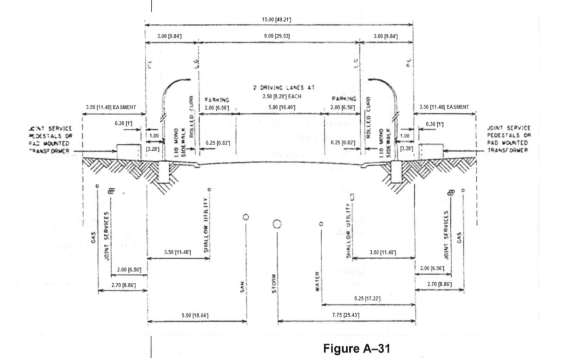

Figure A–31

Daily Traffic Volume (vehicles/day)	# of Lanes	Right-of-way Requirement	Minimum Intersection Spacing
<1,000	2	49.21' (min.)	196.85'

Function
- To provide direct access to properties.
- To collect and distribute traffic from residential properties to Collector and Residential streets.

Access Conditions
- Direct access is permitted to abutting residential properties.
- Access is not permitted to commercial properties.
- Residential streets might intersect with other Residential streets, Residential Entrance streets, Collector streets, and Primary Collector streets.

Traffic Features

Posted Speed (mph)	30	On-street Bikeway	Signed Bicycle Route
Parking	Yes	Bus Route	No
Sidewalk	1.1 mono walk on at least one side, preferable on both sides	Truck Route	Yes
Traffic Signals	No	Sound Attenuation	Yes
Pedestrian Crossing	At Grade		

Note
- Undivided roadway with intersections controlled by signage.
- Parking is permitted on both sides but might be restricted under special circumstances.
- Sidewalk is normally only required on one side but is preferable on both sides. Refer to Section E - Sidewalks and Walkways for more details.

Typical Cross Section	

Classification	Design Speed	Intersection Design
Urban Local Divided (ULD) 50	30 mph	

Horizontal Alignment

Minimum Stopping Sight Distance	Minimum Radius of Curvature
Residential ULD 50 = 213.25'	Residential ULD 50 = 262.47'

Median and Left Turn Bay
- Minimum median width is 11.48'.
- Left turn bays and intersection channelization are not required.

Note
- Same requirements as Residential streets.
- Standard curb with 0.82' gutter is to be used on the median and low profile curb with 0.82' gutter on the outside edges, except in areas adjacent to parcels which do not contain residential developments where standard curb is to be used.

Vertical Alignment

Minimum and Maximum Grades
- Maximum grade: 8.0%
- Minimum grade: 0.6%

Grade at Intersections
- The grade line of the intersecting street (maximum approach grade of 4%) shall tie to the property line grade of a Residential Entrance street.

Vertical Curves and Superelevation
- The length of vertical curve is calculated based on the stopping sight distance.
- Superelevation is not required.

Project Explorer

Civil 3D is a data-rich program. The various Civil 3D objects are both graphical and informational. Traditionally, gaining access to the information within a Civil 3D object was rather arduous and convoluted, differing on the type of Civil 3D object.

Project Explorer simplifies accessing and reviewing such data through a single interface. You can edit Civil 3D objects, validate design assumptions, and create reports and tables in one place.

In this appendix, you will inspect your Civil 3D data through the Project Explorer interface and make some design edits. Then, you will produce an AutoCAD table from Civil 3D object data.

Learning Objectives in This Appendix

- Study the Project Explorer.
- Edit Civil 3D objects.
- Produce AutoCAD tables with Civil 3D data.

B.1 Introduction to the Project Explorer

Project Explorer is an entitlement to the Autodesk 2022 AEC Collection and runs inside of Civil 3D 2022. When it is installed, the Project Explorer icon is featured prominently on the *Home* tab in its own Explore panel, as shown in Figure B–1.

Figure B–1

Hint: If Project Explorer is NOT installed, there may not be an Explore panel on the *Home* tab.

The Project Explorer can be thought of as a one-stop shop for mining data from various Civil 3D objects. Thus, it facilitates reviewing, editing, and reporting on content stored within these objects and the overall Civil 3D project.

Traditionally, such embedded data within Civil 3D objects was available from a variety of locations, such as right-click menus, the branches of the *Prospector* tab, the object's contextual ribbon, Panorama vistas, geometry editors, the object's Civil 3D properties, and/or the AutoCAD Properties palette. Project Explorer makes all of this data accessible in one window, where it can be viewed and, in some cases, edited and reported on.

The Project Explorer provides both graphical and tabular data, as shown in Figure B–2.

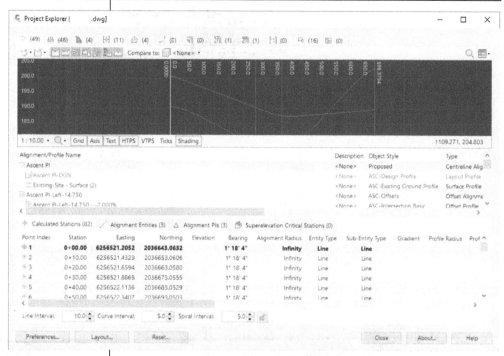

Figure B–2

There are many options to customize the Project Explorer interface to suit your needs. There are keyboard shortcuts, right-click menus, and tabs within the Project Explorer window. These allow access to a large variety of Civil 3D objects and their data in a "one-stop shop" type of environment. Each object and sub-object can easily be found within the Civil 3D Model Space.

B.2 Project Explorer User Interface

The Project Explorer interface window is mode-less, which means it can remain open while you continue to work in Civil 3D. Since it can be open all the time, it is an ideal candidate to be moved onto an auxiliary screen and kept open.

The interface is divided horizontally into four sections, as shown in Figure B–3:

1. Object category tabs
2. View pane
3. Object tabular pane
4. Sub-object tabular pane (with multiple tabs)

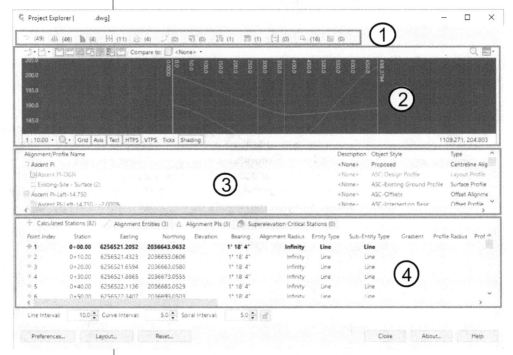

Figure B–3

Object Category Tabs

Each tab represents a Civil 3D object type:

- Alignments (and profiles)
- Assemblies
- Corridors

- Point groups
- Surfaces
- Feature lines
- Parcels
- Pipe networks
- Pressure pipe networks
- Sample line groups
- AutoCAD blocks
- Object sets

Within each tab is a number in parenthesis representing the count of each object that exists in the Civil 3D model.

View Pane

When an object is selected in the Object tabular pane, it is displayed in the View pane. Within the View pane, you can navigate similarly to the AutoCAD Model Space with the mouse buttons for zooming in and out and panning.

In the upper portion of the View pane is the **Viewer toolbar.** The tools present depend on the Civil 3D object being examined, as shown in Figure B–4.

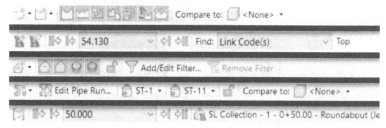

Figure B–4

In the bottom portion of the View pane is the **status bar.** In the left corner are toggles for controlling the display of the **Grid**, **Axis**, **Text** items (labels), and **Shading**, as shown in Figure B–5. Other toggles present depend on the Civil 3D object being viewed. There is also a zoom drop-down list and, in some cases, a control for the vertical exaggeration.

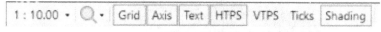

Figure B–5

Positioned at the far right of the status bar are coordinates for the pane.

A right-click menu is available for additional tools.

The objects in the View pane update automatically when values are edited in the other panes.

Hint: For alignments, the view is actually in profile, not in plan. Thus for alignments, all you see is the stationing.

Object Pane

The Object pane lists all the Civil 3D objects of the current tab contained within the drawing in a tabular format. If there are more columns and rows available that fit within the pane, horizontal and/or vertical scroll bars appear.

Clicking on the **Layout** button at the bottom left of the Project Explorer window opens the Layout Options window, where you can customize the column layout, order, and visibility, as shown in Figure B–6.

Figure B–6

In the Object and Sub-object panes, you can also rearrange the column order by dragging and dropping the column headings.

In the Layout Options window, you can toggle which columns are displayed. You can rearrange the order by using the arrows on the right-hand side. There are tabs for the control of the Object pane for the various Civil 3D object types.

Note that some of the text is purple. This indicates that you can edit that text, meaning you can rename the column titles in the Object pane. The last tab is for Display Options settings for the Project Explorer, where you can control the following options:

- General
- Bearing
- Station / Chainage
- Grade / Slope
- General Labels

Once your preferred layout options are established, you can save them in an external .XMPT file for reuse. You can also open an existing .XMPT file or create a new one. There is also the option to restore the defaults.

For alignments, you can specify the intervals and what geometry points to display, as shown in Figure B–7.

Figure B–7

There is a similar *Sampling Interval* choice for other linear objects, such as pipes and pressure pipe networks.

Within the Object pane (and Sub-object pane), there are extensive options through the right-click menu, depending on the Civil 3D object type. Warnings and violations are also displayed in the Object pane, and the text color of these objects is orange.

In the Object and Sub-object panes, anything with purple text on a white background can be edited through various fashions, which will be explored later in this chapter.

Sub-object Pane

When you select an object in the Object pane, its details are displayed as sub-objects in the Sub-object pane. Often there are multiple tabs in the Sub-object pane, along with horizontal and vertical scroll bars when necessary.

Keyboard Shortcuts

The connection between the objects and sub-objects being examined and the Civil 3D Model Space is vital. Often a variety of commands and options are available through the right-click menu.

There are also keyboard shortcuts available. Unlike with the regular AutoCAD or Civil 3D software, these shortcuts are a single character and are immediately activated upon keystroke without the need to press <Enter>.

When a particular object or sub-object is highlighted, the following keyboard shortcuts are available:

<Z>	Zoom to the selected item in Model Space.
<P>	Pan to the selected item in Model Space.
<S>	Select the selected item in Model Space.
<C>	Clear the current selected item.
<A> or <E>	Open the Civil 3D properties dialog box for the item.
<Ctrl>	Highlights the item in Civil 3D to identify its location in Model Space.

Practice B1

Project Explorer Interface

Practice Objectives

- Gain familiarity with the Project Explorer.
- Configure the Project Explorer interface.

In this practice, you will open the Project Explorer. You will examine the various tabs and panes and make some slight configuration changes.

1. Open **PEX1-A.dwg** from the *C:\Civil 3D Projects\Working\ Project Explorer* folder.

2. Select the preset view **Corr-QTO**.

3. Open the Project Explorer by clicking [icon] (Project Explorer) in the *Home* tab>Explore panel, as shown in Figure B–8.

Figure B–8

4. The Project Explorer opens, as shown in Figure B–9. If you have multiple screens, move the Project Explorer window to a secondary monitor; otherwise, move it to the side of your screen.

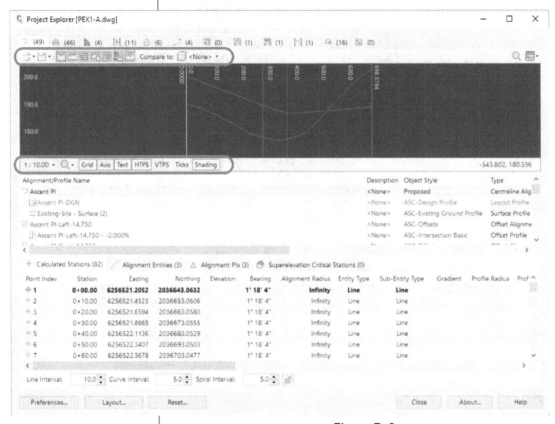

Figure B–9

5. Check out the tabs at the very top for the different Civil 3D objects, as shown in Figure B–10.

Figure B–10

6. Note that there are 49 alignments, 46 assemblies, etc. Click through each tab and note how the displays in the three main panes change. Also note how the Viewer Toolbar and the Status Bar change with the different tabs.

7. In the *Alignment* tab, note the different colors of the text, as shown in Figure B–11. The orange text has warnings that are displayed when hovering over the text, while the purple text indicates that the objects can be edited by double-clicking.

Figure B–11

8. Click the **Layout...** button at the bottom left corner of the Project Explorer window.

9. In the Layout Options window, ensure you are in the *Alignment* tab. Click the down arrow to select **Set Column Layout for Alignment/Profile Calculated Stations** from the drop-down list, as shown in Figure B–12.

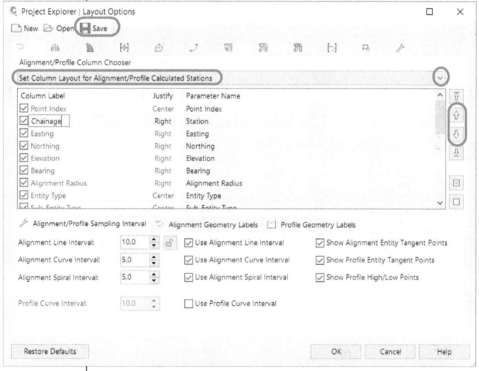

Figure B–12

10. Change the **Stations** text to **Chainage** by double-clicking on the purple text and typing in the new name.

11. Use the **Up** and **Down** arrows on the right side to move the **Northing** column above the **Easting** column.

12. Click ⊟ (Save) to save your configuration. Browse to the *C:\Civil 3D Projects\Ascent-Config* folder and name the file **XXX-Fundamentals.xmpt** (substituting your initials for XXX).

13. Click **OK** to close the Layout Options window.

14. You do not have to close the Project Explorer window. It can remain open for the next practices.

B.3 Civil 3D Object Management

In the traditional Civil 3D interface, it is a bit confusing where to go to get the data embedded in the various Civil 3D objects. At the very least, each type of Civil 3D object has its own dedicated way of displaying or editing the information, be it through its own contextual ribbon, its object properties panel or the AutoCAD properties, the vistas of the Panorama, etc.

A strong benefit of the Project Explorer is the "one-stop shop" environment. Through the tabs and panes within the Project Explorer environment, many of the Civil 3D objects can be displayed, studied, explored, and even edited, all in the same environment and with similar workflows and methods.

Identifying Objects

When an object is selected in the Object pane or Sub-object pane, it is highlighted in the View pane. When <Ctrl> is pressed, a marker flashes on and off in Model Space identifying the object.

You can select multiple objects with the standard windows selection methods, such as using <Shift> and <Ctrl>. With <Ctrl> pressed, each object you click will be selected, whereas pressing <Shift> will enable you to select all objects between the first and second selected objects.

There are various ways of zooming and panning to the object in Model Space:

- Right-click menu

- Keyboard shortcuts (<Z> and <P> respectively)

- Status bar drop-down list in the View pane

You can also select the object directly in Project Explorer to do any of the regular Civil 3D or AutoCAD commands in Model Space through the right-click menu or the <S> keyboard shortcut.

Editing Objects

In general, any object in the Object or Sub-object panes that has a white background with a text color of purple or orange can be edited in some form or another. Most of the time, a simple double-click on that cell will open a pop-up window for the content to be edited.

Names, descriptions, northings, eastings, elevations, etc. can be renamed directly by typing in new values in the pop-up Set Value window, as shown in Figure B–13.

Figure B–13

Other cells upon double-clicking will open windows with drop-down list choices, such as the Set Style window for picking a new style for the object, as shown in Figure B–14.

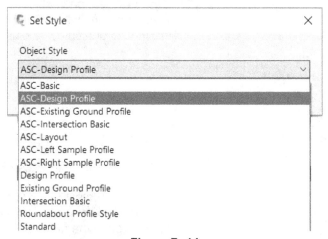

Figure B–14

In addition, a variety of editing choices pertinent to the particular Civil 3D object selected are available through the right-click menu.

Pipe Object Pane

For pipe networks, by default you see the entire pipe run in profiles in the View pane. However, you can select which portion of the pipe run to be displayed by selecting the starting structure and the ending structure, as shown in Figure B–15. Now the View pane will only show the pipe run between these two picked structures.

Figure B–15

Once the selected range is established, you can edit the pipe run by clicking 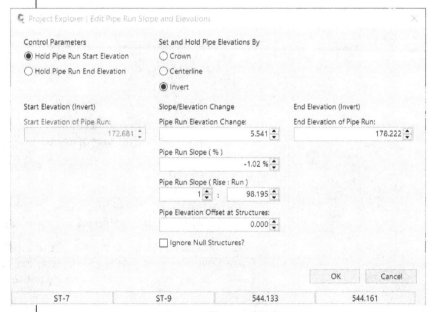 (Edit Pipe Run). In the Edit Pipe Run Slope and Elevation window, you can control the elevations and slopes of the selected pipes, as shown in Figure B–16.

Figure B–16

You can control which elevations and slopes to hold and how the elevations and slopes are applied.

Sub-object Pane Tabs

Not all objects have Sub-object panes. The ones that do often have tabs in the Sub-object pane that drill down to the sub-objects to a greater degree.

In the *Alignments* tab, the *Calculated Stations* tab in the Sub-object pane allows you to view the alignment/profile data in predefined segments for *Line*, *Curve*, and *Spiral* increments, as shown in Figure B–17. You can set the intervals at the bottom of the panel.

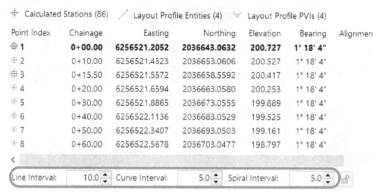

Figure B–17

You have the same linear increment option for the *Pipe Run* tab in the pipe network Sub-object pane.

Compare To

Many of the Civil 3D objects can be juxtaposed against surfaces. In the View pane of the Project Explorer, you have the ability to

view such surfaces by using 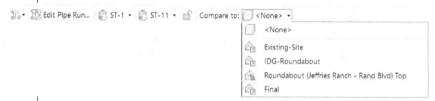 (Compare to...) in the top right corner, as shown in Figure B–18. Use the drop-down list to select the surface you want to study in the View pane.

Figure B–18

When a surface is selected for comparison, the Sub-object pane (with the appropriate tab) will list the comparison surface and the differences, as shown in Figure B–19.

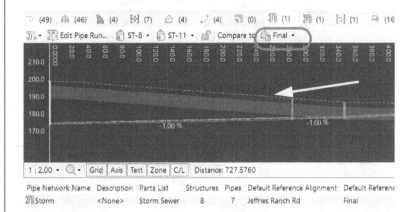

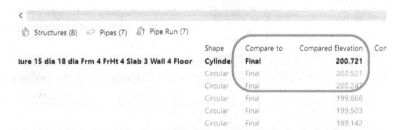

Figure B–19

Practice B2 | Edit Civil 3D Pipe Objects

Practice Objectives

- Study pipe branches within Project Explorer, including the structures and pipes.
- Make adjustments to the tabular data in Project Explorer.

In this practice, you will examine the pipe branches in the Project Explorer and make some preliminary adjustments to tweak the design.

Task 1 - Adjust the outfall pipe.

1. Open **PEX1-A.dwg** from the *C:\Civil 3D Projects\Working\ Project Explorer* folder, if not already open.

2. Select the preset view **Corr-QTO**.

3. Open the Project Explorer by clicking ▣ (Project Explorer) in the *Home* tab>Explore panel, if needed. Go to the *Pipe Network* tab.

4. Click ▢ (Compare to...) in the top right corner of the View pane, as shown in Figure B–20. In the drop-down list, select **Final**.

Figure B–20

5. On the *Pipes* tab of the Sub-object pane, select the first row (**PI-1**). Note how the pipe highlights by turning yellow in the View pane. Use the <Down> and <Up> arrow keys on your keyboard to select other rows and note how the View pane updates. PI-5 and PI-6 are not displayed in the View pane.

6. Go to the **PI-6** row and type <Z> to zoom to the pipe in Model Space. Press <Ctrl> a few times and note how the pipe is highlighted in Model Space.

7. Go to the **PI-5** row and type <P> to pan to that pipe in Model Space. This is the outfall pipe into the basin. Its inverts are incorrect, as can be seen on the *Pipes* tab of the Sub-object pane, as shown in Figure B–21. Also note the *Start* (**ST-6**) and *End Structure* (**ST-7**) this pipe is connected to.

 Structures (8)   Pipes (7)   Pipe Run (11)

Pipe Name	Description	Pipe Style	Start Invert	End Invert	Slope	Start Structure	End Structure
PI-1	12.0 inch PVC Pipe	ASC-Double Line (Storm)	197.503	192.240	2.00 %	ST-1	ST-2
PI-2	12.0 inch PVC Pipe	ASC-Double Line (Storm)	192.140	189.557	1.00 %	ST-2	ST-8
PI-5	24 inch Concrete Pip [...]	ASC-Double Line (Storm)	-0.500	-0.500	0.00 %	ST-6	ST-7
PI-6	12.0 inch PVC Pipe	ASC-Double Line (Storm)	175.224	172.681	1.00 %	ST-8	ST-7
PI-7	12.0 inch PVC Pipe	ASC-Double Line (Storm)	178.222	175.324	1.00 %	ST-9	ST-8

Figure B–21

8. On the *Structures* tab of the Sub-object pane, note the *Rim Elevation* of ST-6, which is near zero elevation. Note the Final Surface Elevation of about **164'**. Also note the *Connected Pipes* of ST-7 (the catch basin), which are **PI-5** and **PI-6**, as shown in Figure B–22.

 Structures (8)   Pipes (7)   Pipe Run (11)

Structure Name	Description	Structure Style	Easting	Northing	Rim Elevation	Connected Pipes	Reference
ST-1	Slab Top Cylindrical [...]	Storm Sewer Manhole	6257036.0092	2036568.6687	201.527	PI-1	Final
ST-2	Slab Top Cylindrical [...]	Storm Sewer Manhole	6256776.9363	2036615.5685	202.285	PI-1, PI-2	Final
ST-6	12 inch Flared End S [...]	Flared End Section	6256268.7387	2036747.2487	0.607	PI-5	Final
ST-7	48 x 48 Rect Two Tie [...]	Catch Basin	6256266.1410	2036648.8573	199.219	PI-6, PI-5	Final
ST-8	Slab Top Cylindrical [...]	Storm Sewer Manhole	6256520.3804	2036643.0819	200.721	PI-7, PI-2, PI-6	Final

Figure B–22

9. Return to the *Pipes* tab of the Sub-object pane and select the **PI-6** pipe. The *End Invert* is about **172.7'**.

10. Double-click on the *Start Invert* cell of **PI-5**, which launches the Edit Pipe Slope and Elevation window, as shown in Figure B–23.

Figure B–23

11. In the Edit Pipe Slope and Elevation window, do the following:

- In the *Control Parameters* area, select **Hold Pipe End Elevation**.
- Type **163.0** for the *Start Elevation of Pipe* (a bit above the Finish elevation).
- In the *Control Parameters* area, select **Hold Pipe Start Elevation**.
- Type **172.0** for the *End Elevation of Pipe* (a bit above the Finish elevation).
- Note the resulting *Pipe Slope* of about **-9**, as shown in Figure B–24, which is acceptable.

Figure B–24

12. Click **OK** to close the Edit Pipe Slope and Elevation window.

13. On the *Structures* tab of the Sub-object pane, select the row of **ST-8**. Type <P> to pan to that structure in Model Space. It is the structure that the Ascent PI pipe branch connects to. PI-7 is the pipe from Ascent PI that connects to the structure.

14. In the *Start Structure for Pipe Run and Profile View* drop-down list, select **ST-6.** Select **ST-8** for the *End Structure for Pipe Run and Profile View*. The View pane updates to show how the outflow pipe now works, as shown in Figure B–25.

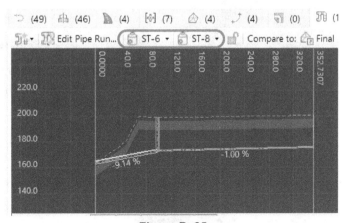

Figure B–25

From here you would need adjust the structure sump depth of ST-8. This is not covered in these practices.

Task 2 - Adjust the Ascent PI pipe branch.

1. In Model Space, note the Structure labels (or the tooltips) upon hovering over the structures are ST-8 and ST-11, as shown in Figure B–26. Enter these values in the *Start Structure for Pipe Run and Profile View* and the *End Structure for Pipe Run and Profile View* drop-down lists.

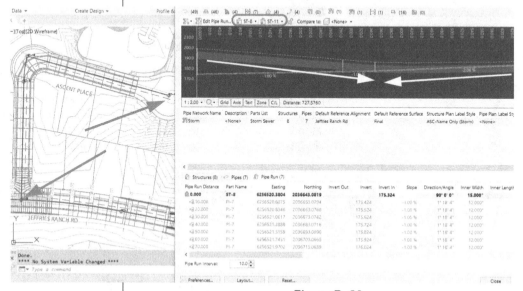

Figure B–26

2. We want to change the flow of the pipes so they flow towards ST-10. Note that the PI-9 pipe is already sloping properly, so you only need to change the slope for the pipes from ST-8 to ST-10.

3. Enter **ST-10** for the *End Structure* from the drop-down list.

4. Click 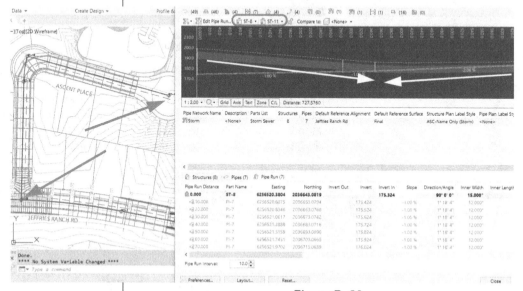 (Edit Pipe Run) to edit the selected pipes within the run.

5. In the Edit Pipe Run Slope and Elevations window, you can control the elevations and slopes of the selected pipes, as shown in Figure B–27. Do the following:

- In the *Control Parameters* area, select **Hold Pipe Run End Elevation**.
- Type **2.0%** for the *Pipe Run Slope.*
- Note the resulting *Start Elevation of Pipe Run*.
- Click **OK** to close the Edit Pipe Run Slope and Elevations window.

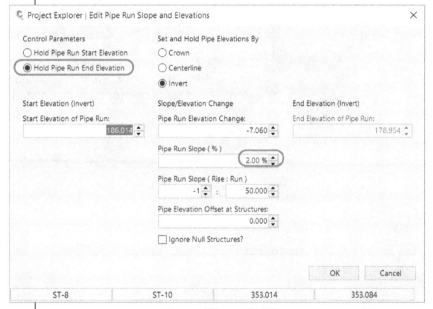

Figure B–27

From here you would need to run another pipe connecting to ST-10 into the basin with an ending headwall structure. This is not covered in these practices.

6. Save the drawing.

B.4 Reports and Object Sets

The use of Object Sets lets you automate the creation of reports, AutoCAD tables, and 2D drawings. You can select a variety of data from different Civil 3D and AutoCAD objects for content. The Object Sets are a collection of such objects, along with a series of steps that are activated, such as what the action is and the format and options for such an action.

Object Set definitions are stored in the current drawing and can contain specific actions that can be used to launch the set.

Create Object Sets

Each Object Set requires a unique name and an optional description. There are a set of predefined actions to pick from, along with the options for such predefined actions and layout styles, as shown in Figure B–28.

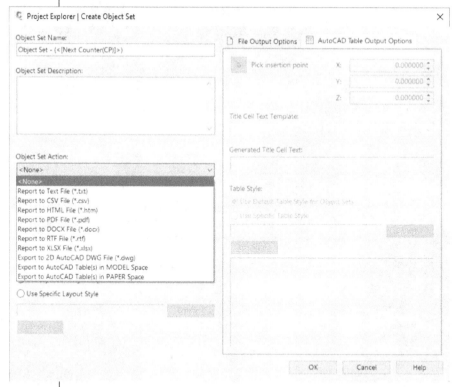

Figure B–28

The **Object Set Actions** are:

- Report to Text File
- Report to CSV File
- Report to HTML File
- Report to PDF File
- Report to DOCX File
- Report to RTF File
- Report to XLSX File
- Export to 2D AutoCAD DWG File
- Export to AutoCAD Table(s) in MODEL Space
- Export to AutoCAD Table(s) in PAPER Space

If AutoCAD tables are being produced, their content can either be dynamic or manual (static). Note that the dynamic feature of the AutoCAD tables is only available when the Project Explorer is open. If the Project Explorer is closed, the tables will behave as static until the Project Explorer is opened, and then the content of the tables will update automatically.

For all other actions, the content is static and does not update as the data within the objects changes.

The **Layout Styles** can be the current layout within Project Explorer, can be edited and saved as a layout style within Project Explorer, or can be loaded from an external file.

For the **File Output Options** (if a report action has been selected), the name and location of the output file is required, as well as the report style.

For the **AutoCAD Table Output Options** (if a table action has been selected), the insertion point for the table and the content for the title cell name is required, as well as the table style.

Practice B3 | Reports and Object Sets

Practice Objective

- Create an AutoCAD table from Civil 3D data.

Task 1 - Create an AutoCAD table from pipe data.

1. Continue working on the previous drawing or open **PEX1-B.dwg** from the *C:\Civil 3D Projects\Working\ Project Explorer* folder, if not already open.

2. Select the preset view **Corr-QTO**.

3. Open the Project Explorer by clicking (Project Explorer) in the *Home* tab>Explore panel, if needed. Go to the *Object Sets* tab, as shown in Figure B–29.

Figure B–29

4. Click (New Object Set).

5. In the Create Object Set window, set the following, as shown in Figure B–30:

   - *Object Set Name:* **Pipes in Mspace**
   - *Object Set Action:* **Export to AutoCAD Table(s) in MODEL Space**
   - *Object Set Action Type:* **Dynamic**
   - *Layout Style:* **Use Layout of Project Exploder Window** (you will change this later)
   - *Pick Insertion Point:* Select a point in Model Space above the profile views
   - *Title Cell Text Template:* **(Object_Name)** (this is the default)
   - *Table Style:* **Use Default Table Style for Object Sets** (you will change this later)

Figure B–30

6. Click **OK** to close the Create Object Set window.

7. On the *Objects* tab, click ✚ (Add/Remove Objects to/from Object Set) to build your Object Set, as shown in Figure B–31

Figure B–31

8. In the Add Object(s) to Object Set window, go to the *Pipe Networks* tab and select **Storm**, as shown in Figure B–32.

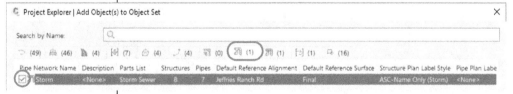

Figure B–32

9. Click **OK** to close the Add Object(s) to Object Set window.

10. Click 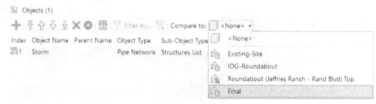 (Compare to...) in the *Objects* tab, as shown in Figure B–33. In the drop-down list, select **Final**.

Figure B–33

11. Note that the point you picked in Model Space for the insertion point of the table now has a table, as shown in Figure B–34. However, it contains too many columns, and the table style may not be up to standard.

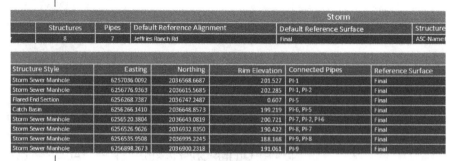

	Storm				
Structures	Pipes	Default Reference Alignment	Default Reference Surface	Structure
8	7	Jeffries Ranch Rd	Final	ASC-Name

Structure Style	Easting	Northing	Rim Elevation	Connected Pipes	Reference Surface
Storm Sewer Manhole	6257036.0092	2036568.6687	201.527	PI-1	Final
Storm Sewer Manhole	6256776.9363	2036615.5685	202.285	PI-1, PI-2	Final
Flared End Section	6256268.7387	2036747.2487	0.607	PI-5	Final
Catch Basin	6256266.1410	2036648.8573	199.219	PI-6, PI-5	Final
Storm Sewer Manhole	6256520.3804	2036643.0819	200.721	PI-7, PI-2, PI-6	Final
Storm Sewer Manhole	6256526.9626	2036932.8350	190.422	PI-8, PI-7	Final
Storm Sewer Manhole	6256535.9508	2036995.2245	188.168	PI-9, PI-8	Final
Storm Sewer Manhole	6256898.2673	2036900.2318	191.061	PI-9	Final

Figure B–34

Task 2 - Edit the Layout Style and Table Style.

1. Double-click on the **Pipes in Mspace** Object Set in the upper pane to edit it.

2. In the Edit Object Set window, in the *Layout Style* area, select **Use Specific Layout Style,** then click the **Edit Style...** button, as shown in Figure B–35.

Figure B–35

3. In the Layout Options window, do the following, as shown in Figure B–36:

    1. Click on the *Pipe Network* tab.
    2. In the *Pipe Network Column Chooser* drop-down list, select **Set Column Layout for Pipes**.
    3. In the lower right corner, click on the blank square to deselect all columns.
    4. Select the following columns:
        *   **Pipe Name**
        *   **Pipe Style**
        *   **Start Invert**
        *   **End Invert**
        *   **Slope**
        *   **Start Structure**
        *   **End Structure**
    5. Select the **Slope** column and use the arrow keys on the right side to move it below the **End Structure** column.

Figure B–36

4. Click 🖫 (Save) and save the set in the *C:\Civil 3D Projects\ Ascent-Config* folder. Name it **XXX-Pipe-table.xmpt** (substituting your initials for XXX).

5. Click **OK** to close the Layout Options window.

6. In the Edit Object Set window, in the *AutoCAD Table Layout Options* area, select **Use Specific Table Style**, then click the **Edit Style...** button, as shown in Figure B–37.

Figure B–37

7. In the Table Options window, do the following, as shown in Figure B–38:

   1. Uncheck **Use Background Colors**. (Note: If you are using a white background for Model Space, do not uncheck this or change the text colors to a dark color.)
   2. Set the *Border Color* to **Red**.
   3. Check **Force all text to UPPERCASE**.

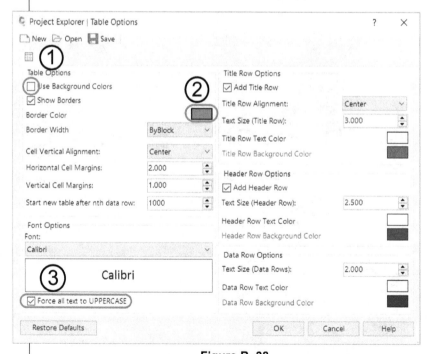

Figure B–38

8. Click 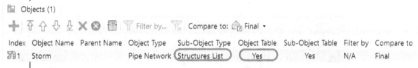 (Save) and save the set to the *C:\Civil 3D Projects\ Ascent-Config* folder. Name it **XXX--Mspace table.xmpa** (substituting your initials for XXX).

9. Click **OK** to close the Table Options window.

10. Click **OK** to close the Edit Object Set window.

11. In the middle pane of the *Object Sets* tab, double-click on **Structures List** (in the *Sub-Object Type* column), as shown in Figure B–39.

Figure B–39

12. In the Select Sub-Object Type window, select **Pipes List** from the Sub-Object Type drop-down list, as shown in Figure B–40.

Figure B–40

13. Click **OK** to close the Select Sub-Object Type window.

14. In the middle pane, double-click on **Yes** in the *Object Table* column, as shown above in Figure B–39.

---

15. In the Object Set Item Output Options window, uncheck **Use Object Table?**, as shown in Figure B–41.

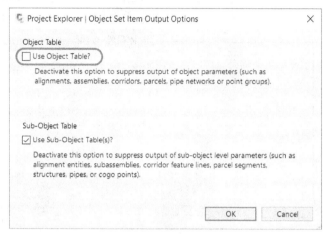

Figure B–41

16. Click **OK** to close the Object Set Item Output Options window.

17. Click **OK** to close the Edit Object Set window.

18. The final table should look like the one shown in Figure B–42.

STORM						
PIPE NAME	PIPE STYLE	START INVERT	END INVERT	START STRUCTURE	END STRUCTURE	SLOPE
P I-1	ASC-DOUBLE LINE (STORM)	197.503	192.240	ST-1	ST-2	2.00 %
P I-2	ASC-DOUBLE LINE (STORM)	192.140	189.557	ST-2	ST-8	1.00 %
P I-5	ASC-DOUBLE LINE (STORM)	163.000	172.000	ST-6	ST-7	9.14 %
P I-6	ASC-DOUBLE LINE (STORM)	175.224	172.681	ST-8	ST-7	1.00 %
P I-7	ASC-DOUBLE LINE (STORM)	180.218	186.014	ST-9	ST-8	-2.00 %
P I-8	ASC-DOUBLE LINE (STORM)	178.954	180.218	ST-10	ST-9	-2.00 %
P I-9	ASC-DOUBLE LINE (STORM)	186.830	179.054	ST-11	ST-10	2.08 %

Figure B–42

19. Close the Project Explorer window.

20. Save and close the drawing.

Chapter Review Questions

1. You can have the Project Explorer window open while you work in the Civil 3D Model Space.

   a. True

   b. False

2. The Project Explorer only manages Civil 3D objects.

   a. True

   b. False

3. Do the tables created from Object Sets in Project Explorer update automatically?

   a. Yes, when set to dynamic.

   b. No, they must be regenerated.

   c. Yes, when set to dynamic and the Project Explorer is open.

4. Which of the following objects does the Project Explorer manage? (Select all that apply.)

   a. Subassemblies

   b. Survey figures

   c. AutoCAD blocks

   d. Dimension styles

   e. Feature lines

Command Summary

Button	Command	Location
	Project Explorer	• **Ribbon:** *Home* tab>Explore panel • Command Prompt: ProjectExplorer
	Compare to	• **Project Explorer View Pane**
	Edit Pipe Run	• **Project Explorer View Pane**

Parcels

In this appendix, you will learn how to create a subdivision plan using specific design criteria. Labels and tables are added to the plan to correctly communicate the design to contractors and other stakeholders.

Learning Objectives in This Appendix

- Create parcels from objects in the drawing or in an external reference file.
- Change the properties and display order of parcels to ensure that the correct linetype and color display.
- Subdivide parcels into smaller lots using various tools.
- Change the parcel numbers so that they are numbered in order.
- Change area, line, and curve labels into tags and display in a table for better readability of the drawing.
- Create predefined reports to share useful engineering data about the parcels created in the drawing.
- Add annotation to parcels to communicate line bearing, distances, and areas for each lot.

C.1 Introduction to Parcels

A site (shown in Figure C–1) is the starting point for defining smaller parcels. The development's zoning agreement or covenants determine the size, setback, and other criteria for the new parcels. If a parcel is residential, there might be restrictions affecting minimum parcel areas, setbacks, and where to locate a house. If it is a commercial property, there might be restrictions or specific mandates for access, traffic control, parking spaces, etc. The **Parcel Layout** commands are used for subdividing larger parcels.

Figure C–1

Sites, parcels, and alignments are closely related. Each can exist by itself and you do not need to have alignments associated with the parcels. However, you often start with a site boundary and then divide the site into smaller parcels by placing alignments within its boundary. In that case, it is recommended the parcels and alignments reside in the same Civil 3D site.

- Parcels are listed in the Toolspace, *Prospector* tab in the Sites branch, as shown in Figure C–2.

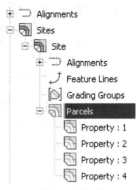

Figure C–2

- When adding alignments to a Civil 3D site, the Parcels list is updated in the Toolspace, *Prospector* tab.

- As in all other Autodesk Civil 3D objects, Parcel object layers are controlled in the *Object Layers* tab of the Drawing Settings dialog box, as shown in Figure C–3.

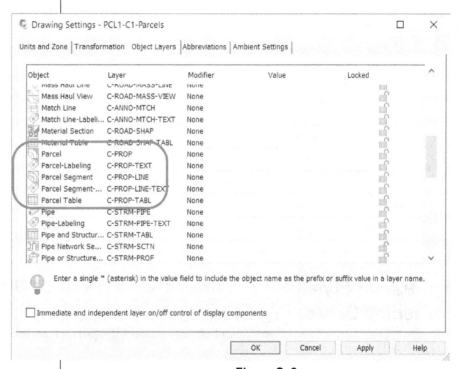

Figure C–3

ROW Parcel

The right-of-way (ROW) parcel is related to the alignment and parcels. This special parcel represents land that is owned, maintained, and used for the community by a regulatory body (usually the local municipality or Department of Transportation). Typically, the ROW contains road, sidewalks, and utilities. The contents of the ROW depend on the covenants or agreements made before the site is developed. For example, in some cases, the sidewalks and utilities might be located within an easement outside the road ROW.

- The Autodesk Civil 3D software contains a **ROW** command, which creates a parcel using offsets from an alignment.

- A ROW parcel can represent the front yard definition of several potential parcels.

- While normal parcels automatically adjust to changes to an alignment, ROW parcels are static as shown in Figure C–4. Therefore, you should only create ROW parcels after determining a final location for an alignment.

Figure C–4

Parcel Style Display Order

Parcel segment display is controlled by parcel styles, and parcel lines can abut parcels with different styles. To open the Site Parcel Properties dialog box, select the *Parcels* collection (under *Sites*), right-click and select **Properties**, as shown in Figure C–5.

Figure C–5

You can select which parcel style should take precedence in the *Parcel style display order* area of the Site Parcel Properties dialog box, as shown in Figure C–6. Placing the style for the overall parent tract (the Site Parcel Style) at the top of the list causes the outside parcel lines to display differently than those inside.

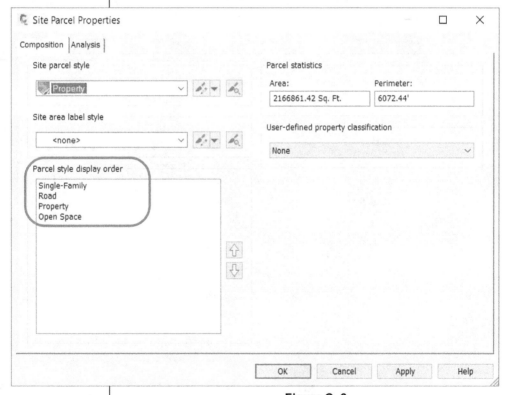

Figure C–6

Parcel Properties

The properties of a parcel include its name, style, and an *Analysis* tab containing the parcel's area, perimeter, and point-of-beginning (POB). The Parcel Property's *Composition* tab displays the label style, area, and perimeter, as shown in Figure C–7.

Figure C–7

The *Analysis* tab contains a parcel boundary Inverse or Mapcheck analysis. In the upper right area of the tab, you can change the POB (Point of beginning) location and the analysis direction, as shown in Figure C–8.

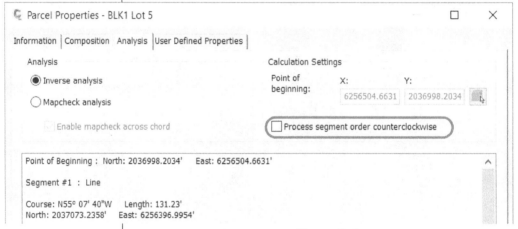

Figure C–8

- The Mapcheck analysis precision is the same as the drawing distance precision.

- The Inverse report precision is set to the precision of the Autodesk Civil 3D software (10 to 12 decimal places).

- The default direction of a Mapcheck or Inverse analysis is clockwise. You can change the direction to counter-clockwise if required, as shown above in Figure C–8.

- A POB can be any vertex on the parcel's perimeter.

The *User Defined Properties* tab contains site-specific details, such as the *Parcel Number, Parcel Address, Parcel Tax ID*, and other properties you might want to define, as shown in Figure C–9. Custom properties can be assigned to a drawing by using the *User Defined Property Classifications* area in the Toolspace, *Settings* tab, under the *Parcels* collection.

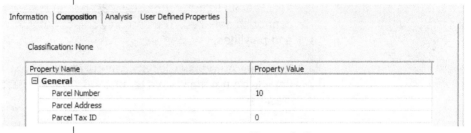

Figure C–9

Parcel Labels and Styles

There are two types of parcel annotation: an area label for the parcel and the segments defining the parcel.

A parcel area label usually consists of a parcel's number or name, area, and perimeter, as shown in Figure C–10. Often, offices define their own parcel label styles. A parcel label style can include several additional parcel properties, address, PIN, Site name, etc.

Figure C–10

Hint: In the Autodesk Civil 3D software, you select a parcel by selecting a parcel area label, not the parcel segments.

Create Parcels from Objects

The Autodesk Civil 3D software can create parcels from AutoCAD objects, such as closed polylines and closed sequences of lines and arcs. Avoid gaps, multiple polyline vertices at the same location, and polylines that double-back over themselves, which might lead to errors in parcel layouts.

These objects can be selected in the current drawing or from an XREF. Note that Autodesk Civil 3D parcel lines in an XREF cannot be selected. You can only select AutoCAD lines, arcs, and polylines.

Note that Autodesk Civil 3D parcels created from AutoCAD objects do not maintain a relationship to the objects after creation.

Creating Right-of-Way Parcels

Once a site contains property that has been defined as a parcel and alignments have been generated, you are ready to start creating subdivision plans. One command that can speed up the process is **Parcels>Create ROW**. It automatically creates Right-of-Way parcels based on alignment setbacks.

ROW parcels do not automatically update when alignments change. Therefore, you may want to create ROWs after you are certain where you want the alignments to be for this alternative.

> ### Hint: Multiple Alternatives in the Same Drawing
>
> Sites enable you to organize alignments, parcels, and related data into separate containers, so that parcel lines from one site alternative do not clean up with parcel lines in others. However, sites do not offer layer or other kind of visibility control. Therefore, if you intend to have multiple parcel layout alternatives in the same drawing, you should consider placing parcel area labels and parcel segments on different layers.

Practice C1

Create Parcels from Objects

Practice Objective

- Create parcels from objects in the drawing or external reference file.

Task 1 - Create a Site parcel from objects.

1. Open **PCL1-A.dwg** from the *C:\Civil 3D Projects\Working\ Parcels* folder.

2. In the *Home* tab>Create Design panel, expand **Parcel** and select **Create Parcels from Objects**, as shown in Figure C–11.

Figure C–11

3. In the model, select the polyline that represent the property boundary, as shown in Figure C–12, and press **<Enter>**.

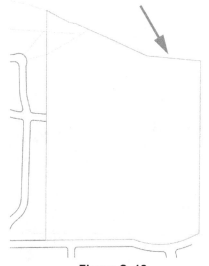

Figure C–12

4. In the Create Parcels dialog box, set the following parameters, as shown in Figure C–13, and then click **OK**.

- *Site:* **Site 1**
- *Parcel style:* **ASC-Property**
- *Area label style:* **ASC-Name Area & Perimeter**
- Select **Automatically add segment labels**
- *Line segment label style:* **ASC-(Span) Bearing and Distance with Crows Feet**
- *Curve segment label style:* **ASC-Delta over Length and Radius** (this is the default)
- Select **Erase existing entities**

One parcel will be created with the parameters entered.

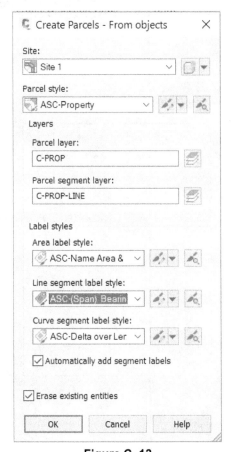

Figure C–13

5. In the Toolspace, *Prospector* tab, expand the current drawing and select the **Sites>Site1>Parcels** node, as shown in Figure C–14. Note that the new parcel is listed in the branch as well as in the preview section of the Prospector.

Note: *If the + is not displayed next to Parcels, press <F5> to refresh the Toolspace, Prospector tab view.*

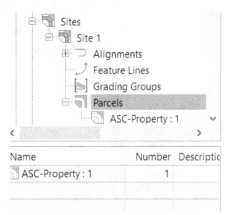

Figure C–14

Task 2 - Create a new site and parcel from referenced objects.

You have received a drawing from the Land Planning department that displays the street layout and different parcels. Using this plan, you will create parcels from XREF objects.

1. Continue working with the drawing from the previous task.

2. In the Toolspace, *Prospector* tab, right-click on the *Sites* collection and select **New**. Type **C3D Training** as the name and click **OK** to close the dialog box.

3. You now need to move the **ASC-Property:1** parcel from *Site 1* to the **C3D Training** site. Expand the *Site1* collection, expand the *Parcels* collection, right-click on the **ASC-Property:1** parcel and select **Move to Site**, as shown on the left in Figure C–15.

4. In the Move to Site dialog box, select **C3D Training**, as shown on the right in Figure C–15. Click **OK** to close the dialog box.

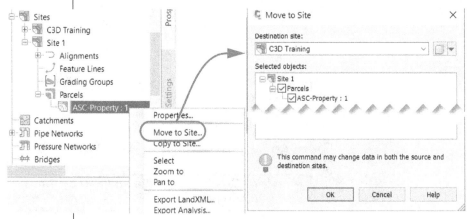

Figure C–15

5. In the Toolspace, *Prospector* tab, expand the current drawing and select the **Sites>C3D Training>Parcels** node, as shown in Figure C–16. Note that the parcel is now listed in the branch and no longer in the **Sites>Site1>Parcels** node.

Note: If the + is not displayed next to Parcels, press <F5> to refresh the Toolspace, Prospector tab view.

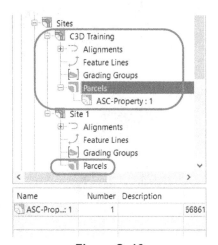

Figure C–16

Note: To save time, the x-referenced drawing **Base-original Property**, has already been referenced. The zone and units for the project drawings were set. This enables you to geo reference the drawings using **Locate using Geographic data**, as shown in Figure C–17. You need not repeat this step.

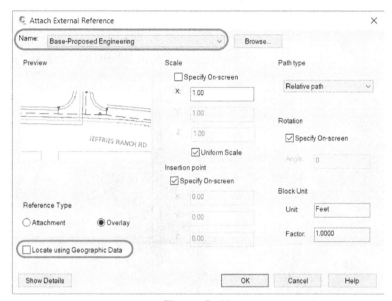

Figure C–17

6. Thaw the layer **Base-originalProperty|C-PROP-LINE-N** and freeze the layer **Base-originalProperty|C-PROP-LINE-E**.

7. In the *Home* tab>Create Design panel, expand **Parcel** and select **Create Parcels from Objects**. Select **Xref** from the command options.

8. Use the AutoCAD Crossing selection or the Lasso Crossing selection method (click and drag the cursor towards the left side of the screen to select all the linework within the green boundary, as shown on the right in Figure C–18. There should be a total of 40 objects. Press <Enter> to end the **XREF selection** command.

9. In the Create Parcels - From objects dialog box, verify that the Site name is **C3D Training**. Clear the **Automatically add segment labels** option and keep the default values in the remaining fields, as shown on the right in Figure C–18. Click **OK** to close the dialog box.

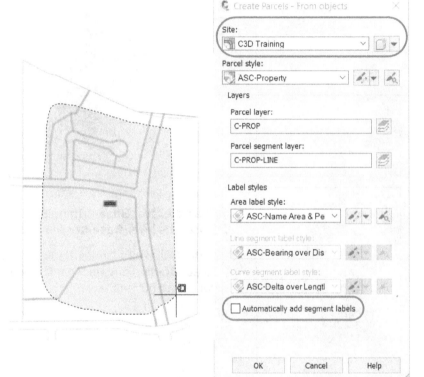

Figure C–18

You may need to refresh the Toolspace by pressing <F5>.

10. The project site now has nine parcels. In the drawing area, select each parcel label and click 🖿 (Parcel Properties) on the *Parcels* contextual tab>Modify panel.

The default parcel numbers may differ because they are randomly numbered.

11. In the Parcel Properties dialog box, in the *Information* tab, clear the **Use name template in parcel style** option, which will allow you to type in a new name for the parcel, as shown on the left in Figure C–19.

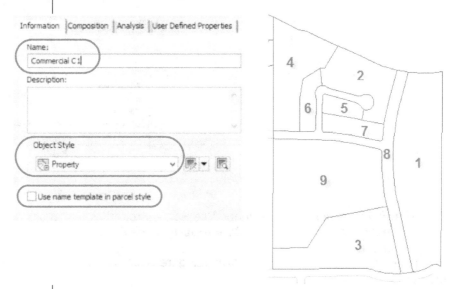

Figure C–19

12. Using the numbering shown on the right in Figure C–19, set the parcel names and styles according to the following table:

Property Name	Style
1. Commercial C1	ASC-Property
2. Multi Family MF	ASC-Property
3. Municipal Reserve MR	ASC-Property
4. Pond PUL	ASC-Open Space
5. Residential BLK2 R1	ASC-Property
6. Residential BLK1 R1	ASC-Property
7. Residential BLK3 R1	ASC-Property
8. Right Of Way	ASC-Road
9. School MSR	ASC-Property

13. In the Toolspace, *Prospector* tab, expand *Sites*, expand the **C3D Training** site, right-click on *Parcels*, and select **Properties**, as shown in Figure C–20.

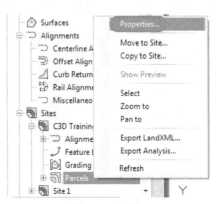

Figure C–20

If the drawing does not look different after completing Step 13, you might need to adjust the draw order so that the XREF drawing is behind the existing drawing linework.

14. In the Site Parcel Properties dialog box, select **ASC-Property** in the *Parcel style display order* area, as shown in Figure C–21. Click 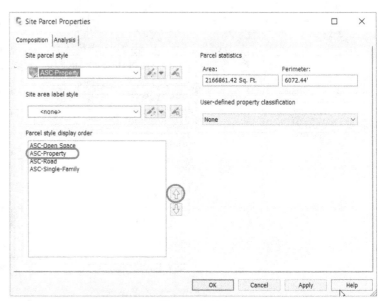 to move it up in the list.

Figure C–21

15. Click **OK**.

16. Save the drawing.

C.2 Creating and Editing Parcels by Layout Overview

In addition to creating parcels from polylines, arcs, and lines, the Autodesk Civil 3D software can also intelligently create (and adjust) parcels using commands in the Parcel Layout Tools toolbar. To open the Parcel Layout Tools toolbar, expand Parcel in the Create Design panel, and select **Parcel Creation Tools**, as shown in Figure C–22.

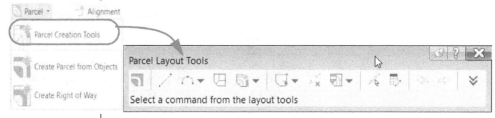

Figure C–22

When drawing parcel line segments, it is essential to use the AutoCAD Object Snaps to ensure that the lines and curve segments touch existing parcel segments so that the enclosures are complete and parcels are created.

- (Create Parcel) assigns parcel creation settings, such as parcel type, labeling styles, and other parameters.

- The (Line) and (Curve) commands can be used to create individual line and curve parcel segments. Segments created with these tools are considered *fixed*.

- (Draw Tangent - Tangent with No Curves) enables you to create a series of connected parcel line segments.

- The Parcel Sizing flyout (shown in Figure C–23), contains a list of commands for creating and editing parcels. The methods used to create parcels include defining the *last* parcel segment by slide direction, slide angle, swing line, or freehand drawing of a parcel boundary. The most frequently used method is **Slide Line**.

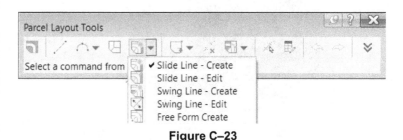

Figure C–23

- The commands at the center of the toolbar (shown in Figure C–24), enable you to further edit parcel segments. These commands include inserting or deleting PIs (points of intersection), deleting parcel segments, or creating or dissolving parcel unions.

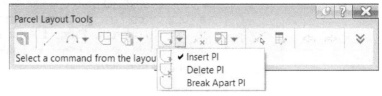

Figure C–24

- 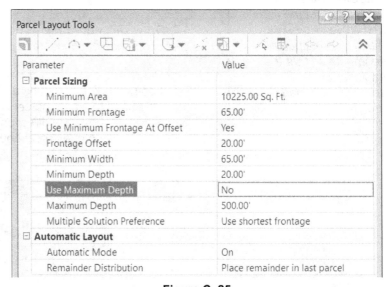 (Pick Sub-Entity) enables you to select a parcel line and display its details in the Parcel Layout Parameters dialog box.

- (Sub-entity Editor) opens and closes the Parcel Layout Parameters dialog box.

- The next two commands enable you to **Undo** and **Redo** parcel edits. These can be used while the Parcel Layout Tools have been opened.

- The drop-down arrow ( ) expands the toolbar to display the Parcel Creation parameters, as shown in Figure C–25 (also accessible through the Command Settings of *CreateParcelByLayout* in the Toolspace, *Settings* tab).

Parameter	Value
Parcel Sizing	
Minimum Area	10225.00 Sq. Ft.
Minimum Frontage	65.00'
Use Minimum Frontage At Offset	Yes
Frontage Offset	20.00'
Minimum Width	65.00'
Minimum Depth	20.00'
Use Maximum Depth	No
Maximum Depth	500.00'
Multiple Solution Preference	Use shortest frontage
Automatic Layout	
Automatic Mode	On
Remainder Distribution	Place remainder in last parcel

Figure C–25

- The *Parcel Sizing* area sets the minimum area for parcels to be laid out. *Minimum Frontage* sets the minimum width of a parcel at the ROW or at a setback from the ROW.

- *Use Minimum Frontage At Offset* specifies whether or not to use frontage offset criteria.

- *Frontage Offset* sets the default value for the frontage offset from the ROW.

- *Minimum Width* sets the default minimum width at the frontage offset.

- *Minimum Depth* sets the minimum depth of new or existing parcels at the mid-point and is perpendicular to the frontage of the parcel.

- *Use Maximum Depth* specifies whether or not to use maximum depth criteria.

- *Maximum Depth* sets the maximum depth for new parcels or when editing parcels.

- *Multiple Solution Preference* specifies whether or not to use the shortest frontage or the smallest area when multiple solutions are encountered.

- *Automatic Layout* affects how parcel auto-sizing subdivides a parcel block.

C.3 Creating and Editing Parcels

The **Create Parcel by Layout** tools can help you to quickly create a subdivision plan. Although these tools can make your job easier and are faster than manual drafting, they are only effective in creating the *last* side of new parcels. Therefore, you might need to create additional (or adjust) parcel lines manually to guide the Autodesk Civil 3D software to the best solution. For example, the area shown in Figure C–26, requires you to create minimum 10,225 sq. ft. (0.23 acre) parcels.

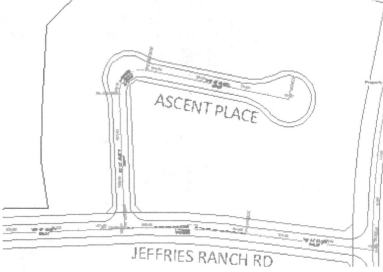

Figure C–26

The back parcel lines (those along the west and south of the cul-de-sac area, and between Jeffries Ranch Rd and Ascent Place) were drawn manually and saved in a separate drawing file. Once inserted, they are used to guide the creation of the parcels next to Ascent Place. If you ask the Autodesk Civil 3D software to automatically subdivide this area, the result is a total of 15 residential lot parcels, as shown in Figure C–27.

Figure C–27

The various creation and editing techniques available in the Create Parcel by Layout toolbar include:

- Freehand tools
- Slide Line tools
- Swing Line tools
- Free Form Create

Freehand

The ╱ (Line), ⌒▾ (Curve), and ▱ (Draw Tangent - Tangent with No Curves) commands enable you to create lot lines without having to specify an area. In contrast, the following commands all create parcels based on a specified area.

Slide Line

The **Slide Line - Create** command enables you to subdivide a larger parcel by creating new parcel lines that hold a specific angle relative to the Right-of-Way, such as 90° or a specific bearing or azimuth. The **Slide Line - Edit** command enables you to modify a parcel to a specified area while holding the same angle from the ROW or a specific bearing or azimuth. The commands are shown in Figure C–28.

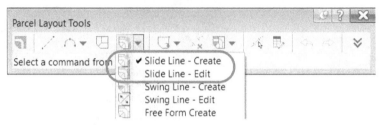

Figure C–28

Swing Line

The **Swing Line - Create** command enables you to create a new parcel by creating a parcel segment that connects to a specified point, such as a property corner. The **Swing Line - Edit** command enables you to resize a parcel while specifying a lot corner. These commands are shown in Figure C–29.

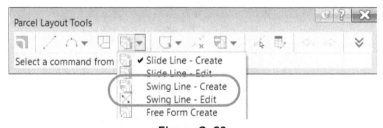

Figure C–29

Free Form Create

The **Free Form Create** command enables you to create a new lot by specifying an area, attachment point and angle, or two attachment points.

Frontage

When using these tools, you are prompted to select a parcel interior point and trace its frontage geometry. This is a critical step. As you trace the frontage, the command creates a jig (heavy highlight) that recognizes the changing geometry of the frontage line work, as shown in Figure C–30.

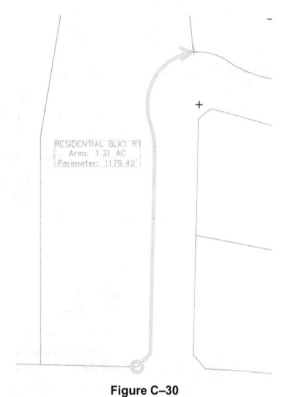

RESIDENTIAL BLK1 R1
Area: 1.31 AC
Perimeter: 1179.42'

Figure C–30

Practice C2 | Create Parcels by Slide Angle

Practice Objective

- Create and edit parcels to maximize the number of lots you can create with the required area and frontage.

You have three parcels zoned as single-family residential: Block1 (1.31ac), Block2 (0.94ac), and Block3 (1.47ac). Your client, the land developer, requires you to maximize the number of lots in these three parcels, while noting the minimum area and frontages as required by the Land Use bylaws.

1. Continue working with the drawing from the previous practice or open **PCL1-B.dwg** from the *C:\Civil 3D Projects\ Working\Parcels* folder.

2. Select the preset view **Parcel-Create**.

3. In the *Home* tab>Create Design panel, expand **Parcel** and select **Parcel Creation Tools**. The Parcel Layout Tools toolbar displays.

4. Click ⬇ to expand the *Parcel Creation Tools* and enter the following values, as shown in Figure C–31:

   - *Minimum Area:* **10225.00 Sq Ft.**
   - *Maximum Frontage:* **65.00'**
   - *Use Maximum Frontage At Offset:* **Yes**
   - *Frontage Offset:* **20.00'**
   - *Minimum Width:* **65.00'**
   - *Minimum Depth:* **20.00'**
   - *Use Maximum Depth:* **No**
   - *Maximum Depth:* **500.00'**
   - *Multiple Solution Preference:* **Use shortest frontage**
   - *Automatic Mode:* **On**
   - *Remainder Distribution:* **Place remainder in last parcel**

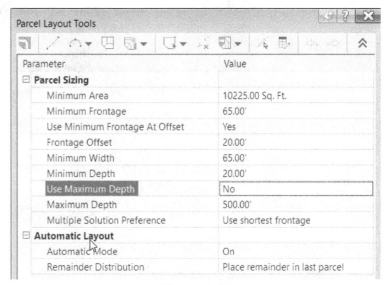

Figure C–31

5. When finished, click ⩘ to collapse the expanded toolbar.

6. In the Parcel Layout Tools toolbar, expand ▦ ▾ and select **Slide Line - Create**, as shown in Figure C–32.

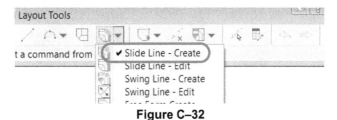

Figure C–32

7. In the Create Parcels - Layout dialog box, set the following parameters, as shown in Figure C–33:

- *Site:* **C3D Training**
- *Parcel style:* **ASC-Single-Family**
- *Area label style:* **ASC-Name Square Foot & Acres**

Figure C–33

8. Click **OK** to accept the changes and close the dialog box.

9. When prompted to select the parcel to be subdivided, select the area label for parcel **RESIDENTIAL BLK1 R1**, as shown in Figure C–34.

Figure C–34

10. When you are prompted for the *starting point on frontage*, select the south end of the corner cut. Press <Shift>, right-click, and select **endpoint** from the right-click menu. Then, select the corner cut, **Pt 1**, shown in Figure C–35.

11. When prompted for the *end point of the frontage*, set the end point of the property line to the north, **Pt 2**, as shown in Figure C–35. Use the same process as the previous step to set the end point.

12. When prompted for the *angle of the property line* that will be used to define each lot, select a point east of the parcel near **Pt 3**, as shown in Figure C–35. For the second point, press <Shift>, right-click, and select **Perpendicular**. Then select the line at Pt 4.

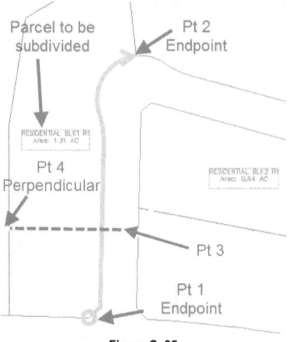

Parcel to be subdivided

Pt 2 Endpoint

RESIDENTIAL BLK1 P1
Area: 1.31 AC

Pt 4 Perpendicular

RESIDENTIAL BLK2 P1
Area: 0.94 AC

Pt 3

Pt 1 Endpoint

Figure C–35

13. When prompted to *Accept results*, press <Enter>.

14. When prompted to select another parcel to subdivide, press <Esc> to end the command.

15. If not already set, on the status bar, set the annotation scale to **1"=40'**.

16. Save the drawing.

C.4 Renumbering Parcels

Creating parcels using the previous methods results in inconsistent parcel numbering. Autodesk Civil 3D parcels can be renumbered individually using Parcel Properties, or in groups using **Modify>Parcel>Renumber/Rename**.

This command enables you to specify a starting parcel number and the increment you want to have between parcels. (It also enables you to rename your parcels based on a different name template.) When renumbering, the command prompts you to identify parcels in the order in which you want to have them numbered. The Renumber/Rename Parcels dialog box is shown in Figure C–36.

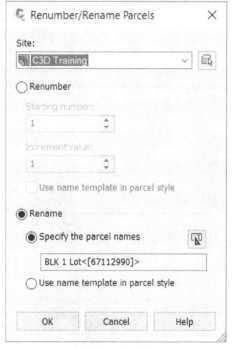

Figure C–36

Hint: Renumber Odd and Even Parcels

If you need to have odd numbered lots on one side of the street, you can set the *Starting Number* to an odd number and the *Incremental Value* to **2**. Repeat the procedure for even numbered lots on the opposite side, setting the *Starting Number* to an even number.

Practice C3 | Rename/Renumber Parcels

Practice Objective

- Renumber the lots created so that they are in sequential order.

Task 1 - Rename and renumber parcels.

1. Continue working with the drawing from the previous practice or open **PCL1-C.dwg**.

2. Select the preset view **Parcel-Create**.

3. Before renaming the newly created parcels, you need to change the label style of the original parcel.

   - Select the parcel label **RESIDENTIAL BLK1 R1**.
   - Right-click, and select **Edit Area Selection Label Style**, as shown in Figure C–37.
   - Select **ASC-Name Square Foot & Acres** as the style and click **OK** to apply the changes and close the dialog box.

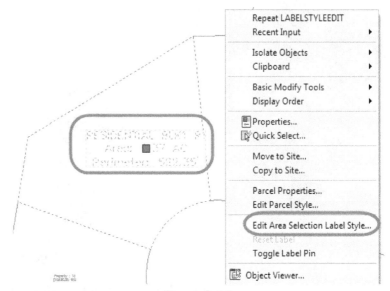

Figure C–37

Do not use the Parcel contextual tab from a selected parcel to select the command because it will only rename the parcel you picked rather than multiple parcels.

4. Rename and renumber the lots so that you have the same numbering system. In the *Modify* tab>Design panel, select **Parcel**. The *Parcel* contextual tab displays.

5. In the *Parcel* tab>Modify panel, click 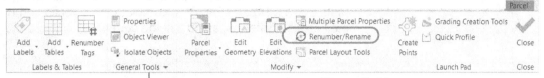 (Renumber/ Rename), as shown in Figure C–38.

Figure C–38

6. In the Renumber/Rename Parcel dialog box, set the following options, as shown in Figure C–39:

   • Select **Rename**.

   • Select **Specify the parcel names**.

   • Click  (Click to edit name template).

Figure C–39

7. In the Name Template dialog box, set the following options, as shown in Figure C–40:

   • Type **BLK1 Lot** followed by a space in the *Name* field.

   • Expand the Property Fields drop-down list.

   • Select **Next Counter** and click **Insert**.

   • Click **OK** to apply the changes and close the dialog box.

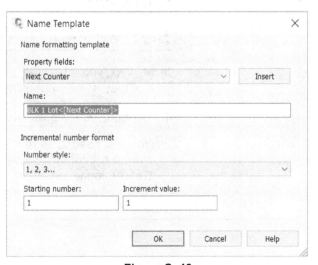

Figure C–40

8. In the Renumber/Rename Parcel dialog box, click **OK** to accept the changes and close the dialog box.

9. When prompted for the points, select the two points shown in Figure C–41. Press <Enter> to complete the selection and then press <Enter> again to exit the command.

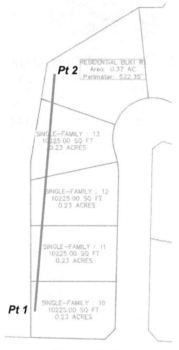

Figure C–41

10. Save the drawing.

Task 2 - Edit parcels using Swing Line - Edit.

In this task, you adjust the last three lots of the parcel suddivision so that they are more marketable.

1. Continue working with the drawing from the previous task.

2. You first need to adjust the Lot line between Parcel 3 and Parcel 4. In the *Home* tab>Create Design panel, select **Parcel**. In the expanded list, select **Parcel Creation Tools**.

3. Expand the Parcel Layout Tools toolbar and ensure the *Minimum Area* is set to **10225**, and the other settings as they were previously, in Figure C–42. Click ⤒ to collapse the expanded toolbar.

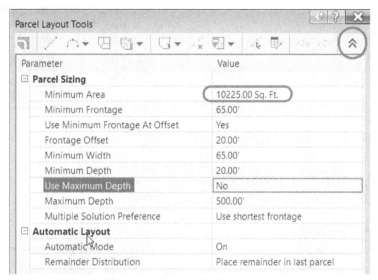

Figure C–42

4. Select **Swing Line - Edit**, as shown in Figure C–43.

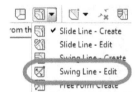

Figure C–43

5. In the Create Parcel - Layout dialog box, set the following parameters:

   - *Site:* **C3D Training**
   - *Parcel Style:* **ASC-Single-Family**
   - *Area Label style:* **ASC-Name Square Foot & Acres**

6. You do not want to label segments, so do not enable this option. Click **OK** when done.

7. When prompted, complete the following, as shown in Figure C–44:

- To select the parcel line to adjust, select the parcel line between Lot 3 and Lot 4.
- For the parcel to adjust, select **Lot 3**.
- For the *start frontage*, select the bottom right corner of **Lot 3, pt1**.
- For the *end of the frontage*, select the top right corner of **Lot 4, pt2**.
- For the *swing point*, select the end point of the rear vertical lot line labeled **pt3** in the figure.
- To accept the results, select **Yes**.

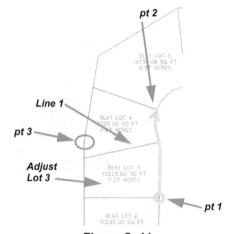

Figure C–44

8. You have the required results for Lot 3. However, Lot 5 is larger than Lot 4. You want to create more evenly sized lots. Display the Parcel Layout Tools toolbar, if it is not open.

9. You could use the **Swing Line - Edit** command, however, you will use a more graphical approach.

10. Erase the parcel line between Lot 4 and Lot 5 using the
    (Delete Sub-entity) command in the *Parcel Layout Tools* toolbar. This causes both parcels to merge into one.

11. Add new parcel line by going to the **Add Fixed Line - Two Points** as shown in Figure C–45.

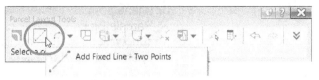

Figure C–45

12. In the Create Parcels - Layout dialog box, leave all the default options as they are. You will correct them after the parcels are created. Click **OK** to close the dialog box.

13. For the start point, select the endpoint of the western lot line.

Hint: Use the <Shift>+ right-click option to bring up the AutoCAD Object Snap overrides menu.

14. For the end point, select (with the AutoCAD **Perpendicular** object snap) the arc of the Knuckle curve, as shown in Figure C–46.

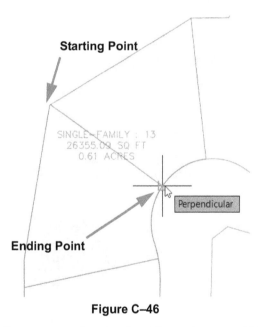

Figure C–46

15. Press <Esc> to stop drawing fixed lines, then type **X** (or press <Enter>) to exit the Parcel Layout Tools.

16. Use the AutoCAD **March Properties** command. You can type **MA** to invoke it.

Not every lot may be updated with the Match command.

17. Select *BLK1 Lot 3 l*abel as the source object and select the two newly divided lots as the destination objects. Hit <Enter> to exit the command.

18. Renumber the two newly created lots as you did earlier in this practice. Remember to set the starting number to 4.

19. If time permits, repeat the steps above to subdivide the Parcels Block 2 and Block 3. If you do not complete the subdivisions for Parcels Block 2 and Block 3, you will need to open **PCL-E1-Parcels** in the next practice.

20. Save the drawing.

C.5 Parcel Reports

The Autodesk Civil 3D software contains several types of parcel reports. Parcel Inverse and Mapcheck data is available in the *Analysis* tab in the Parcel Properties dialog box, as shown in Figure C–47. The report can be generated clockwise or counter-clockwise, and the point of beginning can be specified.

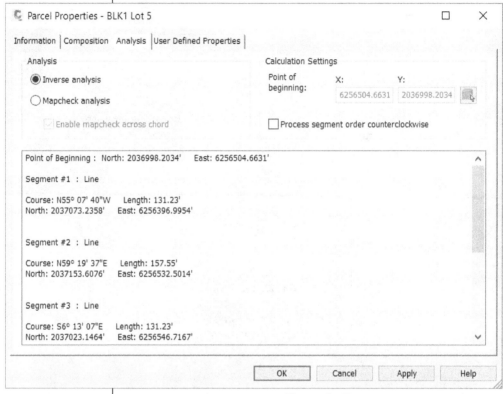

Figure C–47

This dialog box does not enable output. You can copy the results to your Windows clipboard and paste them into your own report. However, if you want to generate a printable report "out of the box," use the Autodesk Civil 3D Toolbox. It includes several stock Parcel-related reports (such as Surveyor Certificates, Inverse and Mapcheck reports, Metes and Bounds), as shown in Figure C–48.

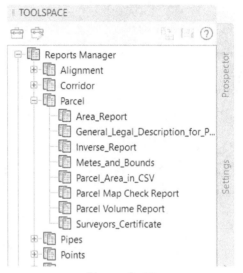

Figure C–48

Once a report is run, it can be opened in a web browser, word processor, or spreadsheet application. Report settings (such as the Preparer's name) can be assigned by selecting **Report Settings** in the Toolspace.

C.6 Parcel Labels

Parcel area labels are a means of graphically selecting a parcel, such as when creating Right-of-Ways. In the Parcel creation and editing examples, the parcel segment labels are created for you automatically. This section explores the functionality of these labels in more depth.

The Add Labels dialog box (**Annotate>Add Labels>Parcel> Add Parcel Labels...**) can be used to assign the required label styles and place labels in the drawing. It enables you to set the line and curve styles, toggle between single and multiple segment labeling, and access the Tag Numbering Table. The dialog box is shown in Figure C–49.

Figure C–49

- Parcel labels, as with all Autodesk Civil 3D labels, are capable of rotating and resizing to match changes in the viewport scale and rotation.

- A segment label has two definitions: composed and dragged state. A dragged state can vary rather significantly from the original label definition.

- The Autodesk Civil 3D software can label segments while sizing parcels.

- Labeling can be read clockwise or counter-clockwise around the parcel.

- Labels can be added through an external reference file using the same commands that label objects in their source drawing. This makes it easier to have multiple plans that need different label styles.

- The **Replace Multiple Labels** option is useful when you want to replace a number of parcel segment labels with another style. However, if you are labeling through an external reference file, labels created in the source drawing cannot be modified.

Parcel Area labels are controlled using Parcel Area Label Styles, which control the display of custom information (such as the parcel number, area, perimeter, address, etc.). For example, you can create more than one parcel area label if you need to show different parcel information on different sheets, as shown in Figure C–50.

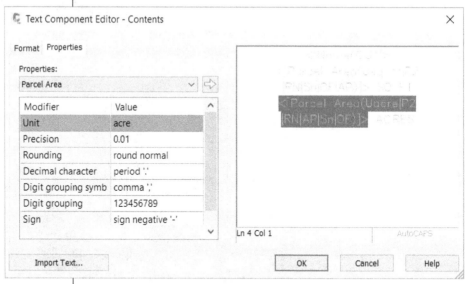

Figure C–50

Parcel Segment labels annotate the line and curve segments of a parcel, as shown in Figure C–51. You can label all of the segments of a parcel with one click or only label selected parcel segments.

Figure C–51

All labels have two definitions: one for the original location, and another when it is moved from its original location. A dragged label can remain as originally defined or can be changed to stacked text. This is defined in the label style definition.

C.7 Parcel Tables

Parcel tables are an alternative to labeling individual parcel areas and segments. An example is shown in Figure C–52.

Parcel Line and Curve Table				
Line #/Curve #	Length	Bearing/Delta	Radius
L2	6.42	N43° 08' 59.63"W	
L1	6.36	S46° 18' 04.79"W	
L3	1.08	S1° 18' 04 79"W	
L4	5 58	N52° 59' 46.62"E	
C1	11.38	19.75	33.00

Figure C–52

When creating a table, the Autodesk Civil 3D software changes the parcel segment labels to an alpha-numeric combination, called a *tag*. A tag with an **L** stands for line and a **C** stands for curve. A segment's tag has a corresponding entry in the table.

- A table can only represent a selected set of label styles.

- The **Add Existing** option (shown in Figure C–53) creates a table from existing objects. New objects are not added to the table. The **Add Existing and New** option creates a table with existing and new objects.

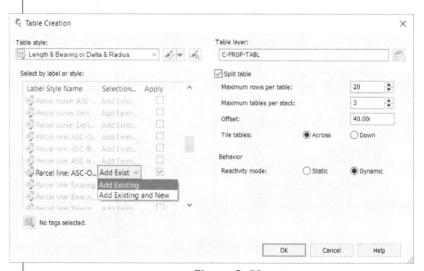

Figure C–53

- A table can have a dynamic link between a segment's tag and table entry. If the segment changes, the table entry updates.

- The Autodesk Civil 3D software switches a label to a tag by changing the *Used In* mode from **Label and Tag Modes** to **Tag Mode**, as shown in Figure C–54.

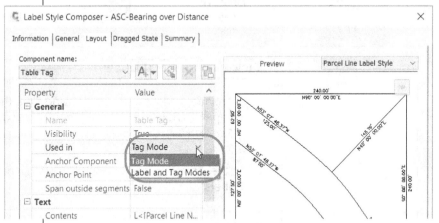

Figure C–54

Hint: Project Explorer

The new Project Explorer offers alternatives to creating tables and reports, providing additional flexibility and improvements. For more information, see *Appendix B: Project Explorer*.

Practice C4

Reporting On and Annotating the Parcel Layout

Practice Objectives

- Add labels, tags, and tables to the drawing to display useful parcel information.
- Create predefined reports to share useful parcel information in a textual format.

Task 1 - Add parcel labels.

1. Continue working with the drawing from the previous practice or open **PCL1-D1.dwg** from the *C:\Civil 3D Projects\ Working\Parcels* folder.

2. In the *Annotate* tab>Labels & Tables panel, click  (Add Labels), as shown in Figure C–55.

Figure C–55

3. In the Add Labels dialog box, set the following parameters, as shown in Figure C–56:

- *Feature:* **Parcel**
- *Label type:* **Multiple Segment**
- *Line label style:* **ASC-Bearing over Distance**
- *Curve label style:* **ASC-Delta over Length and Radius**
- Once the parameters are set, click **Add**.

Figure C–56

4. When prompted to select the Parcels that you want to annotate, select the single-family parcel labels in the BLK1 lot area.

5. When prompted for the label direction, select **Clockwise**.

6. Continue selecting single-family parcels and labeling them clockwise until all of the single-family parcels are labeled, including the parcels in BLK2 and BLK3.

7. Press <Enter> when finished labeling the parcels.

8. Click **Close** in the Add Labels dialog box to close the dialog box.

Parcels can also be labeled in an XREF file.

9. Save the drawing.

Task 2 - Create line and curve segment tables.

The labels are overlapping in a number of locations, making the drawing difficult to read. In this task, you try two methods to fix this. In the first method, you drag the label to a location in which there is no conflict. In the second method, you add a label tag and an associated table.

1. Select the preset view **Parcel-Tag1**. You may have to reset the Annotation scale back to what it was prior to changing the view.

2. Select the label **11.70'**, select the square grip, and drag to place the label in a location in which there is no conflict. Do the same for the label **21.48'**, as shown in Figure C–57.

Figure C–57

3. You will now add tags and a table. In the *Annotate* tab> Label & Tables panel, expand ⬜ (Add Tables) and select **Parcel>Add segment**, as shown in Figure C–58.

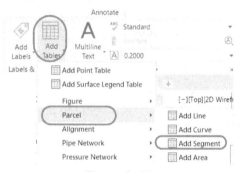

Figure C–58

4. In the Table Creation dialog box, click ⬛ (Pick on screen) and select the labels shown in Figure C–59. Press <Enter> when done.

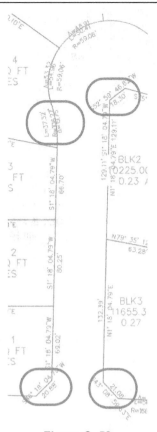

Figure C–59

5. When prompted to convert labels to tags or to not add labels, select **Convert all selected label styles to tag mode**.

6. Click **OK** to close the Table Creation dialog box.

7. When prompted for a location for the table, select a location in an open space, as shown in Figure C–60.

Parcel Line and Curve Table			
Line #/Curve #	Length	Bearing/Delta	Radius
L2	21.08	N43° 08' 59.63"W	
L1	20.88	S46° 18' 04.79"W	
L3	3.58	S1° 18' 04.79"W	
L4	18.30	N52° 59' 46.62"E	
C1	37.32	19.75	108.27

Figure C–60

8. Save the drawing.

Task 3 - Create a parcel area table.

1. Continue working with the drawing from the previous task or open **PCL1-D2.dwg**.

2. In the *Annotate* tab>Label & Tables panel, expand (Add Tables) and select **Parcel>Add Area**.

3. In the Table Creation dialog box, leave the *Table style* as **Area Perimeter Length and Bearing** and in the *Select by label or style* area, select the style name **ASC-Name Square Foot & Acres**, as shown in Figure C–61. All parcels with this style will be selected. Click **OK** to close the dialog box.

Figure C–61

4. Select a location to insert the table into the drawing, as shown in Figure C–62.

Parcel Area Table				
Parcel #	Area	Perimeter	Segment Lengths	Segment Bearings
3	12156.55	470.43	131.23 157.55 131.23 50.41	N55° 07' 40.10"W N59° 19' 36.65"E S6° 13' 06.61"E S59° 19' 36.65"W
5	11296.21	427.15	78.21 113.57 19.73 86.92 128.72	S79° 24' 32.62"E S6° 37' 06.81"W S52° 30' 45.23"W N79° 24' 32.62"W N16° 50' 42.05"E
9	10227.70	407.80	47.65 11.70 36.39 123.83 4.70 70.72 29.81 82.99	N79° 24' 32.62"W N79° 35' 12.54"W N79° 35' 12.54"W N10° 24' 47.46"E S75° 18' 31.56"E S56° 35' 41.15"E S52° 20' 32.14"E S9° 48' 22.81"W

Figure C–62

5. Save the drawing.

Task 4 - Create a parcel report.

1. If the Toolspace, *Toolbox* tab is not displayed, go to the *Home* tab>Palettes panel, and click  (Toolbox), as shown in Figure C–63.

Figure C–63

2. In the Toolspace, *Toolbox* tab, expand the *Reports Manager* and *Parcel* collections. Right-click on *Surveyor's Certificate* and select **Execute**.

3. In the Export to LandXML dialog box, click (Pick from drawing), located at the bottom left of the dialog box.

4. When prompted to select a parcel, select one of the single-family lots that you created earlier and press <Enter>.

5. In the Export to XML Report dialog box, note that only the Lots you selected now display a checkmark. Click **OK** to close the dialog box.

6. In the Save As dialog box, stay in the default folder and type **ASC-Parcel-Report** for the report. Click **Save** to close the dialog box.

7. Review the report (as shown in Figure C–64) and close the web browser.

Parcel BLK1 Lot 4

SURVEYOR'S CERTIFICATE

I, Preparer Registered Land Surveyor, do hereby certify that I have surveyed, divided, and mapped

---

more particularly described as:

Commencing at a point of Northing 2036905.451 and Easting 6256502.548 ;
thence bearing N 79-12-46.378 W a distance of 132.282 feet ;
thence bearing N 9-40-41.250 E a distance of 145.091 feet ;
thence bearing S 55-7-40.098 E a distance of 131.233 feet ;
thence along a curve to the LEFT, having a radius of 59.055 feet, a delta angle of 53° 19' 14.83",
and whose long chord bears S 8-12-42.487 W a distance of 52.996 feet ;
thence along a curve to the RIGHT, having a radius of 108.267 feet, a delta angle of 19° 44' 59.72",
and whose long chord bears S 8-34-25.067 E a distance of 37.135 feet ;
thence bearing S 1-18-4.794 W a distance of 3.580 feet to the point of beginning.

Said described parcel contains 14198.535 square feet (0.326 acres), more or less, subject to any and all easements, reservations, restrictions and conveyances of record.

Figure C–64

8. Save the drawing.

9. (Optional) Save the drawing as **<Your Initials>-Parcels-Complete.dwg** in the *C:\Civil 3D Projects\References\ DWG\Proposed* folder.

10. Update the relative paths of the referenced drawings in the alert box.

Chapter Review Questions

1. Where are parcels listed?

   a. Under the *Survey* collection, in the Toolspace, *Prospector* tab.

   b. In a site under the *Sites* collection, in the Toolspace, *Prospector* tab.

   c. Under the *Figures* collection, inside the Survey Database.

   d. In the Layers panel, in the *Home* tab.

2. What does a parcel style assign in the *Display* tab?

   a. Layer to which parcel segments are assigned.

   b. How big the parcel can be.

   c. The label text that describes the line segments.

   d. The label text that describes the area and name of the parcel.

3. What is the default direction of a Mapcheck or Inverse report?

   a. Clockwise

   b. Counter-clockwise

   c. Always starts going north.

   d. Always starts going south.

4. How do you adjust parcel display order?

   a. Select the parcel segments, right-click and select **Draw Order**.

   b. Move the parcel up or down in the parcel preview list in the Toolspace, *Prospector* tab.

   c. Select the parcel area label, right-click and select **Draw Order**.

   d. Under Sites, right-click on *Parcels* and select **Properties**.

5. How do you create or subdivide parcels interactively?

   a. Draw parcel segments at each location in which you want a parcel line.

   b. **Create** and **Edit** tools in the Parcel Layout toolbar.

   c. Select the parcel, right-click and select **Subdivide**.

   d. Used the AutoCAD **Measure** or **Divide** commands to help place lot lines and even intervals.

6. Which **Parcel Create** command enables you to hold a specified angle relative to the Right-Of-Way?

   a. Slide line-create

   b. Swing line-create

   c. Free Form create

   d. Use the **Add fixed line** command.

7. What are the types of Autodesk Civil 3D Parcel labels that can be set up in the *Setting* tab? (Select all that apply.)

   a. Parcel Line

   b. Parcel Area

   c. Parcel Curve

   d. Parcel Perimeter

8. What does the Add Labels dialog box do?

   a. Creates label styles.

   b. Add or change labels interactively after parcel creation.

   c. Add or change labels during parcel creation.

   d. Creates static text describing what you want to label.

9. What are parcel tables an alternative to? (Select all that apply.)

   a. Drawing the parcels.

   b. Creating tags.

   c. Labeling parcel areas in an already crowded drawing.

   d. Labeling parcel segments in an already crowded drawing.

Command Summary

Button	Command	Location
	Add Labels	• **Ribbon:** *Annotate* tab>Labels & Tables panel
	Add Tables	• **Ribbon:** *Annotate* tab>Labels & Tables panel
	Create Parcel From Objects	• **Ribbon:** *Home* tab>Create Design panel • **Command Prompt:** ParcelFromObjects
	Create Reverse or Compound Curve	• **Ribbon:** *Home* tab>Draw panel • **Command Prompt:** ReverseOrCompound
	Parcel Creation Tools	• **Ribbon:** *Home* tab>Create Design panel • **Command Prompt:** CreateParcelByLayout
	Rename Renumber	• **Contextual Ribbon:** *Parcels*>Modify • **Command Prompt:** EditParcelNumbers
	Slide-Line Create	• **Toolbar:** Parcel Layout Tools
	Swing-Line Edit	• **Toolbar:** Parcel Layout Tools

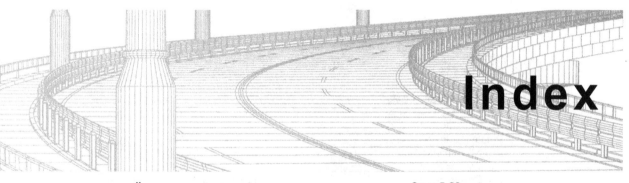

Index

#

2021 Enhancements
    Pressure Pipe Networks **10-54**
    Pressure Pipes
        Allowable Deflection **10-56**
        Appurtenances **10-57**
        Styles **10-58**
2022 Enhancements
    AutoCAD Web App **12-37**
    Autodesk Desktop Connector **4-24, 4-29**
    Autodesk Docs **4-24**
        Data Shortcuts **4-31**
        Notifications **4-29**
        Project Teams **4-30**
        Projects **4-27**
    Pressure Pipes
        Add/Remove Bends or PIs **10-60**
        Alignments **10-58**
        Branch Fittings **10-57**
        Compass **10-59**
        Different Materials for Parts List **10-14**
        Pipe Runs **10-58**
    Project Explorer **B-2**
        Compare To **B-16**
        Keyboard Shortcuts **B-8**
        Object Pane **B-6**
        Pipe Object Pane **B-15**
        Reports and Object Sets **B-24**
        Sub-object Pane **B-8**
        User Interface **B-4**
        View Pane **B-5**
    Share Command **12-37**
    Start Tab **1-4**

A

Alignments
    By Layout **5-20**
    Criteria-Based Design **5-6**
    Edit **5-18, 5-22**
    From Objects **5-10**
    Introduction **5-4**
    Label Set
        Import **5-30**

        Save **5-30**
    Labels **5-27, 5-31, 5-35**
        Dialog Box **5-28**
    Layout Tools **5-16**
    Pressure Pipes **10-58**
    Properties **5-25, 5-34**
    Table **5-33**
    Types **5-7**
        Segment **5-8**
Appurtenances **10-57**
Assembly
    Attach Subassemblies **7-8**
    Create **7-14**
    Detach Subassemblies **7-11**
    Management **7-25**
    Mirror **7-11**
    Sharing **7-26**
    Types **7-2**
Attach command **A-3**
AutoCAD Web App **12-37**
Autodesk Desktop Connector **4-24, 4-29**
Autodesk Docs **1-4**
    Design Collaboration **4-24**
    Folder Selection **4-29**
    Update Notification **4-29**

B

Branch Fittings **10-57**

C

Compass **10-59**
Corridor Contextual Ribbon **8-9**
Corridors
    Create **8-2, 8-18**
    Feature Lines **8-8**
    Intersection **8-25, 8-29**
        Corridor Regions **8-27**
        Geometry Details **8-27**
    Slope Patterns **8-8**
    Surfaces **8-56, 8-60**
        Surface Boundaries **8-57**
    Visualizing **12-33**

D

Data Shortcuts **4-26**
    Create Data Shortcuts **4-38**
    Create New Shortcuts Folders **4-33**
    Data-reference **4-40**
    Promote **4-29**
    Synchronize **4-28**
    Update Notification **4-28**
    Workflow **4-29**
Description Key
    Rotate Parameter **2-40**
    Scale Parameter **2-39**
Design Development **5-2**
Design Development Phase **4-2**
Design Surfaces **9-19**
Drawing Settings **1-37**
    Abbreviations **1-41**
    Ambient Settings **1-42**
    Object Layers **1-40**
    Parcels **C-3**
    Transformation **1-39**
    Units and Zone **1-38**
Drawing template **1-37, 4-3**

F

Feature Line **9-4**
    Elevation Editor **9-5**
    Labels **9-34**
Final Design **12-21**
Fittings **10-56**

G

Grading **9-2**
    Create **9-21, 9-24**
    Creation Tools Toolbar **9-23**
    Criteria **9-34**
        Set **9-35**
    Infill **9-28**
    Modify **9-37**
    Styles **9-34**
    Volume **9-38**
        Tools **9-36**

I

InfoCenter
    Autodesk App Store **1-9**
Infrastructure Parts Editor **10-5**
Interim Design Grade **9-19**

L

Label styles **2-8**

N

Navigation Bar **12-23**

O

Object Viewer **3-49**

P

Panorama **1-27**
Parcel
    Analysis **C-6**
    By Layout **C-17, C-20**
    Display Order **C-4**
    Free Form Create **C-22**
    From a Legal Description **2-81**
    From Objects **C-8**
    Frontage **C-23**
    Labels **C-39, C-44**
    Labels and Styles **C-7**
    Pick Sub-Entity **C-18**
    Properties **C-6**
    Renumber **C-29**
    Report **C-49**
    Right of Way **C-8**
    ROW **C-4**
    Sizing **C-19**
    Slide Line **C-17, C-22**
    Swing Line **C-22, C-32**
    Table **C-45**
Pipe Runs **10-58**
Pipes **10-2**
    Annotate **10-48**
    Catalog **10-5**
    Connect to Structures **10-29**
    Connect/Disconnect From Part **10-38**
    Create Network from Object **10-23**
    Draw in Profile View **10-34**
    Edit **10-37, 10-39**
    In Sections **10-46**
    Network Layout Tools **10-28, 10-30**
    Network Parts Lists **10-6**
    Pipe (and Structure) Properties **10-37**
    Pipe and Structure Rules **10-10**
    Pipe Network Labels **10-45**
    Pressure Network parts **10-8**
    Reapply Pipe Rules **10-12**
    Reports **10-47**
    Structure Catalog **10-5**
    Swap Part **10-38, 10-60**
    Table **10-47, 10-50**
Places **1-13**
Plan and Profile Sheets
    Create **11-19, 11-27, 11-33**
    Create View Frames **11-10**
    Edit Sheet Sets **11-37**
    Match Line **11-6**
        Geometry Edits **11-9**
    Sheet Set **11-35**
        Manager Properties **11-39, 11-41**
    View Frame **11-6**
        Geometry Edits **11-8**
        Groups **11-6**

Point Cloud **A-3**
  Attach **A-3**
  Create Surface from Point Cloud **A-8**, **A-13**
  Crop **A-6**
  External References **A-3**
  Object Snap **A-3**
  Transparency **A-5**
  UCS **A-3**
Points
  Create **2-35**
  Description Key Sets **2-37**, **2-41**
  Edit **2-59**
  Overview **2-12**
  Point Groups **2-67**, **2-74**
  Reports **2-61**, **2-66**
Points Overview **2-12**
Pressure Pipe Networks **10-54**
  Appurtenances **10-57**
  Create **10-62**
  Fittings **10-56**
Pressure Pipes **10-54**
  Add Bends Automatically **10-55**, **10-70**
  Add/Remove Bends or PIs **10-60**
  Alignments **10-58**
  Appurtenances **10-57**
  Branch Fittings **10-57**
  Compass **10-59**
  Editing **10-55**
  Fittings **10-56**
  Parts Lists **10-14**
Profile
  Band Elevations **6-33**
  From Surface **6-12**, **6-19**
  Horizontal Change Alert **6-29**
  Label Sets
    Import **6-36**
    Save **6-36**
  Labels **6-34**
    Dialog Box **6-35**
  Layout Tools **6-29**
  Overview **6-2**
  Segment Types **6-34**
  View
    Reposition **6-3**
    Wizard **6-14**
Profile View **6-24**
Project Explorer **B-2**
  Compare To **B-16**
  Keyboard Shortcuts **B-8**
  Object Pane **B-6**
  Pipe Object Pane **B-15**
  Reports and Object Sets **B-24**
  Sub-object Pane **B-8**
  User Interface **B-4**
  View Pane **B-5**

Projects
  Create Drawings **4-25**
  Multiple Drawings **4-23**, **4-24**
  Share Data **4-25**, **4-26**, **4-29**
  Single-Design Drawing **4-23**
Prospector
  Preview Pane **3-50**
Prospector Tab
  Master View **1-20**

Q
QTO
  Define Materials **8-75**
  Earthwork Volumes **8-73**, **8-76**
  Mass Haul **8-74**
  Material Volumes **8-74**, **8-80**
  Pay Items **12-10**
    Assign **12-11**, **12-12**
    Compute **12-17**
  Quantity Takeoff Criteria **8-74**
Quick Access Toolbar **1-9**, **12-37**, **12-43**

R
Report Settings **1-25**
Roundabouts **8-41**
  Creating **8-41**
  Heads Up Display **8-45**
  Standards **8-41**

S
Sample Lines
  Create **8-68**
  Create Sample Line Group **8-64**
  Modify **8-67**
  Sample Line Tools toolbar **8-65**
  Sample More Sources **11-28**
Section Views **11-24**
  Wizard **11-24**
Settings **1-24**
  Command **1-46**
  Feature **1-45**
  LandXML **1-44**
  Overrides **1-47**
  Pipe Network **10-4**
  Point **2-33**
Share **12-37**
Sites **5-3**
  Create a New Site **C-11**
  Parcels **C-2**
SteeringWheel
  Full **12-26**
  Mini **12-26**
  Rewind **12-27**
  Settings **12-28**
Styles **2-7**
  Apply Style to Points **2-31**
  Figure **2-3**

Import **3-76**, **4-4**
Label **1-43**, **2-8**, **A-17**
Multi-Purpose **11-26**
Object **4-10**, **4-16**
Page **11-26**
Pipe and Structure **10-9**
Plan and Profile Sheet Objects **11-7**
Point Label **2-18**, **2-28**
Point Marker **2-13**, **2-25**
Profile
   View **6-4**
Purge **4-6**
Reference **4-6**, **4-15**
Section **11-26**
   View **11-25**
   View Band **11-25**
Surface Contour **3-24**
Subassemblies
Attach **7-8**
Detach **7-11**
Select Similar **7-12**
Subassembly Composer **7-6**
Flowchart **7-6**
Multi-use Panel **7-7**
Preview **7-6**
Properties **7-7**
Toolbox **7-7**
Superimposing Profiles **6-30**
Surface
3D Solid Surface **A-14**, **A-16**, **B-24**
Analysis **3-49**, **3-69**
Boundary **3-30**
Breaklines **3-27**, **3-33**
   Survey Figures **3-29**
Contour Data **3-19**
Create **3-18**
DEM Files **3-16**
Drawing Objects **3-16**
Edit **3-41**, **3-53**
   Copy Surface **3-47**
   Line Edits **3-43**
   Point Edits **3-43**
   Raise/Lower **3-47**
   Simplify **3-44**
   Smooth Contours **3-45**
   Smooth Surface **3-46**
   Surface Paste **3-47**
Labels **3-65**
Point Files **3-16**
Point Groups **3-17**, **3-23**
Process **3-2**
Properties **3-8**, **3-48**
Quick Profile **3-52**
Rebuild **3-10**
Volume Calculations **3-67**
Survey

Database **2-50**
Figure **2-3**
Figure Prefix Database **2-4**, **2-6**
Import **2-49**
Open a Survey Database **2-53**
Workflow **2-2**
Swap Pressure Parts **10-60**

T
Template **4-3**
Toolspace
Anchoring **1-20**
Prospector Tab **1-20**, **1-29**
   Active Drawing View **1-20**
Settings Tab **1-23**, **1-30**
Survey Tab **1-24**, **2-49**
Toolbox Tab **1-24**
Transparent Commands **2-80**
Bearing and Distance **2-78**
Point Number **2-78**
Profile Grade and Elevation **2-79**
Profile Grade Elevation **6-33**
Profile Grade Length **6-33**
Profile Station and Elevation **2-79**, **6-33**
   From COGO Point **6-32**
   From Plan **6-32**
Profile Station at Grade **2-79**, **6-33**
Profile Station from Plan **6-32**
Station and Offset **2-79**
Zoom to Point **2-79**

U
User Interface **1-7**
Application Menu **1-8**
Command Line **1-12**
InfoCenter **1-9**
Quick Access Toolbar **1-8**
Ribbon **1-10**
Status Bar **1-12**

V
ViewCube **12-23**
Settings **12-25**
Views
Backgrounds **12-32**
Named **12-29**
Named Views **12-29**
   Create **12-30**
Parallel **12-24**
Perspective **12-24**

W
Workspaces **1-5**
2D Drafting & Annotation **1-6**
3D Modeling **1-6**
Civil 3D **1-6**
Planning and Analysis **1-6**

CPSIA information can be obtained
at www.ICGtesting.com
Printed in the USA
LVHW021311100722
723139LV00006B/229

9 781956 032048